GRANDMOTHERS AT WORK

DISCARD

Grandmothers at Work

Juggling Families and Jobs

Madonna Harrington Meyer

NEW YORK UNIVERSITY PRESS
New York and London

NEW YORK UNIVERSITY PRESS
New York and London
www.nyupress.org

References to Internet websites (URLs) were accurate at the time of writing.
Neither the author nor New York University Press is responsible for URLs that
may have expired or changed since the manuscript was prepared.

Library of Congress Cataloging-in-Publication Data

Harrington Meyer, Madonna, 1959-
Grandmothers at work : juggling families and jobs / Madonna Harrington Meyer.
pages cm
Includes bibliographical references and index.
ISBN 978-0-8147-2923-6 (cloth : alk. paper) — ISBN 978-0-8147-2947-2 (pbk. : alk. paper)
1. Work and family—United States. 2. Grandmothers—United States. I. Title.
HD4904.25.H385 2014
331.4084'60973—dc23

2013045558

New York University Press books are printed on acid-free paper,
and their binding materials are chosen for strength and durability.
We strive to use environmentally responsible suppliers and materials
to the greatest extent possible in publishing our books.

Manufactured in the United States of America
10 9 8 7 6 5 4 3 2 1

Also available as an ebook

to Jeff

to Sam, Maureen, and Ellen

CONTENTS

Preface   ix

Acknowledgments   xi

1. Balancing Care and Work   1

2. Joys and Second Chances   32

3. Intensive Grandmothering   62

4. Juggling Work and Grandchildren   98

5. Financial Ebbs and Flows   131

6. Containing Carework   153

7. Emotional Ups and Downs   174

8. Social and Health Pros and Cons   207

   Conclusions: Grandmothers at Work   230

   Appendix   239

   Notes   259

   References   265

   Index   275

   About the Author   281

I never really had a grandmother growing up. My mother's mom, Kathryn, died decades before I was born. My mom was just 18. My father's mom, Anna, died when I was very young. I have only two memories of Anna. In one, she was at our home for a holiday. The house was filled with family and I had asked Grandma, whose hair was always in a tight white bun, if I could brush her hair. She allowed me to do so and while I was probably nowhere near gentle enough, I was enthralled by her long and silky fine hair. In the other memory, we were visiting her at the nursing home. My dad, mom, and several of my siblings were all there chatting with her and she had little idea who we were. At one point she encouraged my mother to marry her son, something she had already done decades earlier, sending the kids, but not our parents, into peals of laughter. I would have liked to have a grandma around much more than I did. My mom would have, too. She would have liked to have some grandmotherly help given that she bore seven children within a fast-paced 10 years. Though she raised us without a helpful grandmother, she became an incredibly helpful and loving grandmother as we had our own children. My siblings and I have been enormously grateful as we watched the joy between our mom and our children deepen each year. We see just how much we missed as we were growing up.

A longing for a grandmother had little to do with why I started this project, however. I began thinking about this project when I was going up for full professorship and my three children were in middle school and high school. I have often described parenting while working full-time as living life within a tightly secured bungee cord. Every minute of every day is accounted for as my husband, Jeff, and I trade off who will teach, write, shuttle kids, help with homework, start the laundry, prepare dinner, walk the dog, and every other thing imaginable. In my mind's eye, our children were nearing graduation and we were nearing an empty nest. I was imagining the bungee cord loosening until it perhaps disappeared altogether. I thought that Jeff and I were about to be sprung free.

Then I went to a conference at the Russell Sage Foundation in New York City and I heard over a dozen women professors, 10 to 15 years my senior, talking at length about how much time and effort they devoted to their grandchildren. They loved their grandkids, and were happy to help, but were feeling the pinch as they were asked by their adult children to use vacation time, travel time, sick time, free time, and even some work time, to help with newly arriving and young grandchildren. What they were describing sounded to me a lot like a bungee cord that was at times fairly tight. I knew all about younger mothers juggling work and children; I had not really considered the lives of middle-aged women juggling work and grandchildren. This was a stage I had not seen coming.

I pondered the project for well over a year and then nearly did not do it at all, save for a conversation with my dear colleague Suzanne Mettler, Professor of Political Science at Cornell. She talked about poor, single women at her church who were also quite tied down by the incredible task of juggling work and caring for grandchildren. I am indebted to her for her insights and encouragement. I knew that as long as I made sure that the sample was diverse, including women of all classes, races, marital statuses, and regions of the country, I would be able to portray grandmothers at work.

There are many grandmothers who do not work, and there are many working grandmothers who do not take care of their grandchildren. This book addresses neither. This book focuses on working grandmothers who care for their grandchildren. How do they juggle their work and carework responsibilities?

ACKNOWLEDGMENTS

This research was partially supported by the Syracuse University Center for Aging and Policy Studies, with funding provided through grant number P30-AG034464 from the National Institute on Aging. I am indebted to many friends and colleagues who helped me find grandmothers who were working, caring for their grandchildren, and willing to be interviewed. You know who you are and you know how much I appreciate your assistance. I cannot name names here as it might undo my efforts at keeping the grandmothers' identities confidential. I am grateful to my amazing graduate students with whom I have had the good fortune to work: Chantell Frazier for assisting with some of the interviews; Yan Liu for analyzing the Health and Retirement Survey (HRS) data; and Ynesse Abdul-Malak and Jessica Hausauer for editing, and commenting on, the entire manuscript.

I am grateful to my mom, Anne, and sisters, Maura and Rose, and my dear friends Karen and Margaret, who helped me in numerous ways during my travels for this book. My husband and I are enormously grateful to his parents, Lyle and Jeanne Meyer, grandparents extraordinaire, who cared for our children many times over the decades so we could go to conferences and take highly treasured vacations. I am grateful to Suzanne Mettler and Jill Quadagno for helping me keep the big picture in focus and for reading portions of this work. I am grateful to Jeanne, Jeff, Ellen, and Maureen Meyer for reading the entire manuscript. Nice to have such smart relatives! I am especially indebted to the 48 women whose stories I tell in this manuscript. I appreciate the efforts of everyone at NYU Press, particularly Alexia Traganas, Caelyn Cobb, and my wonderful editor, Ilene Kalish. And for all of the joy they have given me along the way, I am most grateful to my husband, Jeffrey, and to our three children, Ellen, Maureen, and Sam. A few of the grandmother's quotes already appeared in my chapter, "US Grand-mothers Juggling Work and Grandchildren," in *Contemporary Grand-parenting: Changing Family Relationships in a Global Context*, edited by Virpi Timonen and Sara Arber. I appreciate their permission to reprint them here.

1

Balancing Care and Work

Legions of working grandmothers across the United States are quietly, almost invisibly, caring for grandchildren so that parents can work or have a break from busy schedules. Deanne is one of 48 working grandmothers I interviewed who is balancing paid work and caring for grandchildren. A 57-year-old, white, married, well-educated, middle-class woman with two daughters, Deanne works full-time as an elected official in a small midwestern town. She also takes care of three of her six grandkids three or four days a week after work and often on weekends. She also checks in on her mother at the nursing home a few times a week. Though she is juggling so many responsibilities, and at times is very tired, she is positively gleeful when she talks about caring for her grandchildren, "Being a grandmother is the best job in the world. Love them, spoil them, and say goodbye."

We tend to think of balancing work and family as something that only relatively young families contend with, yet many middle-aged grandmothers are employed and providing routine child care for their grandchildren. Grandmothers are prized daycare providers because often the quality is very high, the cost is very low, and the flexibility is maximal.[1] Grandmothers often have very special bonds with their grandchildren. Many young working families report that they feel that the best possible care providers for their children would be the grandmothers. Many grandmothers may agree.[2] One phone survey of adults ages 40 and older found that when grandparents live nearby, more than half provide some amount of child care every week, and one half of those provide more than 12 hours a week. Another study found that as many as 43 percent of grandmothers care for grandchildren regularly, and 20 percent of children with working mothers are regularly cared for by their grandmothers.[3]

But as the age at retirement increases, many grandparents may be feeling more of a pinch between paid and unpaid work.[4] Any lingering images of grandmothers in aprons or rocking chairs are being replaced by grandmothers who need to set down their briefcases so they can bathe little ones. One-half of Americans are grandparents by age 50 and three-fourths of those in their early 50s are still employed.[5] The average age at retirement has increased by two years for men and for women since the mid-1990s, with men now retiring at an average age of 64 and women at an average age of 62.[6] Figure 1.1, based on 2010 US Census data, shows that about 70 percent of women in their early 50s, and nearly 65 percent of women in their late 50s, are employed. Studies show that working grandparents are just as likely to provide care as those who are retired, and one-third change their work schedules to accommodate grandchild care.[7] Grandmothers may well be the most desirable source of child care, but increasingly women in that age group are themselves employed. This study analyzes how working grandmothers balance paid work and unpaid carework.

The numbers of single parents and of working women have risen steadily for decades, but neither the US government nor employers have responded with policies that would help working families balance work and family obligations. The US welfare state does not provide young working parents, or middle-aged working grandmas, with guaranteed paid time off for sick days, vacation days, family leaves, or flex time; universal health insurance; low-priced, high-quality daycare; or universal access to preschool programs. As a result, many families are turning to grandmas for help.

According to my analysis of the Health and Retirement Survey (HRS) 2010, of all the women ages 51–70 who are employed and who have grandkids, 46 percent are providing at least some hours of grandchild care per year.[8] For this book, I conducted in-depth interviews with 48 working grandmothers who care for their grandchildren, and I learned that some watch the grandchildren occasionally, maybe once a

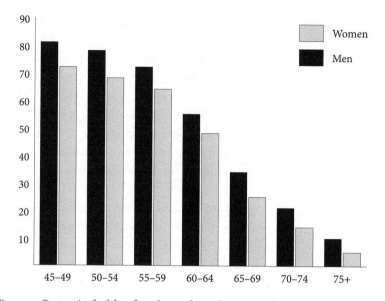

Figure 1.1. Percent in the labor force by gender and age, 2010. *Source*: US Bureau of Labor Statistics 2011a.

week or once a month, while others care for them for several evenings a week and most weekends. Taking care of grandkids is a tremendous source of joy and provides many with a second chance for raising children without as many responsibilities and pressures as the first time around. Deanne, whose eyes fill with happy tears at the mere mention of her grandkids, says being a grandmother is better than being a mother because it is only part-time. You get to say goodbye. As a grandmother, Deanne can postpone housework to play with the grandkids because they do not come to stay every day.

> When you have your own kids you are busy with all the other things you have to do. But with your grandkids you can just sit. If the dishes get done the next day, who cares? I can take that walk.

Caring for grandchildren is fairly intense work. In fact, it appears that just as motherhood has intensified in the United States, becoming very centered on the strategic development or purposeful cultivation of children,[9] so has grandmotherhood. For many grandmothers

I interviewed, the work is very demanding. Deanne has been working and caring for grandchildren for 10 years. Currently she is focusing on her newly divorced daughter's three sons, who live just a few minutes away. Deanne's daughter is working full-time and attending night classes to earn a bachelor's degree. Deanne said that she and her daughter both agreed that it was best for the daughter's long-term earnings to complete the degree now. Nonetheless, that agreement means that Deanne provides many more hours of care to her grandchildren than she, or her husband, ever expected.

> When my daughter was in college . . . I left work early and picked the grandkids up from school. Sometimes the boys walked here and waited in the office for me to finish. . . . I give them 55 cents for the candy machine. They have their treats, play on my computer, and then we head to their house, or maybe to my house to change and get toys. I would take them home and fix supper, play time, bath time, and to bed.

Deanne works daily from 8:00 to 4:00, then on three or four nights a week she takes the boys from 4:00 until 11:00. She dozes on the couch, waiting for her daughter to get home from her class. Like many of the grandmothers, Deanne feels she is constantly on call to provide ever more assistance for the grandchildren. Her work day is peppered with calls and requests about whether she can do more. Two calls came in during our one-hour interview.

> I have lots of phone calls at work, daily, several a day, from my daughters. "Can you pick this one up, run this one over there?" Almost every day.

Many grandmothers frequently rearrange their work schedules to be readily available for the grandchildren and this may adversely affect earnings, savings, and private pensions and Social Security contributions. For some it is a matter of choice. But for many it is because their own jobs are more secure and flexible than their adult children's jobs. Deanne explained that she has been at her job for years, but her recently divorced daughter's new job situation is precarious. So Deanne changes her work schedule almost daily to care for her grandchildren. She comes in late, leaves early, takes days off, and minds the grandchildren while at her office. Her daughter has not yet built up any sick leave or vacation time, so Deanne has ramped up the amount of care she provides.

> She started a new job last spring and doesn't have much time built up for family time, so Grandma is here. She is an accountant, for less than one year. Once it is April she will have two weeks of vacation, but now she has nothing. Her old job was talking layoffs, and she could not risk being without a job, so now has a new job. . . . I am fortunate being an elected official; I am paid whether I am here or not. . . . But I don't have a set schedule. I can come and go as I need to.

Deanne responds to nearly constant requests from her daughter for help. She nearly had to postpone our interview due to a last-minute request. She occasionally declines the requests, but more often she says yes and then returns to work later to complete her projects.

> I nearly missed our interview today because I had to babysit. . . . My daughter just cannot risk missing work. . . . I sometimes have to tell my daughter . . . I am too busy at work. And sometimes I will take care of them and come back to work after, if the work really has to get done.

Many middle-aged women are also providing a substantial amount of financial support to their adult children and grandchildren, some because they want to spoil the grandkids and others because the grandkids do not have basic necessities such as clothes, food, or diapers. Particularly if their adult children are single parents, grandmothers tend to provide a great deal of help with money. Deanne and her husband had nearly paid off their own home in preparation for their retirement. But when their daughter divorced and nearly lost her house, Deanne and her husband bought it. Deanne's daughter is unable to make the monthly payments because she is trying to complete her college degree.

> When my daughter divorced, they nearly lost the house to foreclosure, so I went on the loan and signed for them. But then they again nearly foreclosed, so my husband and I bought it.

Deanne's husband is self-employed and disabled. The economy is bad for construction workers, so he is rarely working and earns very little in income. Additionally, Deanne and her husband took a second mortgage on their own home to further assist their daughter during the divorce. Given that her husband's earnings have dwindled near zero, Deanne is now paying three mortgages: the first and second mortgage on her own home, as well as her daughter's mortgage.

> And my husband has such poor health that he has had to reduce his work. The construction business has taken a downslide in the last few years. There is almost no new construction. He is mainly just a handyman now. So now I have to make the payment on my own house and most of the payment on my daughter's house, and that is hard, a bit tight. I hope she will be able to pay her share again soon. I think we will be alright when I retire. Our house will be almost paid for. But we had to get a second mortgage to help our daughter with some things.

Many grandmothers divert money from their savings and investments and, as a result, do not get to build up a nest egg. Some even take on new debt, including loans, second mortgages, and withdrawals from their 401Ks, to provide money to the younger generations. Deanne and her husband have done this and more. Deanne is optimistic that her daughter will eventually pay back this money and that she and her husband will be financially secure when they retire. But her husband is much less certain. Deanne says he feels taken advantage of and very worried about their finances.

> I am hoping to get that money back from our daughter, to quell my husband's sense that the kids are all just taking and no one is ever giving back. He sometimes feels used and abused. He is more worried about the money than I am. He thinks he will not get this money back. But I am the optimist. I like knowing that we helped her and that our grandsons had a nice roof over their heads.

Because so much of Deanne's paycheck goes toward the mortgages, they are not saving for their retirement at this time. She had hoped to work for just one more four-year term in office before retiring. That plan will likely have to change because they will not have paid off their own, or their daughter's, home by then. At a time when they are supposed to be accumulating a nest egg for their own retirement, Deanne and her husband, and many other grandparents, are accumulating debt.

Though every grandmother I interviewed talked about the joy she feels spending time with her grandchildren, some find ways to limit grandchild care either because they are overwhelmed or they resist gendered expectations that as women they should do this work and absorb the costs. Deanne is one of several grandmothers who are clear in stating that they need limits to the amount of grandchild care they are expected to provide. Like several others I interviewed, she uses her job to reduce her availability. Deanne likes having employment in part because she loves her job and her colleagues, and in part because the job helps to set some boundaries. She said she was concerned that if she was not working she would be asked to take care of the grandchildren even more.

> I could not do full-time grandkids. I need the job, the adult connections. I would not want to do the child care full-time. Much as I love them. It is fun to have them come but fun to see them go.

Some grandmothers limit grandchild care because their partners are either unable or unwilling to help. Deanne's husband does not help.

> My husband does not take care of the grandkids, not his thing. He will help me a little bit. Normally he just stays away, and just goes to bed, and stays away. He avoids the whole situation.

Many grandmothers are also caring for frail older relatives, caught up in a new kind of sandwich generation in which they are providing support for their grandchildren, adult children, and parents. For some, working, caring for grandkids, and caring for a frail older parent is routine. For others it is utterly exhausting. Deanne is somewhere in the middle. In addition to full-time work and 15–20 hours of grandchild care a week, she cares for her 80-year-old mother. As the only child living nearby, she feels duty bound.

I also have responsibilities with my mom in the nursing home. I am the only child in town; I go to the nursing home three or four nights a week to check on her and visit with her. I have been doing this pace forever.

Many grandmas are providing more support than they ever intended, or in some cases wanted, to give. Though many feel well appreciated for all of the support they provide, some feel underappreciated. Deanne is one of many working grandmothers who feel their efforts are warmly appreciated. She says that her daughters say thank you constantly and often they repay her efforts in kind.

> They always tell me, they hug and kiss. My daughter does so many nice things for me. She brings me garden produce, tomatoes and cucumbers, bakes, sends home dinner for me and my husband. At least once every other week she sends home supper. She just made stew the other night. They came over when we were on vacation and stripped my wallpaper and painted. They will do fun surprises; make sure I get nice things for my birthday. They call, ask what I am doing and how I am. They call and say thanks. I feel very appreciated. When we are in Florida for the month of March she does my mail, my bills.

But like some other grandmas, Deanne worries about sibling rivalry. Deanne helps her daughter who lives nearby, who has recently divorced, by paying the mortgage and sitting for the boys after school most days and weekends. She worries that her other daughter, who lives farther away and is married and needs little help, is getting short shrift. Deanne makes a point to visit for long weekends and had just returned from a weekend in which she watched the grandkids so the parents could rebuild a deck. She has not yet heard complaints that things are unfair but worries that she might.

Some grandmothers worry that they are providing entirely too much support and enabling their adult children to be irresponsible parents. Though I never raised the topic of enabling, fully one-third of the grandmas I interviewed did. Deanne does not worry that she is providing too much grandchild care or financial support, but her husband certainly does. She says that he resents her being gone so often to help with the grandkids. He is worried that Deanne is giving the kids and grandkids too much money and spending too much time helping them. He wishes she were home to do things for him, like housework and dinner, and with him, like go out with friends. She told me that he feels that she is not keeping with the plan they made for their own middle age.

> He does mind that I do too much. He feels I let things with him slide. I was just gone all weekend. He misses me doing the housekeeping but he really misses my company. He never says anything to me, but I hear from others that he says that I put the grandkids first. And I guess some days I do. After 34 years, we must have done something right. It makes me feel bad that he thinks that I don't care about us. I do. But there are times they need me and I want to be there to help.

Every spring Deanne and her husband take a month off work and live in Florida with a big group of friends. She said he is very protective of that time. He does not want the grandkids there. She told me, however, that she plans to start bringing the grandkids to Florida as soon as they are a bit older.

The impact of working and caring for grandchildren hinges mainly on the intensity of the care and the access to resources. Many take multiple roles in stride, finding this to be among the most joyful stages of their entire lives. They lead active, healthy lifestyles. Others find that multiple roles lead to stress, depleting their resources, leaving them busy or too tired to maintain social activities or properly care for their own health. Deanne says working and caring for the grandkids keeps her young, and though she gets very tired, this is how she wants it to be.

> I have aches and pains but I stay young. I can't imagine doing nothing. . . . I sometimes just want a day off. Yesterday I would have loved a nap but I had to take care of the granddaughters and do the dishes. I had supper ready for them and left.

No matter how difficult it is at times, juggling multiple roles, being bone-tired, or disagreeing with her husband about how much help is appropriate, Deanne, like many of the grandmothers I interviewed, would not give up her time with the grandkids for the world.

I thoroughly enjoy where I am at. I like my job and the people I work with and yet I am available to be there with the kids. I have the best of both worlds and I hope it lasts.

Increasing Need for Grandmother Care

Several sociodemographic trends contribute to the reliance on grandmothers. The United States has relatively high levels of single mothers raising children, and relatively high levels of employment, particularly full-time employment, among women with children.[10] Despite the recent recession, neither the US welfare state nor US employers offer much support to working families with children.

The United States has experienced a retreat from marriage and a dramatic increase in single-parent families. In 2008 the US Census Bureau reported that the share of women who are married had dropped from 66 percent in 1960 to 53 percent.[11] This drop has been more pronounced among black women. In 2008, 55 percent of adult white, compared to just 34 percent of black, women were married. The US fertility rate has hovered near the replacement level, 2.1 births per woman, for decades. Increasingly these births are to single women. Figure 1.2 shows that in the 2010 US Census data, 41 percent of all births in the United States were to unmarried women, up from 29 percent in 1980.[12] Andrew Cherlin points out that many single mothers, particularly those with less education, are actually cohabiting.[13] Thus, more than half of births to unmarried mothers may have been births to cohabiting mothers, but the US Census does not record those relationships and nonmarital relationships tend to be more fragile. Asians had the lowest proportion of births to single mothers, while blacks had the highest.[14]

Families headed by single mothers are much more likely to be poor. The US Census reports that among families with a child under 18, 19 percent of all married couples, compared to 41 percent of female-headed households, are poor. Single parenting is especially difficult for black and Hispanic mothers; 43 percent of Hispanic and 48 percent of black single mothers live in poverty.[15] Many of these single mothers continue to be poor as they reach old age; the Administration on Aging

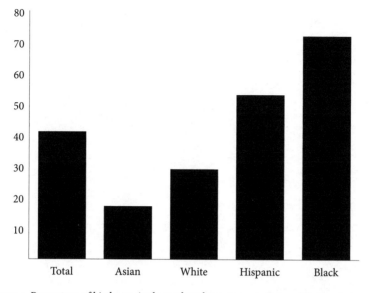

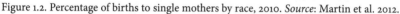

Figure 1.2. Percentage of births to single mothers by race, 2010. *Source*: Martin et al. 2012.

has found that 41 percent of single older Hispanic and 32 percent of single older black women who live alone are poor.[16]

Americans are working more hours than workers in any other country, even Japan. US women, particularly those with young children, are increasingly likely to work and to work full-time.[17] Figure 1.3 shows that more women, especially more mothers of younger children, are working than ever before. Notably, the percentage of working women with children under age 3 also rose, from 34 percent to 61 percent between 1975 and 2010. Such demographic changes have reshaped US families. Sarah Jane Glynn reports that only 20 percent of children currently live in a family with a traditional male breadwinner/female homemaker, compared to 45 percent in 1970. Mothers are now often the main or only family breadwinner.[18] In 2010, the mother was the single or primary breadwinner in 41 percent of families, up from just 11 percent in 1970. In 2011, among families with children, 40 percent were headed by two working parents, and another 32 percent were headed by a single parent. Young families have an increasing need for policies and programs that help them balance work and children. But in the United States there are not many options, prompting many to call for Grandma.

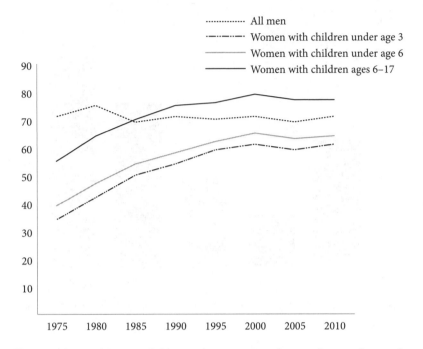

Figure 1.3. Among those 16 and older, employment status of men and women by age of youngest child, 1975–2010. *Source*: US Bureau of Labor Statistics 2011b.

A key economic factor may be increasing reliance on grandmothers as well. The Great Recession of 2007–2009 has hit many working families hard and there has not been a lot of recovery during the subsequent recovery period. I conducted my interviews from 2008 to 2012 and though I did not ask questions about the recession, many respondents brought it up. The Pew Research Center shows that median household incomes decreased about 4.1 percent during the two years of the recession and another 4.1 percent in the two years following.[19] Moreover, the poverty rate rose from 12.5 percent in 2007 to 15 percent in 2011. Median household wealth fell from $131,016 in 2007 to $79,431 in 2010, a loss of 39 percent. The percent of families that reported at least one unemployed member nearly doubled, from 6.3 percent in 2007 to 12 percent in 2009, and remained at 11.5 percent in 2011. Certain groups were especially hard hit. For example, the median wealth of white households in 2009 was 20 times that of black households and 18 times that of Hispanic households, the largest wealth gap on record.[20] Many of the families I interviewed were not impacted by the recession, but several took glancing blows and a few took direct hits. No wonder they turned to Grandma for assistance.

Support from the US Welfare State and Employers

Neither the US welfare state nor US employers have been very responsive to the needs of young working families.[21] Compared to most European nations, the US welfare state provides little support for families as they grow, and this explains part of the reliance on grandmothers. Comparisons of different country policies have found that where state supports are more extensive, grandparents provide less care; where state supports are meager, grandparents provide much more support.[22] The United States provides no federal guarantees for paid vacations, paid sick leave, flexible work schedules, paid family leave, universal health insurance, affordable daycare, or universal access to preschool programs. Many workers receive some benefits through their employers, but these benefits are more readily available to full-time workers with higher salaries and lengthier tenure on the job. Moreover, such coverage has been shrinking in recent years.[23]

Although 127 countries guarantee paid vacations, the United States has no federal vacation policy. The net effect is that paid time off is unequally distributed for US workers. One-third of female workers and one-quarter of male workers do not earn any paid vacation days. In fact, among all working parents, only about 60 percent receive them.[24] Latinos are only one-half as likely as whites, blacks, and Asians to have those benefits. Lower-income families are the hardest hit. Of working parents in the bottom quintile of earnings, only 27 percent have paid vacations. By contrast, of working parents in the top two earnings quintiles, 76 percent have paid vacations. Vacations have been linked to higher employee satisfaction and productivity, better physical and emotional health, and stronger family bonds. Additionally, many working parents and grandparents use paid vacation days to schedule time off on days the children would otherwise need child care.[25] Those without paid vacation time have one less option for providing child-care coverage throughout the year.

Similarly, the United States does not guarantee workers any amount of paid sick leave. Workers receive more or less generous packages through their employers. Ultimately, 44 million US workers do not have paid sick days. Among working parents, only about 60 percent have paid sick leave, and for Latinos that rate is only about 30 percent.[26] Of working parents in the lowest earnings quintile, only 24 percent receive paid sick days, compared to 75 percent in the upper two earnings quintiles. Workers use sick days to cover their own, and their children's or grandchildren's, illnesses. Those without paid sick days must either go to work when they or their children are ill, or they take time off with lost wages.

Moreover, the United States does not guarantee flexible work schedules and, as a result, few women are able to negotiate such arrangements. Even the best-educated and highest-paid women are often unable to negotiate a flexible schedule when they have children. Only about 50 percent of US workers have flexible hour plans that allow them to rearrange their work schedules, 40 percent have flexible day plans that allow them to alter which days they work, and 25 percent have flexible location plans that allow them to work from home or another location.[27] These types of flexible work rules allow parents or grandparents to rearrange their work time to accommodate their children's or grandchildren's snow days, vacation days, early release days, sick days, and all other sorts of irregularities without losing pay or losing their jobs.

The United States does little to regulate the work week. Many people work much more than a 40-hour work week. Recent time-use studies suggest Americans work more than employees in any other country, and this makes balancing carework and paid work all the more difficult. By contrast, Great Britain has taken steps to regulate the work week and to make more reduced and part-time work available; children have fared better in terms of health, education, and welfare under these types of national regulations.[28] On the internationally comparative scale of the well-being of young people, Britain moved from 17th place in 2001 to 12th place in 2006.

The lack of guaranteed paid maternity leave may be what hits US families hardest. Figure 1.4 shows the weeks of guaranteed paid family leave that are available in 21 countries. Only the United States has zero weeks of federally guaranteed paid leave. Jody Heymann and her colleague Kristin McNeill found that of the countries they studied, 180 offer paid leave to new mothers and 81 offer paid leave to new fathers.[29]

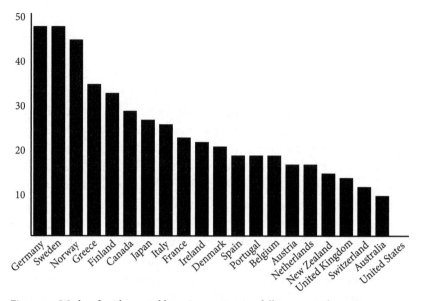

Figure 1.4. Weeks of paid parental leave in 21 countries, fulltime equivalents. *Source*: Boushey and Glynn 2012.

The only federal US provisions for family leave fall under the umbrella of the US Family and Medical Leave Act, which offers 12 weeks of unpaid leave. However, less than one-half of US workers are able to make use of it either because an employer is exempted for being too small, they have not worked at that firm for a full year, they do not work enough hours, the care recipient does not meet the qualifying criteria (same-sex partners or in-laws are not covered), or they cannot afford time off without pay.[30]

Those with lower incomes and who are single parents, who are least likely to be able to afford time off without pay, are least likely to take the leaves. Only 39 percent of workers earning less than $20,000 a year are covered by this law, compared to 74 percent of those earning more than $100,000.[31] Although some women are offered paid maternity leave by their employers, this has dropped from 27 percent of working women in 1998 to only 16 percent in 2008.[32] Coverage for paid maternity leave varies markedly by the worker's education. The US Census reports that between 2006 and 2008, 66 percent of new mothers with at least a bachelor's degree were able to take paid leave, up from just 15 percent in the early 1960s.[33] By comparison, just 19 percent of new mothers with less than a high school diploma were able to take paid leave, the same rate of coverage as in the early 1960s.

The United States and South Africa are the only industrialized nations without a universal health insurance program; thus, access to health insurance is difficult for many families to sustain. Families are pressured to obtain health insurance through their jobs. The trouble is, access to health insurance through jobs is on the decline, leaving some 18 percent of those under age 65, or over 40 million Americans, uninsured and many more stuck in jobs that make it difficult to balance work and family.[34] Whenever Americans change jobs, end marriages, or develop preexisting conditions, their access to health insurance is at risk. To the extent that it may make employment precarious, taking time off from paid work to care for children or grandchildren may also increase the likelihood of becoming uninsured. To the extent that working parents and grandparents feel compelled to take jobs that offer health insurance, rather than jobs that offer the flexibility to care for family members, the lack of universal health care may impede their ability to provide care.

Despite the increasing demand, there has been little increase in the supply of flexible, affordable, high-quality child care. In 2005, about one-fourth of children of employed mothers were in organized child-care facilities, and one-fifth were cared for regularly by grandparents.[35] Child care is often difficult to find, expensive, and of variable quality. Harriet Presser points out that those with irregular work patterns, who may require child care during late afternoons, evenings, or on only a part-time or rotational basis, often find that there are few organized child-care options available.[36] Moreover, when children are sick, they are not permitted at daycare and working parents have to make other arrangements or stay home from work. Or call Grandma.

The costs for child care can add up, eroding family earnings. Most families struggle to cope with what Jonathan Cohn calls the "bruising financial burden."[37] According to Linda Giannarelli and James Barsimantov, family daycare expenses are often the second largest household expense, after the house mortgage.[38] High-quality daycare through the private market is so expensive that families are increasingly being encouraged to pay for it through bank loans.[39] The state provides some supports for families. Middle-income families may be eligible for tax subsidies through the dependent care tax credit. Low-income families may be eligible for tax credits and subsidized child care, but only about 15 percent of those entitled to subsidized daycare actually receive assistance. Waiting lists for subsidized daycares and preschools are often so long that some children would be of high school age by the time they would be admitted.[40]

Finally, concerns about the quality of child care persist. Deborah Lowe Vandell and Barbara Wolfe show that care is variable and often only fair to poor in quality.[41] The National Institute of Child Health and Human Development established standards for care and reported that most daycare settings do not meet them.[42] Only 10 percent of the daycare settings that the institute evaluated provided what it deemed high-quality care. Some of the grandmothers I interviewed are so disturbed by the quality of daycare that they provide grandchild care to keep their grandchildren out of daycare.

Although many experts have called for universal, full-day, preschool for all children ages 3 or 4 and older, little progress has been made on this front. Advocates suggest that universal preschool is cost-effective for kids and parents, may increase academic performance, and may reduce reliance on welfare, teen pregnancy, and criminal behavior. President Barack Obama promised federal dollars to states that would expand their preschool programs. The RAND Corporation, using an experimental design, showed that the investment of $12,000 per preschool student provided benefits of $25,000 over a 20-year period. These benefits included higher grade retention and high school graduation rates, less of a need for special education, lower arrest rates, better employment rates, less welfare use, and higher earnings.[43] Preschool provides parents with high-quality, low-cost daycare that enables them to work. Some states have universal preschool, and to implement one that covers 3- and 4-year-olds nationwide is estimated to cost between $40 and $50 billion dollars annually.

The paucity of paid vacation, paid sick leave, flexible work schedules, paid maternity leave, universal health insurance, affordable daycare, or universal preschool—either through the US welfare state or through employer benefit programs—leaves many families turning to grandparents for assistance with child care. Ben Bernanke points out that the situation may be even more dire for some because the US economy has been weak for the past decade.[44] In the wake of high unemployment and layoff rates, workers who try to take time off for their kids may be particularly vulnerable. While grandmothers are not likely to have particularly good benefits, many of the grandmothers I interviewed noted that they have often been in their jobs longer and may be better able than their daughters to negotiate work and family responsibilities without risk of losing their jobs.

Theoretical Images of Grandmothering

Several theoretical perspectives are useful in analyzing how working grandmothers balance work and grandchild care. No matter how much fun it may be, caring for grandchildren is a form of work. Grandmothering is unpaid carework that is best understood from a lifecourse approach. There are many rewards to grandchild care, but it is still the case that it is women who are primarily expected to juggle roles of paid and unpaid work. For some, these multiple roles lead to role enhancement and, for others, to role stress. In the end, the consequences of carework generally, and grandchild care specifically, are mixed in terms of financial, emotional, social, and physical well-being. Those with the most resources and those providing the least intensive forms of support fare best; those with the fewest resources and those providing the most intensive forms of support would benefit most from federal policies that would support working families at all stages across the lifecourse.

Carework. Theories of carework are central to our understanding of how many women, and a growing share of men, of any age balance work and family responsibilities. Indeed, all of us need care at certain points in our life: when young, ill, disabled, or frail in old age. Responsibility for caring varies over time and by country.[45] Grandparents are increasingly becoming the caregivers. One study found that the second most important reason grandparents were caring for their grandkids was to spend more time with them.[46] The most important reason was that they were needed to provide care so the children's parents could work. For some, providing care was a necessity, not a choice. And with that carework comes a variety of joys and frustrations.

Lifecourse Approach. To fully assess the positive and negative impacts of being a working grandmother who cares for her grandchildren, I

employ a lifecourse perspective that emphasizes the long-term implications of factors such as historical events, cohort differences, timing
and sequencing of personal decisions, and structural opportunities.[47]
An emphasis on the lifecourse highlights the cumulative effects of various choices, opportunities, policies, and programs at different stages of
life. A lifecourse approach allows us to analyze the sort of every-day
juggling between paid and unpaid work that women undertake across
the lifecourse.[48] Each stage may present different issues. Young mothers,
who may be newly employed or just establishing careers, face different sets of issues than grandmothers, who may be more secure in their
positions or are more willing to trade flexibility for lower pay and fewer
benefits. Similarly, a lifecourse approach allows us to analyze not just
the immediate impact of carework, but also the long-term impact of
carework on financial, emotional, social, and physical well-being.

Some women may have a single stage of life where they are providing care for others; some women seem to be sequential careworkers,
providing care to others at every stage of their lifecourse. The working
grandmothers I interviewed had all already cared for their children as
they raised them and now were caring for their grandchildren as they
helped to raise them. While some described breaks between the epi-
sodes, many described a lifetime of carework, caring for the generations
before and after them in an endless sequence. The costs incurred at any
one stage may not seem like much, but the cumulative impact of carework over the lifecourse may become substantial in the form of reduced
savings, limited social lives, emotional stresses, and physical limitations. This book demonstrates that while many working grandmothers
are readily able to absorb these impacts, others struggle to find enough
minutes and dollars to cover the needs of so many generations.

Rewards of Carework. Carework may well be the single most rewarding form of work many humans ever perform. Given that it is rarely
externally rewarded, Nancy Folbre points out, it is mainly prompted by
intrinsic rewards.[49] What makes carework different from other sorts of
work, such as raking the leaves or flipping burgers, is that often, though
certainly not always, the careworker has strong feelings of love or affec-
tion for the care recipient. Thus while it is work to cook, clean, bathe,
or change diapers, the drudgery of repetitive tasks is often offset by the
warm feelings of knowing you are doing it for someone whom you love.

Spending time together, taking care of daily needs, and handling problems as they arise may strengthen bonds and deepen joy.[50]

Care provided by grandparents may be particularly rewarding because many grandparents feel such powerful feelings for their grandchildren and because those feelings are often exuberantly mutual. It is one thing to love your granddaughter so much and quite another to know just how much she loves you right back as she leaps into your outstretched arms. This book tells many stories but the central story is one of joy. Though there are some limits and complications, every grandmother I interviewed loves spending time with, and taking care of, her grandchildren. But I only interviewed grandmothers who were providing some care for their grandchildren. I did not interview grandmothers who did not provide care for their grandchildren. Their stories are likely very different.

Gendered Expectations. Though men have increased carework in virtually all venues, most studies still show that women do about twice as much carework for children, the disabled, and the frail elderly.[51] When it comes to grandparenting, the ratio is also about two to one. The gendered expectation that women will provide care more so than men remains stubborn. So does the gendered expectation that women will absorb the financial, emotional, social, and physical costs of providing carework.[52] Folbre suggests that though the pressures on women to perform caring labor have dissipated somewhat, many still tend to perform this intrinsically motivated, but poorly rewarded, work because of our lingering ideas about women's roles and the proper care of families.[53] Indeed very few of the women I interviewed ever mentioned or complained about the expectation that as women they were expected to perform what society still mainly defines as women's work.

But not all women are suited to the prevailing images of motherhood—and not all grandmothers are suited to the prevailing images of grandmotherhood.[54] Andrew Cherlin and Frank Furstenberg found that while many grandparents are either companionable or highly involved, many grandparents are remote and uninvolved.[55] The National Association of Child Care Resources and Referral Agencies (NACCRRA) found that, even among those who live in the same neighborhood as their grandchildren, one-half of grandparents did provide grandchild care but fully one-half did not provide any grandchild care.[56]

When First Lady Michelle Obama's mother moved into the White House to help raise Obama's two daughters, Joanne Kaufman wrote an article for the *New York Times* about grandmothers who did not want a hands-on role.[57] She reported that one grandmother had told her daughter that she did not like newborns. Another grandmother had encouraged her daughter to bottlefeed and then, when she continued to nurse, went to the porch for another cigarette. One daughter reported that she purposely lived near her mother with the expectation that she would provide grandmother care. She did not. Though all of the grandmothers interviewed for my book were actively providing grandchild care, some made comments that were similar to those in the *New York Times* article. Despite the rhetoric of choice, many careworkers feel obliged, needed, even forced, to provide care.[58] While some of the grandmothers I interviewed readily adopt an intensive grandmothering posture, even when doing so is decidedly disadvantageous by some measures, others balk at taking on these unpaid, gendered labors that interfere with their own financial, emotional, social, and physical plans.

Intensive Grandmothering. Just as motherhood has become more intense in the United States,[59] grandmothering may be intensifying. Numerous scholars have noted that as mothers of younger children have increased paid work hours, they have also actively increased purposive child nurturing and cultivation to better prepare their children as competitive adults.[60] Rather than playing outside, US children are increasingly being shuttled from piano lessons to soccer camp and Spanish lessons.

Historically, the role of grandmothers has been traditionally defined very differently than that for mothers. Certainly, most of the grandmothers I interviewed thought the roles should be defined differently. Grandmothers, they told me, are supposed to take kids for ice cream, bike rides, and fun walks while mothers are supposed to worry about proper nutrition, good manners, and algebra. Typically, grandparents were meant to augment childrearing and not be responsible for the basic daily care of children.[61] Traditionally, then, role differentiation was quite high.

But over the past few decades the job descriptions have become more similar. The role of grandparenting may be looking more like the role of parenting. All of the women interviewed in this book are providing basic daily care for their grandchildren—driving, feeding, bathing, dressing—at least several times a year, if not several times a week. While the intensification of mothering may be fueled mainly by changing cultural expectations, the intensification of grandmothering may be fueled, at least in part, by unmet need. Given the rise in the numbers of working parents and single parents, and the paucity of federal programs that provide job security or paid time off for family responsibilities, grandmothering may be intensifying because young working families need the help.

With only four exceptions, the grandmothers I interviewed are providing more care than their own mothers did and more care than they expected to provide. In addition to feeding, bathing, and tucking in, grandmothers are driving kids to lessons and camps, helping with homework, and watching kids for weeks, months, and even years at a time. Those helping grandchildren with special needs take on even more intensive carework, including therapies, physician visits, and medications. Developmental disabilities are on the rise in the United States, up 14 percent between 1997 and 2008, with a nearly 300 percent increase in autism.[62] Of the 48 grandmothers I interviewed, seven were caring for grandchildren with disabilities. Given the increase in working, and also single, mothers, more families are turning to grandmothers for assistance with special needs. Many are taking the intensification of grandmothering duties in stride while some are wishing they were doing a lot less mothering and a lot more traditional or old-fashioned grandmothering. Some ache to replace daily care with the fun things they had hoped to do as grandmothers, such as taking children on trips to the library, zoo, or beach.

In its most negative form, intensive grandmothering may be enabling. I never asked any questions about enabling, but one-third of the women brought up the issue during the interviews. It is important to remember that this is not a random sample and therefore it does not represent the incidence of enabling nationwide. It is also important to remember that this means that two-thirds did not bring up enabling. Two-thirds felt that they were providing the appropriate amount of support and that their adult children were responsible, even admirable, parents. But one-third worried they were providing too much support, enabling their adult children to be irresponsible parents. Some grandmothers say they are providing entirely too much support for their adult children and grandchildren.

They are quick to say their own parents never would have helped them in this way. They say they know they are enabling, and their partners and friends and coworkers remind them about this constantly. But they are unable or unwilling to stop, even though they can see that their constant bailouts are permitting their adult children to behave irresponsibly. Why don't they stop? Because they do not want their grandchildren to do without or to suffer the consequences of their parents' inadequacies.

Role Stress or Role Enhancement. Different carework roles present different challenges and generate different impacts.[63] Those who care for young children face very different rewards and challenges than those who care for chronically or terminally ill adults. Those who work and provide care face multiple responsibilities. The impact of being both employed and carers for grandchildren is not well studied or understood. The growing share of working grandmothers who provide care for their grandchildren may find that competing responsibilities are impacting their financial, emotional, social, or physical well-being. By assessing the impact of multiple social roles over time, role stress theory suggests that roles conflict and may lead to overload, with adverse impacts on finances or health. Thus, grandmothers who are employed, caring for grandchildren, and perhaps also caring for frail parents may face more financial difficulties or health complications.

By contrast, role enhancement theory suggests that roles such as employment may buffer the impact of roles such as carework or vice versa.[64] Grandmothers who juggle multiple roles may find that the variety of their duties minimizes the adverse health effects of any one of the duties. Those with multiple roles may enjoy better finances and health. The grandmothers I interviewed reported plenty of both role stress and role enhancement, often simultaneously. Ultimately the impact depends on what resources they have and what level of support they are providing. Grandmothers with better health and more resources, including helpful partners, and those who are providing less intensive support, are more likely to find that the roles enhance each other.

The Sandwich Generation. One particular incidence of role stress that social theorists have focused on often is that of women in the middle, or the sandwich generation. Generally, this group is defined as women who are caring for both their adult children and their own parents. Research shows that their efforts to balance unpaid carework and paid work may lead to more negative financial and health impacts.[65] Little attention has been paid to a different sort of sandwich generation: women who are in the middle of caring for their own parents, adult children, and grandchildren. This is a club sandwich of carework. While it is not particularly common, the interviews in this book show that balancing this many roles and paid work can be all-consuming and exhausting.

The Impact of Work and Grandchild Care

In general, research shows that the impact of any kind of carework on women's finances, and emotional, social, and physical well-being, is mixed. Some studies show positive outcomes, others show no significant outcomes, and still others show negative outcomes.[66] To the extent that careworkers juggle competing responsibilities by reducing work hours, passing up opportunities for training and advancements, or leaving work altogether, we are concerned about the economic impacts of carework. To the extent that careworkers have less time to care for themselves and become exhausted by caring for others, we are concerned about the emotional, social, and health impacts of carework. Though grandmothers may love spending time with their grandchildren, they may find that juggling paid work and frequent intensive care for grandchildren puts too big a strain on their economic and health resources. Providing the right amount of the right types of care for grandchildren may leave working grandmothers rejuvenated and fulfilled; providing too much of the more intensive types of care may leave working grandmothers depleted and exhausted.

Economic Impacts. There are two main ways that carework may negatively affect financial security for careworkers: reducing hours of paid work and giving money to those in other generations. While some studies show few economic impacts of carework, others show that working women caring for family members, particularly those caring for multiple generations, may reduce hours, refuse or limit travel, switch to more flexible jobs, decline promotions, lose benefits, and even leave the labor force.[67] In the short run they are more likely to have reduced hourly wages, reduced annual wages, greater reliance on public assistance, and depleted savings. In the long run, caring for those who need care may lead to smaller Social Security pensions, fewer and smaller private pensions, less private savings, and greater reliance on public assistance in old age.[68] The short- and long-term economic consequences of caring for a frail older relative tend to hit poor, single, and black and Hispanic women hardest. They are more likely to provide care, provide more hours of care, and reduce work hours.[69] Indeed, the cumulative life-course impact of many small decisions that help balance work and kids or grandkids may grow quite large by middle and old age.

The economic impact on careworkers is compounded when they give money to those in other generations. In addition to giving hours of care, many careworkers also give dollars to those they are caring for, covering a wide variety of expenses. For example, those who care for older family members spend an average of 10 percent of their annual income to provide financial support to the older generation; 34 percent use savings to provide support.[70] Whether or not they are providing child care, many grandparents provide financial support for their adult children and grandchildren.[71] Grandparents typically give gifts, even lavish gifts. Some help with one-time expenses like college, a first car, or a first home. Others help with daily and monthly expenses, such as rent, electricity, food, clothes, diapers, calculators, child care, and much more. For those who are simultaneously cutting back on paid work to provide grandchild care, and providing support for routine expenses, the financial repercussions may be enormous. Those with greater resources and supports may be better able to absorb such expenditures while those with fewer resources may become impoverished or go into debt. Studies suggest that the amount of financial support, and the impact of that support, may vary by gender, race, class, and marital status.[72] Among the working grandmothers I interviewed for this book, some sail through the competing demands of employment and grandmothering with few economic concerns while others find that the needs and demands of their children and grandchildren have outpaced their resources. Some have given all, and even more than, they have.

Emotional, Social, and Physical Well-being Impacts. Research on the impact of carework on working women's emotional, social, and physical well-being is also mixed. Some studies show few negative impacts while others show substantial negative impacts.[73] The literature is difficult to untangle because many studies do not clearly differentiate between working and nonworking care providers or custodial and noncustodial grandparents. Some studies suggest that caring for grandchildren, regardless of employment status, may have many positive effects on grandparents, including feelings of being needed and useful, a more active and involved social life, and better mental and physical health.[74] But many studies suggest that working and caring for grandchildren, whether custodial or not, may lead to stress on the job; less free time for exercise, rest, and proper health care; and competing demands between generations for care. Caring for grandchildren is also linked to higher rates of a variety of health problems, including heart disease, high blood pressure, diabetes, and depression.[75] The negative consequences of grandchild care on health may be more pronounced for grandparents who are women, black or Hispanic, less educated, poorer, and custodial or coresidential.[76] Recent work shows that most of the negative effects occur during the transitions into and out of grandchild care and are linked to differences that preceded the carework, gender, race, class, and coresidence.[77]

In the end, caring for grandchildren while employed may affect economic security, and emotional, social, and physical well-being, in ways that are mixed and that vary by race, class, and marital status.[78] Folbre points out that the mixed findings on the impact of carework may be due to the fact that the impact of carework truly is mixed.[79] The positive rewards of carework are often offset or balanced by the stresses and burdens generated by carework. There are simultaneously pros and cons. Moreover, Folbre suggests that those who choose to provide care are probably quite different from those who choose not to provide care, so the mixed impacts are also linked to matters of selectivity.

Among the grandmothers I interviewed, many were bone-tired after a weekend with the grandkids and yet they were facing an evening's worth of neglected laundry and dishes before they went to work the following morning. But they were also elated at having spent time in the park, or reading a book, or sharing a meal with their grandchildren. For some, notably those with better health and more resources, greater income, and willing partners, the joys of grandmothering outweigh the exhaustions. But for others, sustaining the work and stresses of multiple roles is detrimental and may well be untenable. Given the lack of federal support on these issues, and given that a growing share of grandmothers remain in the labor force, it is important to more fully understand the links between employment, grandchild care, and financial and health security.

Methods and Data

Grandmas at Work Survey. To write this book, I needed to talk with working grandmothers who also cared for their grandchildren. I designed a survey that would enable me to ask a series of questions. I wanted to determine how middle-aged women balance hours of work and hours of grandchild care. I interviewed 48 women across the United States who were employed (for any number of hours) and who cared for grandchildren (for any number of hours). The Grandmas at Work Survey is described in more detail in the appendix. Table A.1 provides a list of the aliases and sociodemographic information for each woman. Table A.2 provides summary statistics for the sample. Of the 48 women I interviewed, 77 percent are white, 67 percent are married, 81 percent have at least some college education, 79 percent live in the northeast, and 81 percent work at least 40 hours a week.

Though an ideal sample would be randomly selected, there was no mechanism for drawing a random sample for this project. I employed a convenience snowball sample, asking colleagues, friends, and relatives to help me find grandmothers who were employed and caring for their grandchildren. Then I asked the women I interviewed for the names of two other grandmothers who did not know each other and who met my criteria. I emphasized variation in race, age, marital status, class, and geographic location. My response rate was 100 percent in the sense that everyone I actually managed to ask to do an interview agreed to do one. Some phones and email messages were never answered, so those grandmothers were never asked to participate. Many were grateful that someone was finally noticing that grandmothers were quietly helping to raise this next generation even as they worked to support themselves. All were happy to talk about the grandchildren who brought so much joy to their lives.

I did not interview custodial grandmothers who were legal guardians of their grandchildren. They face a special set of challenges and are the focus of many other studies. The percentage of custodial grand-parents has been rising. The US Census Bureau American Community Survey reports that in 2007 about 6.2 million grandparents lived with their grandchildren and about 2.5 million of them were responsible for the care of their grandchildren. Roughly 2 percent of US children are being raised by their grandparents. My sample does not include cus-todial grandmothers, but my sample does include some grandmothers who live with grandchildren and even a few with temporary custody.

Most of the interviews were done face-to-face in the grandmothers' homes, workplaces, or coffee shops of their choosing. Some were done by phone when I could not arrange to fly to them or if they preferred a phone interview. Each interview lasted about one hour and I tran-scribed as we talked, typing the words on my flamingo pink Dell laptop. The questions were all open-ended except a few multiple-choice ques-tions that I asked everyone at the end. My first objective was to get a sense of their work, marital, and childrearing histories. How did they balance work and children when their own children were young and how did they balance their current work and grandchild duties? My second objective was to get a sense of the impact of being middle-aged and working and caring for grandchildren on their financial, emotional, social, and physical well-being. How did they think these responsibili-ties affected their workouts, free time, marriages, friendships, and travel or retirement plans?

Few of the grandmothers were interested in confidentiality, but I offered and delivered it nonetheless. Grandmothers signed a standard consent form at the interview and in it I told them that I would protect their identities. In my analysis, I gave each grandmother an alias, and I have been purposefully vague about where each lives and works. In the interest of simplicity and confidentiality, I have replaced the first names of family members with their relationships to the grandmother. So "George" becomes "my husband," "Kelly" becomes "my daughter," and "Ari" becomes "my grandson." Otherwise, words appear here verbatim.

Health and Retirement Survey 2010. Because the grandmothers I interviewed were not randomly selected and did not provide a nation-ally representative picture, I also analyzed the HRS 2010 data to provide a sense of how many grandmas in the United States were working and tending grandchildren, what determines who did so, and the impact of balancing both roles. Though the quantitative data only address some of the themes addressed in the qualitative data, I wove these data in with the individual stories to provide a sense of how common a particular theme is and to identify when relationships are statistically significant.

Grandmothers at Work

Using qualitative data from 48 in-depth interviews with working grandmothers who care for their grandchildren, and nationally representative data of grandmothers ages 51–70 from the HRS, I explore how working grandmothers juggle their roles and the impact of that juggling. Chapter 2 focuses on the main theme of every interview: joy and second chances. For many grandmothers, the rewards for providing care are tremendous. The grandmothers I interviewed, to a person, felt tremendous happiness when spending time with, or even talking about, their grandkids. Regardless how difficult the circumstances or demands, they loved this time with the grandkids. As a lifecourse perspective reveals, for many it provided a second chance to enjoy raising kids without so many competing pressures or concerns about shortcomings.

Chapter 3 describes how grandmothering in the United States, like mothering, is becoming more intensive. Though the roles of grandmothers were traditionally clearly differentiated from the roles of mothers, those boundaries are blurring. Nearly all of the grandmothers described doing more than their own mothers did, and more than they had intended to do. While mothering may be more intense due to evolving cultural expectations, grandmothering may be becoming more intense due to a combination of cultural expectations and unmet need. Younger families that struggle to make ends meet or balance multiple responsibilities may ask grandmothers for assistance with child care, and grandmothers often say yes. They are often prompted by family legacies, a sense of duty, or the need for their intervention. I found that when the demands get tough, so do the grandmothers.

Chapter 4 explores how working grandmothers balance paid work and unpaid carework. Some have understanding bosses and lax workplace guidelines, while others have to proceed with much more caution. In either case, however, nearly all frequently rearrange their work schedules, use paid vacation and sick days, and bring work home or return to work late to be available to provide grandchild care. Some even change jobs, exchanging higher pay and better benefits for greater flexibility. Such rearranging of work schedules may lead to lower income and fewer fringe benefits in the short run, as well as fewer savings, assets, and pensions in the long run. Working grandmothers would benefit if they, and their adult children, had more generous federally guaranteed paid time off for vacation, sick time, and family leaves. Working grandmothers would also benefit if universal health care, high-quality and low-cost child care, and universal preschool were more readily available.

Chapter 5 explores the delicate matter of finances. Though none of the grandmothers I interviewed are paid for their services, nearly all provide financial assistance to their children and grandchildren. Some limit their contributions to gifts and splurges but many also cover monthly bills and daily necessities. Some can readily afford these contributions but many are diverting money from their own retirement funds, depleting their nest eggs, or incurring new debts in their efforts to support the next generations. The financial implications of intensive grandmothering are more pronounced for grandmothers who earn a lower income or are single.

Chapter 6 looks at factors that limit grandchild care. Some grandmothers have actively taken steps to reduce how much care they are providing. Some are protecting their time, interests, and plans. A few resist the gendered expectations that as women they should provide care and absorb the impact on their financial, emotional, social, and physical well-being. Some cleverly work more than they want, or need, to with the goal of being unavailable for grandchildren. Others have partners who cannot or do not or will not assist in caring for the grandchildren. Often there are resentments when one grandparent wants to provide more care than the other. Finally, a small percentage of the grandmothers limit grandchild care because they are caring for frail older relatives. They are in a new sort of sandwich generation in which they care for their adult children, young grandchildren, and frail older parents. For the most part, their energies and resources are exhausted.

Chapters 7 and 8 explore the impact of balancing paid employment and unpaid grandchild care on emotional, social, and physical well-being. Multiple roles may lead to stress or they may enhance each other.

Indeed, I found that the impacts are mixed. Many, though certainly not all, of the grandmothers report very positive emotional rewards. They feel richly appreciated and their spirits soar with the knowledge that they are providing much-needed and highly valued care. Some see little appreciation expressed by their adult children. About one-third struggle with the worry that they are providing too much care and enabling their adult children to be irresponsible. A few worry that that their adult children are fighting with each other over whether grand-mother care is equal or proper. Finally, the social and health impacts of working and caring for grandchildren are also mixed. Some integrate grandchild care into hectic social lives while others eliminate nearly all social obligations to focus exclusively on the grandkids. Similarly, some integrate active grandchild care into an already healthy and active life-style while others forego their own proper diets, exercise regimes, or doctor visits to focus on the grandchildren. Ultimately, a few are simply too exhausted by the demands of paid work and unpaid carework to do anything else and, as a result, neglect their own emotional, social, and physical health.

Few of the grandmothers complained about, or even mentioned, the presence or absence of national policies that would support working families. Most saw the problems, and the solutions, as family matters. But given the increases in single parenting, working women of all ages, and the intensification of mothering and grandmothering, national policies that ensure that all workers have paid time off for vacation, sick days, family leave, and flexible scheduling, coupled with universal health insurance, readily available and low-cost daycare, and universal preschool, would enable parents to rely less on grandmothers for child care and would permit grandmothers to serve more as grandmothers and less as mothers.

2

Joys and Second Chances

Much is said about the negative aspects of carework, but the working grandmothers I interviewed who care for their grandchildren reap tremendous positive rewards. Indeed, to talk to these 48 grandmothers is to talk to 48 women who know joy. To a person, the grandmothers I interviewed are happy to spend time with their grandchildren. Many, but certainly not all, like the balance of work and grandchild care, feeling that the roles enhance rather than stress them.

Paula, a 48-year-old, divorced, black woman from a northeastern city with four children and seven grandchildren, balances many roles. But when it comes to caring for her grandchildren, she sums it up with just a few words: "It's joy. Pure joy." Similarly, Lucinda is one of several grandmothers who rearranges her life to spend as much time as possible with the grandchildren because she enjoys it. A white 52-year-old, who works full-time as a physical therapist, a job she absolutely loves, Lucinda feels great happiness when with her granddaughter. When her only granddaughter was born, she rearranged her schedule to take every Wednesday off. For the last two years she has been a Wednesday grandma. Every Wednesday Lucinda, and her elderly mother, drive an hour and spend the day caring for Lucinda's granddaughter. They attend classes, take walks, supervise baths, read books, and play all day. While the granddaughter naps they clean, vacuum, and prepare meals. But they don't do laundry. Ever. Sometimes on weekends, Lucinda and her husband keep their granddaughter for the evening or for overnights. Lucinda has planned to use a week of vacation to watch her granddaughter so that her daughter and son-in-law can go on a trip. She spends as much time with her granddaughter as she possibly can.

> I enjoy being able to take care of my granddaughter. A lot of grandparents don't have the option, either due to proximity or finances. I feel fortunate that I am able to do it. I have the best of both worlds. I have a career, a family, and I can tend to them when I want, and I still have leisure time. I am wondering where to fit sleep in! I think it makes me feel younger.

Lucinda's daughter and son-in-law tried to buy a house nearer Lucinda but prices were too steep. They finally purchased a home near his parents. Initially his parents took care of the granddaughter one day a week and occasionally on weekends but, for reasons Lucinda does not know, they are no longer willing to do so. Lucinda and her husband are happy to fill in. She knows this time with her young granddaughter is fleeting and she grabs every opportunity.

> She will be going to school soon and then I will not have those days. It changes so quickly. My advice to grandparents is just go ahead and put things on the back burner while the babies are young. You will have more than enough time later. They grow up fast. . . . My mom and my husband always try to get their time with her but I tell them to step away from the baby. We fight over time with her. My daughter does worry about me in that she wants to be sure I get my time with my granddaughter. So she says: I am offering this up before I ask someone else. She knows I want to take care of her. And so she offers me the opportunities. She makes sure I get first chance, but she has other options.

As soon as they are financially able to do so, Lucinda and her husband are going to reduce from full-time to part-time work so that they can spend more time with their granddaughter. There is talk of a second child and for Lucinda that baby can not come soon enough. She would like to sell her house and move closer to the grandchildren and care for them three days a week and work only two days a week.

For those who accept the position, providing care to grandchildren may provide many positive rewards.[1] Grandmothers tend to love their grandchildren. No matter how hard they work at the office, no matter how frustrated they are with their adult children, no matter how tired they are at the end of the day, the grandmothers I interviewed typically want time with their grandkids. For many, grandmothering is more fun than mothering ever was; often it provides a second chance to make up for some voids earlier in their lives. Whatever the situation, for many grandmothers in the United States the main reward of caring for grandkids is joy. Not all grandmothers provide care for their grandchildren, but for those who do, this chapter explores the rewards of carework when the recipients are their own grandkids.

Who Provides Grandchild Care?

To understand who is more likely to provide care on the national level, I analyzed the Health and Retirement Survey (HRS) 2010 data. I used the portion of the survey that provides a nationally representative sample of men and women ages 51–70 who were grandparents who cared for their grandchildren while employed.[2] Figure 2.1 shows the total for men and women combined, excluding those who are living in an institution or who are custodial grandparents. Among all those ages 51–70, 27 percent were not grandparents, 41 percent were grandparents who did not provide any hours of care for their grandchildren during the preceding two years, and 32 percent were grandparents who provided at least some care for their grandchildren.

Figure 2.2 shows that among all men and women combined, of those who have a grandchild, 53 percent were not working, 5 percent were working fewer than 20 hours a week, and 41 percent were working 20 or more hours a week. Finally, of those who had a grandchild and were employed, 13 percent were working fewer than 20 hours a week and 87 percent were working at least 20 hours a week. As Figure 2.3 shows, among those who are employed and who have grandchildren, 45 percent provided care for their grandchildren for at least some hours during the preceding two years.

Because this book focuses on grandmothers, and generally grandmothers are more likely to provide care and to provide more hours of care, I reexamined the HRS 2010 data by looking just at women. Figure 2.1 shows that among women ages 51–70, who were not living in

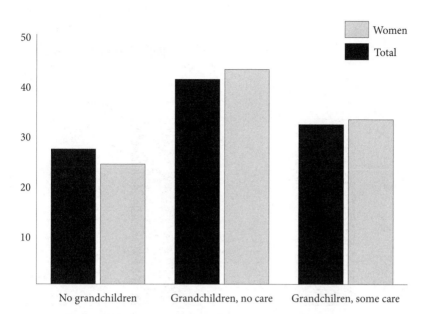

Figure 2.1. Percentages for those providing grandchild care, men and women, ages 51–70, who are noninstitutionalized or noncustodial. *Source*: HRS 2010, weighted.

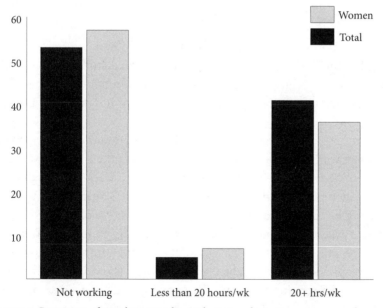

Figure 2.2. Percentage of grandparents who work, men and women, ages 51–70, who are noninstitutionalized or noncustodial. *Source*: HRS 2010, weighted.

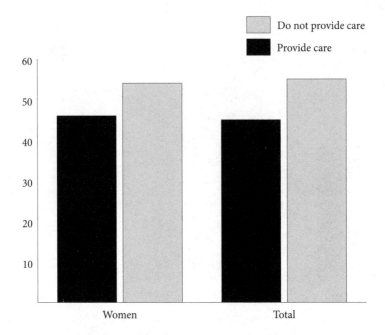

Figure 2.3. Percentage of grandparents with jobs who provide some care, men and women, ages 51–70, who are noninstitutionalized or noncustodial. *Source*: HRS 2010, weighted.

an institution or were not custodial grandmothers, 43 percent were grandmothers who provided zero hours of grandchild care during the preceding two years, and 33 percent were grandmothers who cared for their grandchildren for at least some number of hours during the preceding two years.

Figure 2.2 shows that of women who have a grandchild, 57 percent were not working, 7 percent were working fewer than 20 hours a week, and 36 percent were working 20 or more hours a week. Finally, of those who had a grandchild and were employed, 15 percent were working fewer than 20 hours a week and 85 percent were working at least 20 hours a week. As Figure 2.3 shows, the finding of importance for the book, among women who have grandchildren and were employed, 46 percent provided care for their grandchildren for at least some hours during the preceding two years. These are the women who are the subject of this book. All of the grandmothers I interviewed are within that 46 percent.

Which sociodemographic groups are most likely to provide grand-child care? Table A.4, in the appendix, evaluates the links between various sociodemographic factors and the tendency for working, noncustodial grandmothers to provide care. Among employed grandmothers, ages 51–70 in the HRS 2010, the tendency to provide care does not vary significantly by many of the factors that the literature suggests might matter. I was surprised to find, for example, that age, race, income, and hours working per week were not significantly related to whether working grandmothers provided care. Moreover, health insurance, self-rated health, the presence of mental health problems, whether they care for aging parents, and health behaviors such as smoking and drinking also did not significantly affect whether working women provided care for grandchildren.

A few factors were significantly related, though the differences were very slight. Those with more education, those who exercised more, those with functional limitations, those with fewer grandchildren, and those who were married were all very slightly more likely to provide care.

Only three factors had substantial impact on whether working grandmothers provided care. Proximity mattered: 54 percent of those who lived within 10 miles of their children, compared to 38 percent who lived farther away, provided care. Residence mattered: 74 percent of those who lived in multigenerational households, compared to 41 percent who did not, provided care. Hours spent caring for aging parents mattered as well. Ironically 62 percent of those who spent more than 100 hours caring for aged parents in the preceding two years, compared to 39 percent of those who spent fewer than 100 hours caring for aged parents, also provided care for their grandchildren. This suggests that people who provide care for one are more likely to provide care for others. Or, caregivers are caregivers.

The Joys of Grandmothering

While all types of carework have the potential to be rewarding because of the intimate relationship with the care recipient, grandmothering may well be the single most rewarding form of carework. The rewards of this type of carework became clear during the interviews.

Grandmothers sparkle when they talk about their grandkids. Their eyes well up with great big happy tears. Grandmothers love their grandchildren and they love just how much the grandkids love them back. Several told me how happy the grandkids are when Grandma walks in the door. Though they are often quite tired, grandmothers are hesitant to say no. They want time with the grandkids, and they want to help their adult children. Moreover, they are aware that these moments of joy with young grandchildren are fleeting. They are only young, and this blatantly in love with their grandmas, for a brief time.

Every grandmother I interviewed spoke of the happiness she felt just being with her grandchildren. The bonds are strong and heartfelt. Janet is a 61-year-old, white mother of two and grandmother of two. She works full-time and provides a lot of financial support, and child care, for her grandchildren. She said that she and her husband love their time with them.

> Having grandkids is the greatest thing in the world. You love them so much. So much joy! They are so fun, so exasperating, so wonderful. We love it.

Many feel lucky that they get this opportunity to be with their grandkids. Reagan is a 60-year-old, white stepmother of one and grandmother of three. She lives in the northwest where she balances full-time work with frequent weeknight and weekend care for her grandchildren. She and her husband both hope to keep up this balance for another 10 years. Like many of the grandmothers, she says she is lucky to live nearby and feels sorry for grandmothers who live far from their grandkids. She has almost daily interaction with her grandchildren.

> I have the best grandkids on the planet and I absolutely think that . . . I adore them, and I am so lucky it's not even funny.

Karen feels similarly. She is a 61-year-old white woman, and though she works full-time, she watches the grandchildren many evenings and weekends. She wishes her husband would help, but he does not. She gets tired watching three boys; one has autism and the others are 2-year-old twins. But she loves her time with them and is well aware it will not last forever.

I feel tired, but I love watching them, and watching them eat and throw food on the floor. I love when they come running to me and want to sit and cuddle. I realize that it will not last forever. They will grow up. Time passes. I want to take advantage of them while they are young and I can. I am so blessed that I have them and can spend time with them. Glad I am part of their life, not an absentee grandparent.

She is clear that she likes being the grandmother but has no desire to be the mother. Being the backup, rather than the first line of response, is her objective.

I like to go to their daycare, go to their programs, meet their teachers, be the backup if there are any problems. I like being the backup.

To a person, the working grandmothers I interviewed are tired, but they are not about to let that get in the way of time with their grand-kids. Meryl has low energy, and that worries her husband. But she does not share his concerns. Meryl is a 54-year-old, white, married registered nurse with three children and one grandson. Because her daughter became a single mother at 18, her daughter and her grand-son lived with Meryl and her husband for the first five years while she completed high school and a bachelor's degree. Meryl takes care of her grandson after work and on weekends and she finds the relation-ship is one of joy.

I feel very rejuvenated and joy-filled when I can spend time with my grandson. He makes me feel younger. He is a smart little boy and engaging. He enjoys being with us as much as we enjoy being with him. It's a mutu-ally rewarding relationship.

Working full-time and caring for her grandson exhaust her, though. Her husband tells her he is worried that she does too much for their daughter and grandson, that he is worried she is being taken advan-tage of. She, however, has no such worries. She assured me she is no doormat and that she is okay with this. In fact, she said she would quit her $70,000-a-year job and spend more time with her grandson if she could afford to do so. The joy outweighs any tiredness.

I feel tired sometimes; he is active. There are Sunday nights when we say "close the door" after they leave. There are times when we are tired. . . . I think he has a positive effect on my health. I am a nurse: I work with a lot of death and dying and my grandson brings balance to my life. He brings joy to my life. It's never too much to juggle or too tired to be with him. I am tired in the evening and if he is coming to my place and be gone by 9, that's fine. I need to have her pick him up by my bedtime as I do get up early in the morning. . . . I never foresaw this, never thought about grandchildren. I would quit work if I were financially able to do so. I love my job and enjoy it, but I would always pick my grandson over my job.

Similarly, Maggie, a 67-year-old, white, widowed mother of three and grandmother of eight, balances part-time work with many hours each week of grandchild care. Like most of the women I talked to, she gets exhausted but loves it.

I had always hoped for grandchildren. I really enjoy the kids. I love their honesty. They are so genuine.

Diane, a 55-year-old, white mother of two and grandmother of one, also gets tired but loves being with her grandchildren. She is currently married to her third husband and lives in the northeast. She works 30 hours a week on commission as an interior designer and cares for her granddaughter many of the remaining hours of the week. She has rearranged her life to spend as much time as possible with her granddaughter.

I get tired sometimes. . . . My job is very physical: I walk miles at work. And then when I babysit her on a work day, especially after work on Saturday, it's exhausting. But it's a euphoria, being a grandmother for me. It's such a gift for me to experience my children again through theirs. When I talk about my granddaughter it makes me feel weepy. I have told everybody, the love of a grandchild is the biggest love you could ever experience. Bigger than for any man, any child. It's all encompassing.

Some grandmothers define their job as having fun and not doing much work. Marta is a 54-year-old, white, married woman who works full-time as an administrative assistant. She lives in the northeast; in addition to providing increasing amounts of help for her own and her husband's parents, she cares for her two grandsons after work and on weekends. She loves her time with them and they love their time with her.

> I just play with them: I'm a leisure grandma. I just play and have fun with them . . . It's positive, because I enjoy being around them and they, I think, they enjoy being around me, too. I took the day off work last month so that my daughter could have some free time. . . . My grandson was having a great time, because he was playing on the slide and everything. Two weeks later when I saw them again he goes, "Gramma, you can take me back to McDonald's any time you want!" It was so funny how he just said that, he still remembered.

Similarly, Dana, a 48-year-old, white, divorced mother of three and grandmother of four, emphasizes fun. But she also loves just how much she helps her kids raise their families. She works full-time as a lab technician and has the grandkids at her house two or three evenings a week. Their parents work and have classes in the evening, so Dana watches them, feeds them occasionally, and otherwise just enjoys her time with them. Dana feels that it is not a duty to care for the grandchildren; rather she feels lucky she gets to spend so much time with them.

> I have them a few times a week, really. I work in the daytime and watch them in the evening. Their mother works during the daytime. And her husband is currently going to school, so he's going to college, to classes and stuff in the evening. So I wind up watching them for part of the time during the week, at night. . . . We feed them occasionally when the parents don't before they come over, but that's rare.

Dana's household income is under $20,000 a year but she has a lot of fun doing inexpensive activities with the grandkids.

> Basically they come here and we play games and that kind of thing. They don't spend the night. It's only a few hours that they're here for, not overnight. Their parents always pick them up about 10 so it's about 4 or 5 hours

a night. I never take them to doctor's appointments or anything. I'm pretty much a play gramma; we just do the fun stuff. We watch a lot of cartoons.

Her adult children have limited funds and are balancing work and school. Dana feels that if she did not care for the grandchildren her daughter and son-in-law would probably struggle to pay for babysitters.

I haven't turned them down much; I doubt they'd be too upset if I did. If they didn't have me, I don't know, they'd probably have to hire a babysitter a lot, and that would just probably be too expensive for them. It's been kind of rough for everybody lately. So, no, I don't think that would work too well if they didn't have me.

Dana rarely misses work for her grandkids because it would cut into her much-needed income. But she would be happy to care for them more during her free time, if she was needed. The days of working and caring for grandkids are long and leave her tired but fulfilled.

I'm usually pretty tired by the time mom and dad come to get them. . . . I get tired, but not stressed. Exhausted, it makes for a long day sometimes. I say it makes me fulfilled; I get to be around children. I miss being around my kids. I like having the grandkids around. It's fun. . . . I teach them to play games. Like the other night, I taught the older one to play a game I used to play with my kids. I don't remember what it's called, but you probably know it, it's the one where you use the string to make shapes with your hands and with each others' hands, you know? Whatever that's called, I taught it to her yesterday and we had a lot of fun doing that.

Dana was raised by her grandparents and she has fond memories of that time. She wants her grandchildren to have similar memories. Dana's boyfriend is also happy to have the children around and helps her care for them. Together, she says, they have a lot of fun.

My parents passed away years ago, when I was 2 and 13, so I was raised by my grandparents. . . . The main one I hang out with is my boyfriend and he's here all the time anyway. He likes it, he likes having the kids around himself, too. He wants to live vicariously through them. If he could just teach them to keep the popcorn in the bowl, he says. We give them popcorn when they come over and they're small, so they tend to make a mess, but it's fun.

Grandmothers are usually helping out two generations at once, and knowing that often increases their satisfaction with the role. Cally loves how much she helps not just her grandson but also her daughter. Cally is a 65-year-old widow who works part-time in the midwest. She has a blended family of six children and one grandchild who she says all get along great. Her daughter and 8-month-old grandson have lived with Cally since his birth because her daughter and husband divorced. Cally has several patched-together jobs that amount to about 30 hours a week, as well as a vigorous volunteer schedule restoring a local theater. But her main focus is the joy she feels helping her live-in daughter raise her son.

> It makes me feel wonderful. I love it. Welling up with tears right now. He is fun and I have fun with him. And he is cuddly and I love that. I love feeding him. The quiet time with him. I love to make him laugh. I know that eventually my daughter is going to move. And she will move far away. . . . I might move with her. . . . I like being close to them. . . . We both know that he and I have a great connection. We have bonded. And she does not want to take him away. . . . I know this moment is temporary.

It is more than the joy of being with her grandson. Cally also treasures the joy of working so well with her daughter. Over the years, Cally has cared for a lot of people as they neared death: her husband, her first partner, and both of her parents. Now she gets to provide care for someone who is well. Thriving. She and her daughter do much of the work together and trade off duties seamlessly.

> We share all the work at home. We often go shopping together. And we take turns with laundry. We just do it all, together. I never feel I am being put upon. His father takes him two afternoons a week but if he can't, then I will step in. If there is a concert, I just take him with me to the theater. He is easy and everybody loves him.

Similarly, Janelle is a 67-year-old, white, newly divorced, full-time secretary who loves time with her grandson. She also loves knowing that she is giving her daughter and son-in-law some much-needed help and some peace of mind.

> He is a happy little kid. To have him around. He is kissing now; there isn't anything better than getting his little kisses. He comes running to me at daycare, laughs and hugs me. A great warming feeling. . . . I feel that I am helping them out. They are not worried about him when I have him, and I know they are right there if I need them.

Like most grandmothers, Vanna is well aware that the grandkids are only young and only wanting to spend time with grandma once. So she watches them every chance she gets. Vanna is a 53-year-old, married mother of three and grandmother of two. She works part-time at a job that is very meaningful—helping needy people through a church—and flexible. She is rarely needed to watch the grandkids while their parents work; instead Vanna and her husband mainly babysit so the parents can go out evenings and weekends. Her daughter appreciates all that they do.

> My daughter and her husband work opposite shifts so that they can take care of them themselves. So I take care of them when they want to go out. We babysit when they go out in the evening or on the weekend. They come to my house, and spend the night, sleepovers. We do whatever they want. When they were little they wanted to play house; now they want to swim or go for walks, or read books. They read to us now.

It is clear that part of why Vanna enjoys her time with the grandkids so much is that her husband is also helpful. They love time with the grandkids so much that they have asked their daughter to always call them first, to give them first rights, so that they can spend as much time with the grandchildren as possible. Their own housekeeping has become a lower priority.

> My husband and I both take care of the kids. It's not hard to keep the house up; the grandkids help us out. They set the table. And my husband is right there with me. He will cook, clean up, set up the bed for the kids at bedtime. He plays chess and checkers with the kids. I don't get behind.

We don't have much laundry or shopping, and that is always secondary because the grandkids are here to play.

Vanna had always planned to work and babysit the grandchildren and she is very happy with her current arrangement. She hopes to keep this balance of work and grandchild care for a long time. She wants to keep her job, which pays less than $20,000 a year, in part because the work itself is so important to her, and in part because she fears that caring for the grandchildren full-time would be too tiring and not as much fun. She said she has gained weight in recent years and it is becoming more difficult to go for long walks, as she used to always do. She appreciates how active she is with the grandkids.

I love having them come over and when they are here. Whenever she asks I always say, sure, I am happy to watch them. I do get tired at the end of the day. They are much more active than me. If I had to do it full-time, that might not be so much fun. For me this is all fun. Makes me feel younger. It brings you back to the day when you were the mother of kids.

She also appreciates being the grandmother and not the mother this time around. She finds it much less stressful.

It was more stress as the mother. But now, as grandmother, you don't have the clothes and dishes to wash, and you can put all of your energy into the kids. Then when they are gone, go to bed and catch up on your sleep. . . . I look forward to having things to keep me busy. I like having something to do.

But her perfect balance of grandkids and meaningful work is about to be upset. Her husband is retiring in a few months and their house is on the market. On the plus side, he has started doing most of the housecleaning, grocery shopping, and cooking. Vanna said she feels guilty but he says she should just enjoy it. They will buy a smaller house or even rent an apartment near their grandkids and will begin spending a month or two in Florida each winter. She said her daughter and son-in-law can easily make other arrangements for the grandkids when they want to go out, but Vanna does not want to cut back on how much time she spends with the grandkids.

Even when the impacts on health and finances are high, so is the joy. Sometimes the demands on grandmothers are much greater than expected, but many choose to rise to the occasion. Gillian, a 61-year-old, black mother of two and her husband unexpectedly had to take in their two grandchildren for eight months. Balancing their jobs and the needs of two small children left them physically exhausted and financially depleted. But they enjoyed it nonetheless.

> Oh, yes, I feel so tired sometimes. I want them to go to bed, and we have to get up early; I want them to go to bed so I can go to bed. I get tired. My husband and I, we both get very tired. You don't bounce back as you get older. You get tired. It makes me feel tired, not younger or older. But I enjoy it. I just did what I had to do. The more you compliment what they are doing, the more they want to do it. They are learning something from us.

They never wanted or intended to raise the grandkids for eight months, but they enjoyed the experience. Now that the grandchildren are back with their mother, and only visiting one or two weekends a month, Gillian wishes they lived much closer.

> No, I did not imagine this at all, I thought we had raised our children and they would raise their own children. I thought the kids would visit and then go home. We did not think we would be mother and father again for eight months. It was an experience and we don't regret it. It was fun times. To sit and color and sing the ABCs again. I wish I could spend a lot more time with the grandkids but I work full-time and live 40 minutes away. I feel envy about their other grandmother who lives right there in the house with them. She isn't working. So she sees the kids all day every day.

Paula, a 48-year-old, divorced black woman who works full-time on the night shift, and then cares for grandchildren during most days and weekends, told me that though her schedule is causing her many health problems and she has been told by her doctor that she must either quit her job or quit caring for the grandkids. She will do neither. She needs the money and she treasures her time with the grandkids. She feels tremendous joy about taking care of them. In part, it is because they help to take care of her. She values the reciprocity.

One born on my birthday is so protective of me. They look out for me. I ask them to do chores and they will help. Help fold the laundry. I do most of it but they will help. If I am sick they do everything, they even try to cook. So they look after me. They are sweethearts.

For one grandmother I spoke with, caring for the grandchildren provides her with much needed joy to help her overcome the grief she suffers since the death of her daughter. At age 69, Leah is a white, widowed mother of two and grandmother of two, who works full-time. Her daughter died a few months ago and the grandchildren are with their father. Leah takes care of them as much as she can.

It's still very fresh. I miss her so much. She has two children, and they are with their father. I see them every week. I help him with the kids. He is having visa troubles.

Leah is worried that if he cannot keep his visa he will move the children with him to another country and she might not be able to see them at all. She is still grieving deeply and cried so hard that we terminated the interview. She says time with the grandchildren is the only thing getting her through her grief.

I wish I could see them all the time. But I can never take the place of their mother. And their father has his own life. I love the kids so much. I have to keep the family together. That is the only thing that keeps me going. They are the joy of my life. I can't wait to see them and they are so happy to see me.

Why does spending time with grandchildren give grandmothers so much joy? When I asked, the grandmothers rolled their eyes and pronounced that I must not have grandchildren. They are correct: I do not. But even so I realize the question is unanswerable. It is like asking why rainbows are beautiful. Grandmothers are diverse and some may feel little to no joy whether spotting a rainbow or being with their grandchildren. But those women were not in my sample. All 48 of the women I interviewed expressed joy and nearly all of their eyes welled up with tears as they did so. For many, that joy was linked to this second opportunity to spend time with children while having fewer responsibilities and stresses than the first time around.

Second Chances

A lifecourse approach to understanding grandmothers at work creates a framework from within which to understand both the motivations and impacts of carework. To understand how they feel as grandmothers it is important to understand how they felt as mothers and to glimpse how they differentiate the roles. Some of the grandmothers are accumulating joy after joy. They loved being mothers and they love the opportunity to relive that joy with grandchildren. They love grandmothering precisely because it is so similar to mothering. Others are enjoying grandmothering precisely because it is so different than parenting. Many of the grandmothers mentioned that they enjoy grandmothering more than parenting in part because they have more time. When they were mothers, they were busy balancing work, housekeeping, and child-care responsibilities around the clock. Some were focused on education and career advancements, including promotions, partnership, and tenure. As grandmothers, their jobs are for the most part secure, their children are for the most part grown and moved out, and they have a second chance to focus more on the fun, and less on the responsibilities, of raising children.

Many grandmothers were just too busy as parents to have a lot of fun. Now with more time on their hands, even though they are still working, they can take time to enjoy the grandkids. Lee is a 60-year-old, married, white mother of two and grandmother of two. She works full-time in the western United States in the court system, provides care to an older neighbor, cleans the church, and watches the grandkids three to four times a week after work and on weekends. She and her husband care for the kids together and though they are getting more tired now that they are older and there are two grandkids, they love it.

> Meals usually we do. And they love to make cookies; we'll make pie crust today. They loved using the cookie press last year so we'll bring that out again. The 3-year-old, she loves painting and Play-Doh. Last year I made some Play-Doh for her. Last year for Christmas we got her a dollhouse and

she's really enjoying it. We had to put all the small things up because her brother is moving around now. She loves setting up the dollhouse. Yeah, I really enjoy bringing out my kids' old toys and seeing them get used again.

Lee mainly spends her time with the grandchildren doing everyday sorts of activities like grocery shopping and reading.

It's fun . . . we go grocery shopping together. My granddaughter likes to ride in the carts. Last week she wanted to walk so that's more challenging. Moving around with two of them, and having to make sure she's all right walking and doesn't wander. She loves reading or to be read to. She can read after I've read the book; she can read it back to Gramma. She remembers it and the pictures. My husband and I notice how smart they are more, where we were too busy to notice how smart our kids were.

Many enjoy grandmothering in ways that they never were able to enjoy mothering. Even though she gets overwhelmed, Estelle likes that she is not as busy this second time around. Estelle is a 63-year-old white woman who works full-time, is well educated, and who divorced her abusive husband 30 years ago and has remained single. She has raised three children and provided care for six grandchildren. Despite the complexities of having her grandson and her single adult daughter move into her home recently, she feels a great deal of joy about being so close to her grandson. She is often bone-tired by the end of the day, and she worries that she is enabling her daughter to be irresponsible, but she treasures this chance to be the grandmother and not the mother.

He is a blessing: happiest cherub you ever saw in your life. I am so happy to have this second chance. I am no longer working on my degrees or holding two jobs. I have time and I watch him. I have time to just watch him. I have a second chance to just play and do things and watch him. It's a joy!

Grandmothers often have more wisdom or hindsight, and more time, than parents to simply enjoy the kids. At 67, Cherry works full-time and takes care of her four grandchildren some days before work, some days after work, and often on weekends. Neither her parents nor her husband's parents helped them when their own kids were young and they wanted to make sure they helped their kids with the grandkids as much as possible. They are tired at the end of the day but that is better than being lonely.

> I feel extremely good, very fulfilled, and very exhausted. I feel very tired from it but go to bed with a smile on my face. The other grandparents live far away and don't get to see them daily and I consider myself lucky. My kids never demand, they always ask. Is it okay, are you doing too much? They look out for me, and they appreciate it extremely. Makes me feel younger. I am on top of things. Still doing the things I did as a parent. One of the worst things older people can do is be by themselves with other older people. I would rent a kid; it's the fun of it. They are so happy when you arrive. They run to me. They call me. We are so darn busy, it's great.

Like many of the grandmothers, Cherry has no desire to be the parent, but she wants to be a very active grandmother. She said she has learned her bounds and to keep her mouth shut. She does not want conflict. Instead she wants as much time with the grandkids as possible. As a grandmother she has more time to simply enjoy the children than she ever did as a mother.

> I felt my mom missed so much by not helping with the kids. I love being a grandmother: a second chance to have your kids all over again. But now you have the time. I look at grandparenting as being a lucky, beautiful part of our lives. I enjoyed my own children but I was young and did not know yet what I really wanted. I learned a lot raising them and now I learn a lot raising my grandkids. I like to pass on all the knowledge and life stories that I have learned. It's important to them as they go forward.

Grandmothers often have more time to enjoy the kids in a way that mothers do not. Miriam is a 67-year-old, white, married mother of three and grandmother of six. She works full-time in the northeast as a secretary, though she is about to join her husband in retirement very soon. She frequently uses her vacation days and sick days to care for the grandchildren. She takes a lot of calls at work to arrange when care is needed. Three of the grandchildren lived in her house for four years with their father and she cared for them all hours except for those she was at work. She has been exhausted by the care but would not trade it for anything.

> I really enjoy being with my grandchildren. They are a lot of fun. I did not have the time to enjoy my kids the way I do my grandkids. The worries are different. When it's your own kids you have to do everything and you are responsible for teaching them everything. When you are Grandma you can enjoy them more. Have more fun, worry less.

Grandmothers have time to see things that parents often do not. Sharon is a 61-year-old, black mother of three and grandmother of five. She has struggled with cancer, worked full-time, and cared for the grandchildren after work and on weekends for nearly two decades. Her partner of 41 years, and her youngest son who lives nearby, help with the grandsons a lot as well. It is a family project that they all enjoy. Even though she is busy, she is not as busy as she was as a mother. She enjoys this second chance even more than the first one because she has time to see things.

> When I had cancer my family stuck by me and I teach my boys that. We take care of each other. We stick together. I love having the grandsons here. I see things I never saw with my own boys. I was so busy then working and taking care of everything. And we had no money. Now I am not so busy. I see things. I love it. But I did a good job. My three boys turned out great and my grandsons are turning out great, too.

Lee, who divides her time between working for the court system, caring for a frail neighbor, and taking care of her two grandchildren, loves being a grandmother even more than she loved being a mother. She has put some considerable effort into trying to figure out why.

> I never imagined that. I never imagined being a grandmother. I think I almost like it better than being a mother. I don't know what that is. I just enjoy grandmothering more than I did mothering, because I had everything else to do at home, I think. I told people if I could have been a grandmother without being a mother I would have done it. I don't know if it's more time or you pick and choose when you're a grandmother.

She would spend a lot more time with the grandkids if she could but she and her husband are both forced to work more hours, and more years, than they had planned. Their financial situation is very precarious. He is currently hundreds of miles away working for a couple of months, so now when she watches the two grandchildren she does so on her own.

> I'd like not to be working but we're into foreclosure right now, so I'm blessed just to have work. My husband really enjoys the grandkids, too. He takes time off, too, to take care of the kids if he can. He works part-time. Right now he's . . . gone for a couple months. When there were two of us and we took care of them it was nice. But it's a bit harder now, with him being gone.

Caring for grandchildren is different than caring for children, Lynn says. She is 59 and she and her husband enjoy the opportunity. A mother of four and grandmother of three, she works part-time and watches the grandchildren every Friday, her day off. She purposely schedules her work so that she is completely available on Fridays as the kids get out of school. She meets the bus and keeps them well into the evening. She would gleefully retire from her $30,000-a-year job and watch the grandkids full-time if she could afford to do so.

> It makes me joyous, I can't wait to see them. . . . Their stuff is so neat, the bouncy thing, and all their toys. I know when we were little our parents thought our stuff was cool, but they really have some neat stuff now. Everything she does is hilarious, the little one. It makes me healthier, makes you feel young again it definitely does. . . . I wish I could retire and watch all three of them all day long. And there's no pay, it's just a reward in itself.

Compared to raising her own children, Lynn says this second time around she feels much more playful and protective.

> It's completely different, leaving your home and going to your daughter's home. I don't know how to describe it other than when you have your own children, you meet them at the bus, make sure they get homework done. With your grandchildren you're doing the same thing but it's completely

different. You're there to play with them and then you go home. You love your grandchildren but you can give them back. Like, there are those little poems that you find, and we gave my mom one that says, "If you could have gotten grandchildren first," you know. And if your grandchild falls on the floor it's the end of the world. But your own kid, they'll be okay. They can get up on their own. I'm way more protective of them than I am of my own kids.

Many grandmothers have more job security now than they did as mothers. They can put their careers on the back burner for grandchildren in a way they did not feel they could for their children. Sarah, at 67, has a lot of job security now in a job that pays well over $150,000 a year. But when her own two children were young she was under the gun to publish or perish. A married, white, grandmother of three, she feels guilty about how much she missed with her own children when she was building her career but she very much enjoys the flexibility she has now to enjoy time with her grandchildren.

Now work does not get in the way because my job is so flexible. I make it a priority to be at their school events. I would say the job got in the way of the parenting. When my own kids were young, I was building a career. . . . I can still feel guilty and list the things I missed when I let my career come first. Now with the grandkids I am at a different stage. I don't have to prove anything to anyone. I can almost always be at their school events.

When her son and his girlfriend had a baby while still in high school, Sarah made it a top priority to help take care of her first grandson. She rearranged her work schedule in a way she had never done for her own children, in part because she is now so secure in her position.

I never wanted to neglect him because he needed us. I had always put work first for so much of my life. And I did not want to shortchange him. You have your own kids at the peak building period of your job, where there's a lot of pressure for publishing and tenure and promotion. For grandkids you are beyond that. It's way easier.

Often the rules for grandmothers seem to be very different than the rules for mothers. Though she did not do so as a mother, Maryann is one of several grandmothers who have given up virtually all social obligations to work and maximize her time with the grandkids. Unlike her own grandmother, she enjoys being very actively involved in their lives. Maryann is a 59-year-old, married mother of two and grandmother of three, who works more than 40 hours a week. She cared for her daughter's children when they were young and now she cares for her son's child about 10–15 hours a week. She is her own boss and while that provides a lot of flexibility, it also entails a lot of responsibility. She has given up nearly all of her hobbies and outside interests so that she can focus on full-time work and the grandkids.

> I used to read a lot; I don't anymore. I am up at 5:30 every morning and asleep by 10 at night. I used to do cross stitch while the babies napped; I don't do them now. I just don't have time. I had a lot more free time when I was a mom. When the grandkids come along you drop everything for those kids. They say, "Come on," and you say, "Where?" When it was my own kids and they said, "Come on," I would say, "Well, wait, I have to vacuum." I did not appreciate the time I had with my kids as much as I do my grandkids. I get older. I figure out mortality. Things like the housework are not as important as the grandkids. I don't volunteer; I don't belong to any groups. I used to be in a painting group, but I stopped because I was caring for grandkids.

Giving up social activities is worth it to Maryann because it means she can do that much more with her grandchildren.

> Every Monday I have all the grandkids over for dinner. And sometimes their parents come, too. Everyone loves Monday nights at Grandma's. So I did not mind giving up the painting class for Monday night dinners.

Though she loves caring for the grandchildren, she feels she may have reached her limit. But as Maryann is quick to point out, grandmothers have no control over how many grandchildren they have at any given time.

> I keep saying no more babies. But if someone had a baby, I would be there to take care of that baby. It would not be any different. I would do just as

much for the next one as I did for the first three. They are my grandkids and I love them dearly.

It is worth it to Maryann to streamline her life and focus on her grand-children so that she can give them something she never had. Her own grandma was frail; by contrast Maryann and her husband are young and in good health. But balancing work and grandchildren leaves her behind on chores at work and at home and, sometimes, very tired.

My grandmother was old when I was born and she never spent time with me actively. So I wanted to be sure that my grandkids would remember fun times with Grandma and Grandpa. That they would tell their kids what we did. We did this with Grandma. Or we did that with Grandma. Yet on the other hand spending all the time with the grandkids means the housework does not get done. My house was a lot cleaner when my kids were younger than it is now. I have learned to live with the dirt. At work I am stressed because I have to go in at 9 at night because I left work early to take my grandson to his game. And I have to get that work done. I enjoy being with him tremendously; they know I am there supporting them. I want to make sure that they remember me. That they remember their grandma was there.

Working full-time and caring for the grandchildren during much of her free time leaves Maryann tired but she is grateful she is young enough to keep it up.

I do feel younger because I have young kids around me. They exhaust me; I am tired. We had a family picnic and they were there from 8 am till 10 at night. I was exhausted. I get tired. Satisfied. Felt good. I don't feel like a grandma. Mine was older and sat in the rocker. I am blessed that I am young enough to keep up. I can run around the yard with them. I can keep up with the music and styles of dress.

Part of the joy of grandmothering comes from the freedom to break the rules in ways that parents feel they must not. While parents may feel pressured to make sure their kids eat healthy balanced meals, Ally is one of several grandmothers who occasionally throws dietary guide-lines out the window. Ally is a 56-year-old, white woman with five children and nine grandchildren. She works full-time and cares for her grandkids a few times a week after work and on some weekends. She often rearranges her work schedule to arrive late so that she can put them on the school bus, or she leaves early so that she can meet the bus after school. The children are all enrolled in school and daycare, but when there is a sick day or a snow day, Ally often takes a day of paid vacation to take care of them. Ally is one of several grandmothers who appreciate this second chance to enjoy small children with fewer competing responsibilities and a more relaxed set of rules. But she gets tired.

> It's less stressful than when I was juggling with my own kids. I have given myself permission to say no. I will say no if we already have plans, or if we are tired. We watched the girls overnight. . . . I ended up taking a day off work. It was a realization that I am too old to do it all, as much as I might enjoy it. When I am doing it I feel young—silly dancing and crayons—and then when they are gone I am tired. There really is less stress. It's your rules. I don't care what they eat for lunch. I just don't care if they want ice cream first.

She likes the mix of working at her $30,000-a-year office job and caring for the grandkids. Each has its own rewards and she would like to continue doing both for at least a few more years.

> I feel lucky that I can do both. Many of my friends don't live close enough to grandkids to care for them. No desire to quit either—there are different rewards. I love the kids but nobody ever says you did a good job. There are rewards you get from work that you don't get from being around kids. But the great reward is to see now how well my daughters are raising their own kids.

To her great amusement, her husband might be even more focused on the grandkids than she. When their children were young he worked and traveled frequently. Today he does not want to be away from the grandkids if he can help it. They plan to retire in three to four years if their long-term investments hold, not so they can travel, but so that they can provide even more grandchild care.

My husband's interactions with the grandkids are much more relaxed and enjoyable than his interactions with our own kids were. He traveled all the time when the kids were young. Now he sees the grandkids and says to me, "Did our kids do this?" He missed so much. . . . We are hoping to retire in two to four years, depending on the market. He wants to retire at 64. He would like to be able to go to the grandkids' school, chaperone the field trips, and do all the things he missed out on. He is just as capable at brushing hair as I am. We all see that he could do it, too.

Ally and her husband appreciate this second chance so much that they have altered their retirement plans to remain closer to, and be more involved with, the grandchildren.

Our first plan was to retire and live in North Carolina for three months per year, but now he says that is too long to be away from the kids. He really feels it's important that we do this. He wants to come along, he wants to do this. He is making up for what he missed before. Our daughters think that this is great that he wants to do this. We are all amused that he thinks it's so great.

Susan emphasizes a different kind of second chance. Her own mother disapproved of her working when her children were young and did not help with the kids at all. Despite working full-time, Susan, a 62-year-old, white, married mother of two, was determined to be the primary babysitter for her daughter's four children. She wanted her daughter to have support she did not have; grandmothering gives her the chance to provide it.

My mother had five kids. She had two little ones at home when I had my first. She did not come and help me when I had my daughter. She could not help me. Everyone else in the neighborhood had grandparents coming to watch the grandkids. My mother never said, "Go to a movie, enjoy yourself." I had to use a babysitter. I resented that my mother did not help me. She did not think I should work; she thought I should be home. She said I needed to raise my own kids. I really did not like that. I think that is why I do so much for my daughter. I want her to have her mother helping her. My mother never helped me, but she did what she could. But I tell my daughter to take advantage of me, but she is always asking if I am sure, if I am okay. She would be happy to get a sitter but I tell her not to. I want to watch them. I call them my babies.

Susan and her husband are almost entirely focused on the grandchildren. They each have a weekly meeting they attend, and they volunteer together at a football concession stand. But otherwise, their social life revolves around taking care of the grandchildren after work, on weekends, during the summer, and on sick and vacation days.

My husband loves the grandkids; he is always saying let's go help . . . he is great with kids, he loves it. I am lucky I married him. We have a nice life together. We can do anything we want. But we find so much enjoyment with the grandkids. That is our social life. I could not enjoy it any more.

Though her friends and coworkers tell her she is too focused on the grandchildren, Susan feels it is her duty to be available to care for them. She is less busy this second time around and can enjoy her time with them even more than she did with her own children.

I think a lot of people think I spend too much time with the grandkids but I love it so much. It's a thrill, I just love it. It's like they are my own. I feel guilty if she gets a babysitter. No one can take care of them as best as I can. I should be available for them. . . . We enjoy it. We don't have a lot of social life. We love family and I love my grandkids and my daughter. If I can't help her it's a shame. I talk about the grandkids all the time. I get such a charge out of them. I just adore them. They come out with the cutest things. I did not get such a thrill out of my own two, but I was busy with the house and work. I seem to enjoy the grandkids more. I make excuses for the grandkids, can't spoil them enough.

Not everyone falls naturally into the grandmothering role, and not every grandmother has a strong relationship with her adult children. Christine is one of a few grandmothers who views being a good grandmother as an opportunity to atone for being gone so much while her daughter was young. In this case, grandmothering presents an opportunity to strengthen her relationship with her adult daughter. Although it has not been easy. Christine is a 74-year-old, white woman who has divorced three times. She has a PhD and a sizable income, much of which she devotes to her daughter and grandchildren. Christine did not stay home to raise her own daughter. She was completely committed to her career. She never even considered staying home for her granddaughters, but her daughter pressures her continually to do more for the girls.

> I went through so much guilt—for not having been home with my daughter as a child when she was growing up because I was so committed to my work and my career. And now it has all come back again. Now my daughter is so unhappy about it. So I have started the self-flagellation again. I feel guilty all over again about not being there for my family. But I love my work. It's important. But I want my relationship with my daughter to be better, to be closer. And I love my granddaughters.

Christine comes from generations of children being raised by nannies. She does not know how to play with her grandchildren. She said the step-grandmother has stepped in and is perfect for the role, teaching the girls to sew, playing dolls, and reading to them.

> I am pretty uncomfortable. I don't know kids. My mother had housekeepers that took care of me—she was there, but they took care of me. My nanny took care of my daughter when she was a baby. I don't know how to be with kids. I never know what to do. This has caused me a lot of angst. It makes me cry, but talking about it's good for me. I really do want to be more engaged with them, more than just the holidays.

Christine and her daughter argued for years about what a proper grandmother should and should not do. According to her daughter, Christine should want to spend as much time as possible with her granddaughters. In addition to arguing over how many of hours of care Christine should provide, they have argued about the quality of that care. Christine's daughter has told her that while she has the girls, there is to be no fast food or television. After a considerable amount of counseling, they have arrived at a creative solution. After work, when her daughter is driving the girls around to their activities and doing other errands, Christine rides along.

What we do now we call ride-arounds. My daughter has big errand trips and I get in the car and ride around with them. Of course I pay for everything, not that she is expecting. I love it and I hear all about everything. We have a great time. We get all caught up. She says I can jump on and off any time. I don't know how to play with kids, but the ride-around, I can do that. I can sit in the car and talk with them all, buy what is needed. That works well for all of us.

Joy Even Sweeter the Second Time Around

To a person, every working grandmother I interviewed described a feeling of joy when caring for her grandchildren: giddy, teary-eyed joy at just spending time caring for them. Without exception, the grandmothers love their grandchildren and love caring for them. No matter how tired they get, they want time with their grandkids. The reward is a joy that they glow about. And that joy is often compounded by the fact that they are helping two generations at once, working together as a family to raise their progeny.

To be clear, many grandmothers may not provide care for, or feel a lot of joy about, their grandchildren. But they are not in this book. Additionally, many grandmothers care for grandkids but are not balancing those duties with a job. They are also not in this book. I interviewed grandmothers who were working and caring for their grandchildren because I wanted to see how they balanced these obligations. We hear so much about supermoms who are juggling work and household and children, but we pay little regard to grandmothers who are doing it all again. Supergrandmothers!

The role of grandmothering brings a different kind of joy than the role of mothering. Typically, there is less pressure and responsibility. And even if older ages mean less energy for chasing grandkids, often they also mean more time for just enjoying them. For some that happiness is augmented by role diversity, because they like being employed and caring for grandkids. For others that joy is impeded by role diversity, when either paid work or care for someone other than grandchildren competes for time and energy. For many the enjoyment is augmented by the fact that they are caring for the kids together with other family members and by the knowledge that they are simultaneously helping their grandkids and kids.

Grandmothering is embedded in the lifecourse. For many, grand-mothering provides a second chance to enjoy raising children with fewer competing responsibilities. For others, it provides a chance to make up for not spending enough time with their own children or for not having a mom who spent time with her children. No matter how tired they get balancing so many responsibilities, most want to care for their grandchildren. They feel needed as well. Their daughters do not have much job flexibility. Daycares do not provide the same high-quality care. There are few options when kids are sick or school is canceled. Perhaps most important, many grandmas provide care for free, bolstering the family income of their children by reducing a key expenditure.

Families in the United States rely much more heavily on grandparents for child care than do parents in countries with federal programs and policies that support working families. If the United States provided federal minimums for paid sick days, paid vacation days, paid family leaves, universal health care, flexible scheduling, good daycare, or universal preschool for all, their daughters and sons would not need them so much. Indeed in countries with more supports for working families, grandparents provide less care.[3] When I presented this work at the International Sociological Association meetings in Gothenburg, Sweden, during July 2010, a European scholar asked, "What is wrong with American grandmothers? Don't they know how to say no?" I responded that I did not think there was much wrong with American grandmothers, but perhaps quite a bit wrong with US welfare state policies. In the absence of programs and policies to help working families, American grandmothers are providing tremendous amounts of care. For the most part, they are repaid with joy. Would they feel just as much joy if they were simply visiting and were not needed for such extensive daycare duty? Perhaps, maybe even more so.

3

Intensive Grandmothering

Much has been said about the intensification of mothering in the United States. Sharon Hays traces evolving practices and suggests that for about three decades we have been in an era of increasingly intensive mothering in which mothers, even if working, are encouraged to invest a great deal of time and energy into raising their children.[1] While mothers of all races and classes are pressured to intensify motherhood, Annette Lareau found that middle-class and upper-class women are most likely to cultivate their children through specific efforts encouraged by parenting experts.[2] In a way that is without historic precedent, modern US families are centered around children and mothers feel obliged to prepare their children for success in a highly competitive world. The image is one of minivans racing from soccer to piano to dance lessons, tutors, summer camps, and any other forms of enrichment available.

Critics sometimes refer to the most intensive of these mothers as helicopter parents who are omnipresent, overly helpful, and addictively complimentary to their children instead of holding them responsible for their actions.[3] Some research suggests that when parents are highly involved in their adult children's lives the result can be lower performance and lower levels of life satisfaction for the adult children.[4] The question then becomes, do intensive mothers expect, prefer, or become, intensive grandmothers?

My interviews with working grandmothers suggest that just as mothering has become more intensive, so has grandmothering. All but four of the 48 grandmothers I interviewed are doing more grandchild care than their own mothers had done as grandmothers. And, between their paid jobs and grandchild care, all but the same four women are working more intensely than they expected to at this stage of life. For some, the role diversity is a source of pleasure. They enjoy the mix of paid and unpaid responsibilities. For others the roles conflict and add to their stress as demands outpace flagging energy levels or hours of the day.

Much of the intensification of grandmothering may be traced to cultural changes in parenting expectations. But some of it is linked to unmet needs. Increases in the rates of working, and single, mothers have not been met by increases in affordable and flexible child-care arrangements. Additionally, increases in childhood disability rates have not been met by increases in accommodative services. Though some types of childhood disabilities are holding constant or even declining, such as Down syndrome, spina bifida, and hearing loss, others types are increasing, most notably developmental disabilities. The Centers for Disease Control reported that between 1997 and 2008, developmental disabilities for children between the ages of 3 and 17 rose by nearly 14 percent.[5] The biggest increases were reported for children with attention-deficit hyperactivity disorder (ADHD), 33 percent, and autism, 290 percent. Of the 48 grandmothers I interviewed, seven were caring for grandchildren with disabilities. Children with disabilities often need more, and more specialized, care. There are often fewer care options available, however, because many providers are unable, or unwilling, to provide care to those who have special needs.[6] Taken together, changing cultural expectations about parenting, the rising rates of working, and single, mothers, and rising childhood disability rates generate a growing need for assistance raising the kids. Grandmothers often step up to provide intensive assistance.

Cherry has provided intensive grandmothering for 17 years. At age 67, Cherry is a white woman who attended some college and works 40 hours a week. She and her husband have helped with each of the four grandchildren daily over the years, before and after work and on weekends.

When the first grandchild was born, they actually lived with us for three months, and then when they worked, we were the evening parents. So four nights a week we had our grandchildren.

After a bit, Cherry and her husband bought a second house and moved their son and his wife and children into a house nearby. For nearly two decades, they have cared for the grandchildren after work almost every evening.

> We had the kids each night after work. We fed them dinner, bathed them, got in PJs, and then the parents took them home around 8. If it was later than 8, we took them to their house to put them to bed. We have been evening parents for 17 years. And we do a lot now, though the older kids can watch themselves more and we mainly watch the 3-year-old.

Cherry described a typical day in which she took care of the grandchildren before and after work. Such a day also includes making and serving dinner to the kids and to her son when he returns from work.

> I get up at 5:30 and get myself ready for my work day. Then I will go to their house by 7:15 am and get the kids ready for school, feed them, drop them at three different schools. My husband often comes to help in the morning, too. I have to take the 3-year-old into her school and get her boots off, etc., and she is very good about it. Then I work 7 ½ hours. Then I go to her preschool and pick her up and take her to her house and then help with the kids. Their dad gets there by about 5:30. I help with dinner, even make it the night before and take it over there. Or their mom will have something ready for me to heat up.

How do they balance their full-time jobs and so much grandchild care? By keeping a simple routine and sharing the workload. Cherry loves her job and time with her grandchildren, but like some of the other married grandmothers I interviewed, she clearly benefits from working as a team with her husband. Those who are single, however, often find that juggling so many responsibilities may be even more challenging.

> We kept our lifestyle as uncomplicated as possible. My husband and I shared the housework and just left the dishes undone if we needed to care for the grandkids. He loved having the grandkids around as much as I did.

We never got out of the routine of having kids, we just kept that routine. You just do it.

In scholarly literature, the role of grandmothering, in the intensification of parenting, has been somewhat overlooked. The intensification of mothering is generally regarded as a cultural trend, with normative expectations about the proper way to rear a child increasing just as hours of paid work among mothers are rising.[7] The intensification of grandmothering may be fueled by similar cultural expectations, but it also appears to be fueled by need. With few exceptions, the 48 grandmothers I spoke with did not want to be mothers or nannies. They wanted to be grandmas who got to love them, spoil them, and send them home. Several mentioned they did not want to be paid because they did not want their adult children to be able to tell them what to, and not to, do. Some of the grandmothers I spoke with are in traditional grandmother roles, spoiling the grandkids and sending them home to their parents.

But for the growing share who are providing regular child care so that their adult children can work, grandmothering begins to look a lot like mothering. One study reported that among those who provide care to grandchildren under age 13, 69 percent said they are currently or have in the past provided backup care, 56 percent sick care, 44 percent before and after school care, and 53 percent summer care.[8]

Grandmothering is intensifying in part because of the increase in single parenting, economic insecurity, and the absence of federal policies that guarantee paid time off for sickness, childbirth, and vacation, or readily affordable child-care options. For the one-half of those who are providing more than 12 hours a week, grandparenting is looking more and more like parenting. Grandmas still bake cookies and take kids to the zoo, but they do much more. Their "to do" lists are long, often propelled by a sense of duty, particularly when they feel a lifeline is needed. These are hands-on grandmothers, providing intensive direct care. Many are sequential grandmothers, caring for one grandchild after another. Many juggle multiple roles seamlessly but others provide care to their own detriment—exhausting themselves physically, emotionally, and financially. They soldier on, not wanting their grandchildren to suffer during hard times. When times get tough, so do grandmothers.

Responsibilities

Some grandmothers have fairly light duty, watching the grandkids one night a week or one weekend a month. But some have much more frequent and heavier duties, caring for their grandchildren nearly daily. And the work itself is nearly as intensive as it would be if they were the mothers rather than the grandmothers. Indeed, many grandmothers are providing the lion's share of nonparental child care even though they are still working. For most of the grandmothers I spoke with, grandmothering duties have come a long way from coloring and walking to the park. They include chauffeuring, bathing, feeding, clothing, tucking in, and doctor visits.

Why? A variety of factors. The US welfare state does not provide most working mothers and fathers with meaningful time off, either through paid vacation, sick time, or family leave. Moreover, the United States does not provide universal health insurance, affordable day care, or preschool. Many families feel they must keep their jobs to keep their health insurance yet they find few child-care options that offer good care at a good price. Additionally, the economy has made some parents' jobs vulnerable and they have to work more hours, overtime, evenings, weekends, or as needed. Finally, some of the adult children became parents at very young ages, some are single parents, others are trying to complete college degrees, and some are recently divorced. They simply need more help. Whatever the combination of causes, in some families the need for help is high.

Perhaps Renee puts it best. "The biggest problem right now is that the younger generation is all working, mom and dad, to survive. The grandparents have to jump in during the tough times." Renee was one of only a few grandmothers who put her family's struggles into the context of the economy as a whole. This 66-year-old, white, married mother of three, guardian of one niece, and grandmother of four helps by providing occasional child care and frequent financial assistance. Other grandmothers provide frequent child care and only occasional financial assistance. Whatever their mix of responsibilities, working grandmothers have only 24 hours in their days.

Some, like Diane, want to concentrate on playing with the grandkids. Like many grandmothers I interviewed, Diane puts all other duties on hold while caring for the grandchildren so she can focus on fun. Diane is in her third marriage and works about 30 hours a week. She has arranged her work schedule so that she never has to deny a request for grandchild care. When she is on duty she provides every type of care for her grandkids. She gets tired but loves it.

> If I babysit I go there. All of her needs are there, all of her toys. She likes to go to bed at 7:30 and I like to put her down. We love to play. She loves to color, she plays the piano. She has a lot of energy. She loves for me to read her books. . . . I get behind on everything when I am caring for her but I don't care. It will all be there tomorrow anyway. When you are a grandmother, you learn, the house can wait. The laundry can wait. They are young for such a little time. That is number one. When I am there I do everything, feed her, bathe her.

Others, like Janelle, have to put all other duties on hold when they are caring for the grandkids for safety's sake. She is not agile enough to multitask with a toddler on the run. Janelle's 32-year-old son lives at her house and sometimes helps with the grandkids, who are his niece and nephew. She works full-time and cares for her two young grandchildren some days after work and often on weekends. Her grandson is nearly two and she has some problems with mobility. She faces quite a challenge keeping up with his pace. Caring for him is all-encompassing.

> I will pick him up from daycare and take him home . . . and we have a snack, make dinner, play a little, feed him, play with him again. . . . Wash him up, brush teeth, read a book, put him to bed. It is hard to keep up with him. He is very physical. He is quick, but he doesn't want to hold your hand. I have to be right on top of him and then he starts running.

Recently he has gotten very fast and has started to dart away from her often, so she is increasingly afraid to take him outside.

> The other day the weather was so nice, I took him out in the yard but he ran off. He doesn't want to hold my hand. He ran a lot and I could not catch him. So we went back in. We did not stay out there long. I felt bad. The weather was so nice. But we could not stay out there. I could not keep

up with him. We took a walk and he wanted to hold my hand so that went well. So I get worried when he runs around, I get worried about the road. I just brought him in.

But even inside the house there are challenges. He is drawn to the stairs and all sorts of other household items that are not safe for him to manhandle.

> My house isn't that big but I do have a stair, and I have to have a gate. I watch him as he runs in my house. But now he can do that step by himself. He doesn't really want toys. He wants the phone, the mouse, the plugs. So now I have to watch all that. I don't do anything else when he is there; I just watch him. I have to put him in the high chair so I can go to the bathroom or get dressed. He is pretty good, and he listens. But he is very active. He climbs—he climbs right up my body. So I have to watch even more. I don't plan anything else—I just watch him, chase him.

Some grandmothers provide intensive grandchild care not so much because they want to, or intended to, but because the care is sorely needed. Patty never expected to provide so much care for her grandchildren. She is a 63 year-old, white, married mother of two and grandmother of four. She has a BA and works about 20 hours a week in the northeast, and has provided intensive, almost daily, care for two different sets of grandchildren for more than a decade. She enjoys the time with the grandchildren. But it has not always been easy to spend time with them. When the older grandchildren were young, Patty took care of them daily, often around the clock, because their mother was struggling with poor mental health. Times with those grandchildren were often quite stressful, particularly when their mother was not well.

> I never imagined I would do this much care for my grandkids. But we have often had full care of our grandchildren, for many hours a day since I retired and became a part-time housecleaner. I have had on and off periods of intense daycare. The relationship is nice with the current grandkids. It is low-key and fun. . . . I get along well with my daughter and son-in-law. But for the older grandkids it was more stressful because their mother was very sick and having a nervous breakdown and the grandkids were angry at me.

There was much more stress for the older set of grandkids because there was so much stress at their home.

Amid the sea of duties they perform, certain tasks may become almost inexplicably challenging, or annoying, for some grandmothers. For Amelia, meal preparation is the Achilles' heel. Amelia is a 51-year-old, married, white mother of four and grandmother of three. Her youngest daughter became pregnant at age 17, while still living at home. That daughter and grandson lived with them for five years, only recently moving out. Those five years were challenging for Amelia, who works full-time as a community college teacher in the midwest. She and her husband would take care of their grandson after work and on weekends, handling meals, baths, clothes, diapers, everything. As their daughter played for her high school basketball team, Amelia and her husband cheered from the stands with their grandson on their laps. Some duties were more difficult than others. Feeding three different age groups often proved challenging.

> The struggle of trying to feed so many age groups and dealing with likes and dislikes was so frustrating. I wanted to deal with adult food and adult likes—not want to deal with chicken nuggets or mac and cheese on a daily basis. . . . She never expected me to make a different dinner but I had this guilt, that there had to be something everyone liked. The thought of having to think of what I would have for the week to meet all those needs was too challenging,

For some, intensive grandmothering combined with a hefty work schedule creates challenges that may in fact be too much. Paula has been warned by her doctor that it is this way for her. Paula has looked after her seven grandchildren, working full-time on three night shifts a week, and has taken care of one grandson who lives with her temporarily while his father is in prison.

> I am also taking care of the other grandkids during the day. When my daughter would work I watched her two kids. And while my other daughter was in school I would watch all these kids. Their parents would leave them with me while they worked and went to school. So I very rarely slept,

because I would work all night and watch the kids all day. I was told to leave the job because it was causing a lot of health problems. But I could not leave the job. I needed the money to pay for my house.

While she has the grandchildren, she does everything from feeding, bathing, reading, homework, and more. But she also makes sure they have fun.

> My grandkids respect me. We wrestle and play around and joke around. I have a great relationship with my grandkids. We still go sledding.

When the child-care schedule is delicately balanced, grandmothers often report to duty no matter what, even when they are sick. I interviewed Patty on her 63rd birthday. She retired from her earlier occupation and now works as a housecleaner part-time so that she can watch the grandkids more easily. She only takes clients who will let her cancel or switch days if she needs to rearrange her schedule for the grandkids. She cares for her four grandchildren every day of the week except Tuesdays. She also cares for her husband, who is 80 and has Alzheimer's disease and cancer, and for her mother, whose health is failing quickly. Her duties are endless.

> On Wednesday and Thursday I go out to my daughter's house, about 20 minutes away, because my granddaughter has preschool. I get there at 7. I help get them ready for school and work, make sure they have eaten, put the baby down for a nap. I get my granddaughter ready for school, walk or drive her to school, put laundry away, collect laundry, cook, put toys away, pick her up from pre-K, then feed everyone lunch. In the afternoon we stay there all day until mom or dad returns around 3:30 or 4. The kids nap, we play games, we all love to be outside. . . . Then on Monday and Friday my daughter brings her two youngest girls here to my home. I don't have to get up so early. But on Monday my daughter teaches gymnastics until 8:30 pm. So in the late afternoon I take the kids back to their home and stay till 6 or 7. I cook, or heat up food, feed them, get the baths started, and then their dad takes over.

Patty is so integrated into the family child-care schedule that she continues to care for the children even when she is not feeling well.

Recently she took a break from the housekeeping work she usually performs and slept when the kids napped. It was nothing serious, she assured me. Had she been seriously ill, she says she would not have gone.

> Last week I was sick and went anyway, and I slept while they did. I was not really sick. If I was, they would take the kids to the other grandma or my daughter would take a day off work.

Intensive grandmothers often pitch in to try to relieve the stress on their adult children. Sometimes they are so busy making sure their adult children get a break that they do not get one themselves. Molly made her own work and child-care schedules even more demanding so that she could help her daughter. Molly, a 50-year-old divorced mother of three and grandmother of five, works full-time in a job that is not very flexible. She cares for the grandchildren before work, after work, on evenings, during weekends, and on her vacation days. She started to help before work when she realized her daughter was having so much trouble getting the kids to the sitter before her own work shift began.

> My daughter would leave at 5 am and she didn't have a car. So when I heard about that I started going every morning to her house at 6:30. I'd take the kids to the sitter for her so she could just go to work, instead of getting up at 4 like she was doing. I'd pick up the kids every single weekend Friday to Sunday, about 6 o'clock and keep them till she'd get off; it'd be 11 at night. I've never liked the whole waking children up in the middle of the night to move them. I enjoyed the kids. I always did. So, you know, whatever I had to do. If they were sick I'd go spend the week at her house to help them.

Molly's daughter had her first child as she was turning 17 and now has two more. A single mom, she is not able to turn to the father for assistance because he has mental health issues. Molly told me he has many times threatened to hurt her daughter and they have had to call the police several times when he was out of control. Molly is determined to help her daughter raise these kids, even though her own mother and sister did not help her with her own children. It is difficult to sustain this schedule of support, but, fortunately, the type of work that grandmothers do changes as the grandkids age. No longer changing diapers, Molly is now navigating sibling squabbles and middle school homework. Her daughter works the night shift, and Molly, whose apartment is just across the hall, is on call for the grandkids every evening.

> Now that they're older, it's really easy, because they clean up and they can cook a little with supervision. My daughter works 11 pm to 7:30 am and leaves for work at 10:30 but my door is literally 10 feet from them, so they come over. Last week one heard a noise, so he was, like, can we stay with you? And I said, come on over, so one was in my bed. They are 11 and 13 now, so they're at the age where they get on each other's nerves. So one of them will come and stay with me. Really it's more supervision than babysitting.

Intensive grandmothers are providing a lot of supervision and assistance with homework. Some are not educated well enough to be able to provide the assistance that is needed, but Molly handles school work readily.

> Homework, yes, my grandson always is, like, "Gramma!" and needs help with math all the time, and mythology, and other things. Probably six hours a week I'm doing that. His science projects, he waited until the last minute and came to my house to get all my bowls and had something to do with artificial dyes, or with oranges and orange juice.

Like many of the grandmothers I interviewed, Molly likes to spoil them a bit with nonessential things and events. It all adds up to a lot of carework and expense, but she loves her time with the grandchildren.

> My grandson asked me if I would help him get his stuff ready for school, so I asked him what he needed and he said, "I just want this one book bag I saw," so I'll get that when I get paid. He's discovered that he's cute so he has to keep his hair a certain way, so he'll ask for $10 to get his hair cut and he'll say, "Can't you take me?" And I'll take him. He being the only boy, he really kind of calls for Gramma's attention. I'm taking him on a cruise with me in

October, but we're not telling him until the day before, the day he needs to pack. He just gets to go because he's old enough. He'll be 14 this year. And he needs to do something special.

The hours of full-time paid work and full-time grandchild care really add up, and though she sometimes needs a break, she would rather not leave them with others. She tried leaving them with another relative in the past (she declined to say who) but said that woman did not have the patience for it. Instead of getting a break from caring for the kids, Molly would just worry that they were not receiving proper care. So she takes care of them herself.

> It's not that many hours a week, if overnight, its 40–50 hours a week. It seems like it's a lot of time, but it's not. I don't think, it's not tiring or wearing me out. It's good. When I had them all weekend or every weekend I would sometimes need a break so I would leave them with someone else. But she has no patience with kids. And then I would worry.

Molly is motivated to help in ways that her mother never did. In addition, she wants to spend time with the grandchildren and she wants to cover them so her daughter can work. Her daughter is saving money to buy a home in a safer neighborhood and Molly is helping to make that dream a reality for her daughter and grandchildren.

Intensive grandmothers maintain schedules that leave them desperately tired, but they feel it is worth it to ensure that the family stays close. Madeline is a 53-year-old, white, married mother of three and grandmother of one. She reduced her work hours from 20 to 12 hours a week so that she could watch her grandson every weekday morning from 7 to 11 am. Then she goes to work and the other grandmother covers from 11 to 5 pm every day. She loves taking care of her grandson, but the level of responsibility and activity is high.

> If he is sick I still go care for him. I have taken him to the doctor. I give him breakfast and his bath and get him dressed every morning. I take him for a walk or we play with his cars. We watch some TV. We walk the new puppy. And sometimes I will bring him to my house and he plays with our dogs

here. . . . Sometimes I take him to breakfast, spoil him like crazy. I clean up whatever mess he and I made while I was there, put the toys away, so that when the next grandma comes she starts from scratch.

Madeline's job involves working with special needs children at a local school and that work, combined with her grandchild care, leaves her tired and ready for the weekends. But often she and her husband take their grandson during the weekends as well.

I do sometimes have him for the weekends. Their house is on the market. He will come here, and he usually doesn't spend the night. We swim in the backyard pool. We walk, we play. He has one bedroom with toys upstairs, and he brings the toys down here to play.

Though she loves being with her grandson, she tries to arrange the schedule so that she does not become overly tired.

I love to be busy. I am not one to sit down. But by the end of the day I am ready to go to bed. It is a good tired usually. I know why we have our children when we are young. My daughter understands though if I say I am tired, I can't do that today. It makes me feel younger playing with him, but I can feel my age as opposed to when my kids were that age. I try to guide activities, so that I don't get too tired.

Between paid and unpaid work, Madeline finds herself pressed to keep her own house clean and pantry stocked. She runs out of time, but even more she runs out of energy.

Sometimes it is difficult, especially when I watch him here. He can destroy a room so fast. So I have to get him back to his house. But then I go to work. So then later I have to clean up. I used to grocery shop in the week. Now I want to get home and relax, so now I usually shop on the weekends. I am at church on Sunday from 7 to 12, then I will grocery shop after.

No matter how tired she gets, Madeline will continue to care for this grandchild and any others that arrive. This is a family tradition. Her own grandmother helped to raise her and she wants the same for her grandchildren.

> I want him to know his grandmothers, and his great-grandparents, seeing him every day. When I don't see him one day . . . I have to call. We are a close family for generations, and my husband's parents also always had grandparents living with him. We both come from that background and we want to keep it going. There isn't anything like family.

When grandchildren have disabilities, grandmothering is sometimes even more intensive. In addition to providing grandchild care, cooking, and cleaning, some grandmothers drive grandchildren to therapy appointments, doctor visits, and more. Connie is a 50-year-old, married, white mother of four and grandmother of three. Her oldest daughter and her oldest grandson are both disabled. Her youngest daughter, only 16, also lives at home with her. Connie works two jobs that add up to full-time work across all seven days of the week. She expected to work and help with the grandkids, though her own mother did not help her when her kids were young. But Connie never expected to help this much. Because his mother is 23 and disabled herself, and according to Connie his mother has no patience with him, Connie and her husband provide almost constant care for her 8-year-old disabled grandson who lives with them.

> My grandson, I do everything. He has doctor appointments scheduled, so I have to take time off to take him. And if he's having problems in school I have to go to meetings at the school for him. On the weekends, I work a part-time job and that's affecting my grandson, but I'm usually home by 3 pm so it works out well. . . . I don't miss much, though. I work my schedule around it. It's not flexible, but I schedule in advance for most things.

Additionally, Connie provides intermittent care for the other two grandchildren. It is a complicated situation and she covers a wide variety of tasks.

> I help them do homework and school stuff. My grandchildren who don't live here come over often, so I babysit. And the 1½-year-old, she's here

almost every weekend. I do the everyday stuff, I do cooking, chasing her around, talking to her. When she's here I do all of that and laundry, too.

Similarly Jamica cares for her grandchild with a disability. In her case, the combination of a parent with a rotating work schedule and a grandchild with autism make grandmothering all the more challenging. At 49, Jamica has already been grandmothering for more than 13 years. She had her children young and her children followed in her footsteps. She cleans houses and only accepts clients who understand that she will reschedule the cleaning if the grandchildren need her. In the early years, she focused on her oldest granddaughter, who lived with her until recently. Since she moved out, Jamica still cares for her younger grandchildren some evenings and most weekends.

> Early on I focused more on the oldest granddaughter. In fact her mom and she lived with me till my granddaughter was 9. They just moved out four years ago. When my granddaughter lived with me, I would cook, do laundry, pick her up from her babysitter, take her to school; the whole family raised her. Read to her, play with her, have tea parties, take her to the doctor, clean, went to school events if her mother could not get there. Cooked with her. Her mom would be at work or at school. They moved out four years ago, but I still help with her. She comes on the weekend. She comes to my house. I will give her sewing lessons, watch movies. She helps me garden. I feed her, tuck her in.

The mother is a firefighter whose schedule fluctuates, causing Jamica's schedule to fluctuate as well.

> Her schedule shifts from mornings to evenings, every four days there is a shift, so all of our schedules have to shift, too. They come to my house, after school or daycare. I pick them up, feed them, we eat, we sleep, we do homework, read, put together Transformers.

Though she has many competing responsibilities, Jamica now focuses on her youngest daughter's boys, especially the one with autism.

> My oldest grandson is autistic and he is very good at Legos and Transformers. We have been lucky; he has a one-on-one at school for first grade. We

mainly are able to take care of him. We work with him. We went through
a lot of therapies. He would line things up and he could tell if anything
was moved just the slightest. It would throw him off. He reads now, he
shares now. It was hard but it is much better now. He spoke early; he was
very able early on. Then at 18 months, like clockwork, he was babbling, he
went backward in language development. It was like the words have been
snatched out of his mouth. He went into the dazed look. I try to talk with
him but he is clearly someplace else.

Similarly, Marsha, a 64-year-old real estate agent, changed careers
and moved to a new city to help with her twin grandsons when one
was diagnosed with Down syndrome and the other with moderate
autism. She rearranges her schedule constantly to care for them days,
evenings, and weekends. She and her husband take them to doctor
and therapy appointments and look after them during sick or snow
days.

When the second was diagnosed it became imperative that we live close.
They needed family. Her parents live cross country. We wanted to be there
for them. So now we see the boys. Every Wednesday I pick them up from
school and take one to therapy. . . . And then my husband and I see them
every weekend, we might keep them overnight on a Friday or Saturday
so the kids can go out, go to dinner. . . . I am the backup if anyone is sick
or traffic is terrible. Normally we go to their house; their things are there,
their space is better for kids, more kid-friendly. We are trying to move out
of our apartment to a house.

Marsha's grandson with Down syndrome needs help with mobility,
feeding, toileting, and communicating.

One grandson has Downs and isn't potty-trained. He is 4½, and he has
no interest yet. He doesn't help with his weight; he is a dead weight in my
arms. You sort of have to move his weight. I have a lifting limit because
of an earlier surgery. I have to physically move him and he is more than
my 25-pound weight limit. Sometimes changing him is a challenge. My
husband is wonderful about helping. Feeding, he needs some help. He is
wonderfully sweet. He is getting speech and physical therapy now, too. He

is communicative but not as much as a typical child. He is a mellow happy-go-lucky kid. Sweet as he can be. He hardly ever cries. He and his brother are interacting more and more these past few weeks. He gets bullied by his brother a bit.

Marsha's other grandson has autism and he mainly needs help with emotional outbursts. She puts a lot of effort into trying to prevent them.

I try to anticipate if things are going to make him angry and try to redirect, we want to avoid a full-blown meltdown. I try to preempt. For example, if you forgot to hand him the keys to unlock the door, that could initiate a pretty big temper tantrum. He likes to lock and unlock. He might have a tantrum. You let *him* push the elevator button. . . . I am lucky; I don't see a lot of full-blown.

She has learned to deal with the outbursts by trying to avoid them altogether and, if that does not work, by making sure he does not get injured.

He tantrumed yesterday a bit. He calls it being sad. I had him after school and we got him a milk shake. He is a very picky eater, he eats about five things. But we got him a milk shake and I don't let him eat in my car. He wanted to come to my house but could not, laid on the floor at his house and cried, had a tantrum for a half hour. As he gets older he doesn't thrash as he used to. He is mild to moderate. I try to anticipate what will set him off and not go there. But sometimes it just does happen. He says now that yesterday he was sad about the milk shake. He is starting to grow out of some of the tantrums.

In addition to caring for the boys, Marsha helps with the housework and meals. While her son and daughter-in-law were on a cruise one week, she shampooed their carpets.

We take the boys to school, therapy, doctor appointments, whatever is needed. I would go with my son to take them to the dentist, hard with two special needs kids, especially because they are so different from each other. One goes 90 miles an hour and is very physical and the other is slower.

Heavens, yes, I do their laundry, I clean their house, I help with meals and mopping the floors.

During the week her adult children were on a cruise, Marsha and her husband moved into their grandchildren's home and grandparented around the clock.

> This week, we have the kids all week so my son and his wife can go on a cruise. We are staying at their house. So this week we are taking them to and from school. Taking them to all the therapies, feedings, bathing, tucking in. We are 100 percent. Doing everything . . . we are determined to shampoo the carpets if we can work it in.

Sense of Duty

Why would grandmothers provide such intense grandchild care when they are still employed? Though all of the grandmothers expressed joy about spending time with their grandchildren, some talked about a sense of duty as well. Some viewed it as their job to help raise the kids, assuring free, high-quality, family-oriented care. They feel responsible. Many were replicating the help their own parents provided, while others made up for the help they, or their own parents, failed to provide. Some are following a family tradition of hands-on grandmothering. Others are providing care because they do not want strangers raising their grandchildren. They feel that family provides the best and safest care. Indeed, Grandma knows best. Still others are providing care to make sure their sons' and daughters' dreams of higher education, job success, or homeownership will come true.

Some intensive grandmothers are motivated by the family legacy. In some families, grandparents are hands-on helpers and they want to keep the tradition alive. Marsha's parents cared for her children and she feels it is her responsibility to care for her grandsons. She has already changed careers, turning to the flexible scheduling of real estate, and moved to a new city to be readily available to care for her twin grandsons who have autism and Down syndrome. She and her husband constantly rearrange their schedules to care for the boys during the week and on weekends. They provide around-the-clock care when their kids travel. And they take the boys to all sorts of appointments and doctor visits. Additionally, when they are at their son's house, they clean, cook, and even shampoo the rugs. They are doing what their own parents did. They feel it is their responsibility to do so.

> My parents were wonderfully helpful and that is what drove me to want
> to be here for my grandkids. My parents loved having their grandkids.
> They loved it when we dropped off the kids for overnight so we could go
> out. They would keep them for us so we could go on vacation. They were
> supreme, wonderful caring grandparents; we are trying to measure up to
> that.

Some provide intensive grandchild care just like their own grandparents did. They are following in big footsteps and want to be sure they give their grandkids what their own grandparents gave them. Molly's plan had been to be a starlet. Instead, she is a 50-year-old, divorced, lower-income grandmother who works full-time and cares for grandchildren another 40–50 hours a week. It is safe to say this was not her plan. But aside from having more money to provide for herself, her three children, and her five grandchildren, she would not change much of what she is doing.

> Never. I never imagined this. I imagined I was going to be a Hollywood
> starlet. The only thing that kept me from posing for *Playboy* was I didn't
> have large breasts. I thought I would be lounging by a pool. But I don't wish
> I could quit, nah, not really. In all honesty if I won the lottery I'd still be
> working. And if I had houses all over the country I would still expect my
> grandchildren would be there, with me. Family is really important to me.

She wants to be the sort of grandparent her own grandparents were for her when she was a child. She treasures those memories and wants her own grandchildren to have similar memories.

> Coming up, my favorite days were when we went to my mom's parents; my
> grandparents were the sweet, loving Grandma and Grandpa on TV. Those
> were my grandparents. And my dad's mom . . . became a stunt pilot in her
> 20s and 30s. She had been a professional dancer, so when she got older she

became down to earth. When we came to the house they'd greet you like they hadn't seen you in years. You could go back the next day and it would be exactly the same. Every morning, there was freshly baked bread. Oh, man, that was the life. I really have a very strong sense of family. So while part of me wanted to be a jet-setter, I always imagined that I'd be a little old lady like that. So I wouldn't change anything. I'd change my financials, but not in terms of the time I put in and helping out.

Some women are prompted to care for their grandchildren because their mothers helped them when their own kids were young; others are prompted to care for their grandchildren precisely because their own mothers did not help them. Molly is of the latter group.

My daughter had my grandson two days before her 17th birthday. I was in denial about it. I was, like, I'm not going to be a grandmother at 36. This isn't happening. And the doctor put him right in my hands, when he was born, and said, "Here, Grandma!" And I fell in love with him. And anything she needed . . . I was trying to convince her to still go to college, she was heart set on Spellman and I told her I'd take care of him so she could go to school. But she didn't want to do that. She thought people would talk about her.

Molly wanted to give her daughter the kind of support she never had from her own mom. Still feeling the sting over her own mother's refusal to help her as a young mother, Molly goes out of her way to be helpful to her daughter and grandchildren.

I was really resentful about one thing though; when I had her my mom wouldn't babysit and help out so I could go to school. . . . When I wanted to go to school I didn't have the help. My sisters wouldn't help me either. I was resentful about that. So I did a lot for my daughter, when she needed it.

Some grandmothers provide intensive grandchild care, even though they do not want to, because their adult children pressure them to do so. Christine, age 73, is the oldest grandmother I interviewed. She has divorced three times and is the mother of one and the grandmother of two. She is white, lives on the West Coast, and has a personal income of more than $150,000 a year. She was raised by a nanny, and her daughter was mostly raised by a nanny, but now her daughter wants Christine to be a hands-on grandmother. When the first grandchild was born, Christine's daughter and husband and the new baby all moved into Christine's home and she took sabbatical and helped the nanny with the baby while the parents were at work.

> I did more at first, the first year and a half, my granddaughter and her parents lived with me at my house. I did a lot then. We all did night feeding. We all took care of her. We had a nanny, too, who came in the day so we could all work. But I was on sabbatical and was here around the clock, helping with the baby. I did everything but bathe her, lots of talking, diapers. But the nanny helped a lot, drove her to things. I would occasionally take the baby to the doctor but I was backup.

Christine's daughter hoped that her mother would help much more with the grandchildren as they grew up. Christine and her daughter fought so much about this that they finally went to counseling. Christine feels that her daughter is trying to make up for not having enough time with her mother when she was a child. But Christine is only semi-retired and very committed to her work, which has her flying about the country speaking at conferences and panels and protests.

> In the early years, when my granddaughter was born, my daughter wanted me to do much more for the kids. And even now she just said to me, "I wish you wanted to be with us more." We had a lot of disagreements, conversations, tears. She ached for me to be more involved. I think it was a longing from her childhood when she wishes I had been with her more. She wanted me to just drop in every day after work and see the girls. Eat with them. We even went to counseling to try to help sort out this relationship.

Though Christine is very committed to her daughter and granddaughter, she is very committed to her career as well. Talking about the tension between what her daughter wants her to do, and what she wants to do with her career, led Christine to cry a great deal during the interview.

I told her that I don't want to apologize about my very meaningful work that is very important to me and to the country. I am needed for this work. I need to do it. I have trained for this work my whole life. And this makes me cry very much.

Christine loves her daughter and her granddaughters. She says she feels buoyed by all the energy the girls have, but she minds the expectation that she will give up her work and care for them. She said repeatedly that we do not ask men to give up their work to care for children or grandchildren, but she is pressured to do so constantly.

This is a trap for women—the expectations that we will just give of ourselves. I have resources and I can spend money. I can pay for daycare and other people to take care of the children and now the grandchildren. But I don't want all of my time to be taken. I have a man's type of work schedule. My time is valuable for the work, the situation we are in in the US, and I am investing in that. It is for the family, but it is for all families. But then I feel bad that I am not meeting her expectations, not giving my daughter what she wants for her family.

Some grandmas provide intensive grandchild care because they do not feel that anyone else will watch the kids as well as they do. Betty feels that taking care of the grandchildren is much more than a joy; it is a duty best not left to anyone but Grandma. Betty is a 59-year-old, widowed, black woman who lives in a city in the northeast. She completed high school and is a licensed practical nurse. When Betty's children were young she did not have help from her mother; instead she was on welfare and stayed home with her children. But she fondly remembers how much her grandmother cared for her when she was young and she is purposely providing similar care for her own grandchildren. She retired from her career job several years ago and now is paid by the hour to work as much as 60 hours a week as a nurse at a health facility. Although she no longer receives employer benefits of health care, private pension, paid sick leave, or paid vacation benefits, she made the switch to hourly work so that she would be able to control her paid work schedule and provide care for the grandchildren. She would like to work fewer hours, but the health facility is understaffed and she is constantly being called to work more shifts.

Like many whom I have interviewed, Betty is a sequential grand-mother, caring for one grandchild after another as they are born over the course of decades. She has four children and 14 grandchildren and has taken care of each of her children's children at various times. Currently, Betty mainly cares for her younger daughter's four children, who live nearby, while their mother works the 7 am to 7 pm or the 3 pm to 11 pm, shift at the hospital.

> Mostly I take care of the grandkids here. They come here after school and then when their mom comes home they go home for bed at 7. If she works till 11, they will lay on the floor on a blanket at my house, and then she takes them home for bed. I feed them dinner most of the time; I cooked some beans yesterday and that is what they will have today with rice. I eat with them—we eat in the kitchen or the living room. It is hard to find time to buy groceries sometimes. . . . Now that I think about it, I am working nine days in a row. And I will take care of the kids probably four of those days when I get home from work.

Betty is working many more hours than she expected to but says she does so out of financial necessity. She is also providing many more hours of grandchild care than she ever expected to, but she sees this work as her responsibility. When I arrived for the interview she was at the door watching kids in the neighborhood and she resumed her post as I left. She feels it is best if she, rather than anyone else, cares for the grandchildren when they conclude their school day.

> I did not imagine I would be doing all of this. I imagined my kids would get grown and take care of their own families. . . . I see so many kids out, and they don't have anybody watching over them and that just bothers me. They just don't have anybody. I don't want my grandkids treated like that. I was not . . . I would not hire anyone to care for the kids, better if I do it myself. You have to be careful about who you leave your kids with.

Diane also feels Grandma knows best. Though Diane says it isn't her duty to watch her only granddaughter, she has reduced her work hours to 30 hours a week and has given up paid vacations and paid sick days so that her schedule is completely flexible. She says she never says no to requests for grandchild care. She never called a sitter for her own children and she does not want her daughter to call a sitter for her grandchild.

> I don't want any strangers watching my kids. When my kids were little, only family watched my kids. It would be scary to have a babysitter. It has to be family. Not a stranger. It is too frightening. I did have a little mother's helper come when my kids were young and after the second visit I found out she was heading for rehab for a drug habit. You just don't know things about strangers. Who wants to leave their kids with a person with a drug problem? Frightening world.

Similarly, Natalie, a married, 50 year-old, white woman, does not want her daughter to hire a sitter unless absolutely necessary. She used babysitters readily with her own children. Now she does not trust babysitters, though she wonders why. So she takes a day a week, and so does her husband, and her mother, with the grandkids. And they watch the grandkids after work every day and during many weekends. She is actively puzzling over the underlying causes of her distrust of babysitters.

> My daughter doesn't use sitters much, and I don't want her to. Why is that? Is there less trust now? . . . They really don't have a babysitter; the kids have seen very few, nearly always family or, now, daycare. When my kids were young I had a handful of babysitters that I would call. But my daughter calls me. Is there less trust? . . . I don't like them with a babysitter. I want them with someone who knows their schedule. I know what they need. I know what puts them to sleep. So she calls and if we are available, we go. Her twin sister also helps with the babies, so a lot of family helps. She is lucky she has family to help. We do say no, but not often. Usually we have been able to do it and we enjoy it.

Though they are tired from providing so much care, and feeling somewhat depleted from providing so much financial assistance to all three of their adult children, they really want to care for the grandchildren as much as they can.

> I am afraid that this sounds contradictory. I would love more time to travel and do hobbies, but we love being with the grandchildren. We are choosing

to do this. They need us and we want to help them. We love to do it. When the grandchildren run into your arms, smile, shout "Grandma is here," it is wonderful.

Some grandmothers provide intensive care to ensure that their adult children meet their objectives. Whether it be completing a degree, succeeding at a career, or buying a first home, grandmothers often put their own retirement or leisure plans, financial needs, or health on the back burner to help their children achieve their goals. Calista provides intensive support with the hope that her daughter will complete college. Despite all of her warnings, Calista's daughter became a young single mother and Calista responded by making sure her daughter completed high school and college. Calista is a 54-year-old, black, divorced woman with three children and four grandchildren. She works full-time as a medical secretary and has severe arthritis in her back from an on-the-job injury when she worked as a nurse's aide. She mainly helps with her daughter's two sons, who live close by. She has watched these boys all of their lives, while their mother went to college and now while she works. She had warned her daughter that having a baby too young would affect her life plans, but once her daughter did have a child, Calista worked hard to make sure that the impact was as minimal as possible.

> I always felt and always taught my kids to stay in school, stay focused, go to college. I told her there's always the deadbeat sitting around waiting to grab you and ruin your life. And she didn't listen. I explained to her then that when you have a child it's a domino effect. It's not just you, by yourself; it involves family members and she didn't believe that until it happened. So my thing was always to make sure her goals were completed. That she didn't say, "If I didn't have kids I could've done . . . ." I took care of her bills and mine, helped with sitters, and when she was going to college my mom helped her all so she could finish.

A decade later, Calista works a full day at the hospital and then meets the boys' school bus each afternoon and watches them till their mother returns from work at 11 pm. She feeds them dinner, helps with homework, and puts them to bed. On Tuesdays, she takes them to Bible study with her. The boys get help with their homework at the church while

Calista studies the Bible. She feels that she must provide the care herself because the quality of care provided by others is uncertain. When her own children were young she had some "bad babysitters" and she did not want that for her own grandchildren. It is important that she provide the care.

> I did have babysitters when they were very young, but they weren't good, which I found out after talking with my kids. I've only had two good babysitters, which is the reason I watch my grandkids. My daughter, after knowing in their lifetime she knows some aren't good, she doesn't want her kids going to babysitters.

But Calista is committed to more than babysitting. She is also committed to prevention. As she did with her own three children, she is determined to keep her grandsons focused on school and away from any of the seedy things that might happen on the corner. She covers a lot of the bills, pays tuition for the boys' football club, takes the boys on several vacations a year, and makes a point of getting them out of the poor neighborhood in which they live to see things in the wealthier parts of the city.

> With the grandkids, I do anything to take them out of the neighborhood. Sometimes with our children that are maybe low income we keep them on the same side of town because the parent can't afford to move. But I like them to see different things. We go to the YMCA in [a wealthy suburb]. I feel if you keep them busy they'll see life differently than standing out on the corner. Our goal is to keep them focused on school, college.

Some grandmothers were intensive parents and they remain intensive as grandmothers. At 61 years old, Pauline, a well-educated mother of four and grandmother of eight, feels she has gone directly from parenting to grandmothering with no break in between. Her oldest grandchild, who is just three years younger than her youngest child, lives with her for now. She works full-time as a computer programmer, earning just under $100,000 a year, and helps with the other seven grandchildren after work and on weekends. When her own children were young, she was divorced, working full-time, and in perpetual search for a babysitter. When Pauline could not find one, she took her children to work with her. Today, she does not take her grandchildren to work. But she often uses sick days or paid vacation days to stay home with them.

> On a normal basis I help my grandson with his homework. When I watch the younger ones we would feed them, of course, cook for them, play with them, help with homework, what you normally do with a child. I have taken them to doctor appointments before but usually their mom does that kind of stuff. Laundry and meals, we've only done that on occasion. But the one who lives with me I do everything for him. When the others come up we cook for them. They usually come out for a weekend.

Pauline usually watches the grandkids at her own house but when needed, she will go to their house. She is often called to care for the grandkids if their mom is busy or if they are sick.

> Occasionally I go down and stay overnight at their house with them if it's needed. Usually if their mom has to work and one of the kids is sick, or if they want to go out, it's "Oh, mom doesn't have a life so she can watch the kids. . . ." In other cases, they'll be sick and their mom is going to work, so I get called in to watch them. It doesn't happen very often, it's not every weekend either, but just sometimes. They live close by so it's easy for me to help them. . . . I've taken vacation days to watch them.

As is the case for many grandmothers, Pauline finds she provides more care for one set of grandchildren than the others. Sometimes the amount of care is decided by logistics; more help is provided to those who live closer. Sometimes the amount of care is decided by age of the grandchildren; more care is provided to those who are younger. Sometimes the amount of care is decided by need; more care is provided to the mothers who are single or the children who are struggling with disabilities. In this case, Pauline helps her divorced daughter's children, sometimes rearranging her work schedule to do so, even though her coworkers tell her she should not do so much.

> Like I say, it's my one daughter more than the other two; I end up watching her children. She's divorced. The other two have husbands who are pretty

good about helping them out, who they can depend on. It's sort of rare for the older two to need me to take time off. I have once or twice over the last couple of years. I have left early, if they're sick at school or needed to be picked up or something. I'm pretty focused while at work, so I'm not distracted by them at all. People at work tell me I should tell my kids they're responsible for their own kids, but I've never gotten into trouble or anything for it. It's not a big thing.

Pauline started grandmothering before she finished parenting her own children and so she has been providing care to children for decades without a break.

It's always been that way; it's not been like I wasn't, and then all of a sudden I was. Because my oldest grandchild is only three years younger than my youngest child. So, you know, it was like I never made the transition from being a mother, to no children, to being a gramma and being around young kids again. There was no, oh, now I have to start taking care of little kids again. My whole life I've had little kids that I have to take care of. If I could quit one, it'd be the working. I enjoy the children much more. Yes, I could quit and you know there would be no real choice between the kids and the job. The kids always come first.

Some provide intensive care to preserve the family tree. At 43, Candi, a divorced black mother of three and grandmother of three, works 50 hours a week as a licensed practical nurse and would prefer not to have to care for her grandchildren virtually every evening and weekend. But she feels she has little choice. She told me that it is her blood coursing through their veins, and she has to do it for her grandkids. She has tried finding child-care places that will provide good care but it is not easy. She was babysitting one grandchild during the interview because they had had to pull him out of an unsafe daycare situation.

Well, to be honest I just take the day and what comes with it. There's no particular system. I just roll with the punches because who knows what's gonna happen each day. For example, the baby is here because he was at daycare and got a gash that required a staple. So he's here now until we get the staple out of his head and try to see about getting him somewhere else to go. At least until we get the daycare place checked out, and they figure out what happened. This was a daycare center, not just someone's house, and he got hurt like that. He hit his head on the table and was hurt pretty badly. But why do you have a table with sharp corners like that with little kids running around. Who was supposed to be watching him?

Candi feels it is particularly important, as a black woman, to help her black son and grandson carry on the family name.

My son is the only one to bring the family name on so until somebody else has a boy he's the legacy. I recognize it's very important to protect him and educate him if for no other reason than to keep our name around. To have someone around . . . and as black people it's really important. So when I look at that responsibility my resentments go out the window because I realize it's a privilege to have something like that, to keep it going.

For Candi, it is part of her Christian duty to help her children raise her grandchildren. Her mother helped her when her children were young, even raising them while she struggled with a drug problem.

I do have a lot of pride because I'm Christian and I don't do all the things I should do yet. But I know God, and I know you will have ancestors to come. And the only way to do that is babies. And I also believe in the promise of if you do what you're supposed to do your kids will never be hungry. They'll be okay but you have to raise them the right way.

Lifelines

Most of the grandmothers I interviewed are providing care that is augmenting what is already a fairly solid family structure. But some grandmothers are providing a lifeline out of a very difficult situation. In some cases, grandchildren have special needs that few daycare situations will accommodate. In other cases, the parents may be partying, doing drugs, serving time in jail or prison, or in some way being irresponsible. Whatever the problems, in these few cases the grandmothers provide supportive interventions that make an otherwise untenable situation much easier. When a lifeline is needed, grandmas jump in for safety's sake.

Grandmothers often provide lifelines for grandkids with special needs. When Janet's first grandchild was born prematurely, and the mother only had six weeks off work, Janet stepped in to care for her full-time.

> Both grandkids were very premature. I actually quit my job and cared for my granddaughter. She was nine weeks premature and on a heart monitor. My daughter got six weeks off with each baby. My granddaughter was only home one week before she had to go back to work. That was heartwrenching. And I took care of her, full-time, when my daughter went back to work. At that time we lived further away and I was driving each day.

Janet is one of only a few grandmothers I interviewed who is vocal about the inadequacies of US maternity leave policies. US federal policy does not provide any paid maternity leave whatsoever and only guarantees 12 weeks of unpaid leave for those in very specific employment situations. The paucity of paid leave for parents of ill or disabled newborns is even more problematic. She was able to find work again once her granddaughter was stable enough for daycare, but she is aware that not all do so.

> The maternity laws in this country are so inadequate. You get no time, have to use sick time. No daycare will take a baby who is that premature and on a heart monitor. I was happy to be there, to take care of her, to help out my daughter. The second was premature, too, but by then his father was a stay-at-home father, so he took care of him.

Grandmothers also provide lifelines when their adult children are not really acting like adults. Sarah has taken her grandson out of many parties at her son's house. A 67-year-old, married, white woman in the southeast, she works full-time and travels a great deal for her very high-pressure, high-visibility position. Though her husband partially retired a few years ago, she has no plans to do so in the near future. She is the mother of two and the grandmother of three. Her son and his girlfriend had a baby while still in high school. Sarah and her husband immediately changed their schedules, and plans, to help with the baby and the down payment on a house.

> We took care of our grandson on weekends, and we saw him four or five times a week. When he went to preschool I would pick him up and bring him to our house. I would not say we raised him but we spent a lot of time with him. . . . I would take him after school and play tennis with him, and take tennis lessons with him. We have put a lot of money into him. We totally spoiled him. He has had a hard life. He is sweet, mature, sensible.

Her son's first marriage ended, and so did his second. Her daughter also now has a 9-year-old and a 1-year-old. Her daughter and her husband separated for five months and now are trying to make it work. Throughout it all, Sarah has cared for her grandchildren evenings and weekends. She often comes to work late or leaves early, or stays home a day, to care for them. She tutored her grandson three nights a week for years, until his grades improved. Recently, she became so concerned about the 9-year-old during the parents' separation that Sarah bought her a cell phone. She felt that her granddaughter was too young for a cell phone but that she needed to able to reach Grandma when she was upset. She said her granddaughter would call and pour her heart out about how much her daddy yelled. But Sarah's focus has remained on the oldest grandson, who is about to turn 18, because her own son has not proven to be a very responsible parent. Even when her grandson was a newborn, Sarah said her son did not see himself as the parent.

> When he is living with my son, they are complete equals. My son doesn't act like his father. He gives my grandson complete freedom. My grandson is sometimes more mature than his father. Many times I have thought that . . . but there have been times, when he was young and they would dump him and leave him, never pick him up on time. I did not want to be frustrated with my grandson, but I was with his parents. They were untrustworthy and they abused us, took advantage. It was not so much conflict with work but aggravation. It was conflict with my life, with my time.

The greatest concern for Sarah was how much her grandson's parents wanted to continue partying when he was a newborn and toddler. She said she would be on the phone with her son and could hear a party in the background and would know that her grandson was there.

Whenever she felt the situation was too unsafe, she would drive over and retrieve her grandson.

> If we had not helped, I don't know what my son would have done. I think my grandson would have been neglected at times. They were so young, not prepared. We stepped in a lot; we were fearful of some of his living situations. They were not good. At times my son was living with lots of people and throwing parties, and my grandson was living there, too. So we would get him and keep him and we would take care of him.

Sarah is very appreciative of how much her son repairs things for her at her house, but she would really like to see him living an independent life and relying on her less.

Grandmothers also provide lifelines when the parents have serious physical or mental illnesses. Gillian never expected to have her grandkids living with her for eight months. But they did when their parents were too ill to care for them. Initially, they kept the two grandchildren sometimes after work and often on weekends.

> Before they lived with me they would come spend the weekend with us twice a month or once a month. On the weekends, we would have our plans, go out for breakfast sometimes, go to the zoo. They love the zoo. Did that year-round. Or the park. I was doing cooking, bathing, we did everything. Bake things. Help breakfast. I loved those weekends, and my husband did, too. We both participated.

Then their father and mother both had serious problems and were unable to care for them. Their maternal grandmother had to have surgery. So Gillian and her husband took them in for a school year. It was not easy. Both children got off to a bad start at their new schools and had to be moved to different schools.

> So they came to live with us for eight months. We had to take them in. For those eight months it was an awakening. They were in school and daycare while here. They love their grandparents but they wanted to stay with their mom. That was rough for them and rough for us. . . . Those eight months were testing. This was starting all over again. We were mother and father

again. Rough. We had to go to school meetings, open house, conferences, fundraisers. We had to cook, clean, clothe. We had to get them up early, at 6 am, get them ready and drop them off and finally get to work myself. When they had their meltdowns I would have to go to school and get them. I have a cousin I could take them to but it was far away. My husband and I stuck together. We were going to do this, see this through. I did not want my grandchildren in foster care. You do what you have to do.

Gillian rearranged her work schedule constantly, and used all of her vacation and sick days, to care for the grandchildren. Her husband, partially retired, did the same. They got very tired balancing work and care of the kids.

I used some personal days and used up all my vacation time to take care of them. Used up all my personal time. My husband is partly retired; he is 64 now but partially retired at 62 so he could take care of the kids at different times than I could. But I had to do all the mornings but some days he could do afternoons. I was very tired, but I got to work on time every day, in spite of it all.

With two more in the house, they spent a lot more time and money on groceries, cooking, cleaning, and laundry.

We had to rearrange the whole house for them. I had to change the bedrooms and offices. We had to make different food; they don't like anything. You have to shop differently, buy things that children will eat. Everything changed. We had to do the laundry a lot more. Help with homework, take time for that, make sure it is done. Many times I had to meet with the teacher, talk about how he was doing. They both passed. Toward the end they really got adjusted. I had to give up going to the gym every morning before work. Now they are back with their mother. I am back at the gym before work most of the time.

Grandmothers also provide lifelines for parents who are in prison or rehabilitation. Paula has done both. She works the night shift three times a week and takes care of the grandkids during the days, often seven days a week. She has maintained this schedule for six years and she gets little sleep. She has been ordered by her doctor to leave the night shift but has not been able to find work on the day shift. One of her grandsons lived with her off and on at first because his mom was in prison, then because his father was in prison and his mother and another relative were abusing him. Paula did not want to discuss the cases but said that she has temporary custody now until her son is released.

> He has lived with me for years, off and on. When he was born, his mom was in prison—she was in prison when she had him so he came right to me at three weeks and was with me on and off. She isn't in prison now but I have had temporary custody for three years. His mother's cousin sexually molested him and his mother was physically and mentally abusing him. He was in a foster home but then tracked me down and asked me to take him.

For now, Paula cares for him around the clock and pays for all of his expenses. But it is difficult to supervise him fully because she works 40 hours a week at night. He is just entering high school and is very appreciative to be living with his grandmother for a while.

> My grandson tells me, "I am so glad you adopted me. You changed my whole life. I am so glad you got me." He had to testify that his mom was abusing him; he stood up and the judge said you look at me and tell me, and he told of the abuse. And now he is with me. He really appreciates what I am doing for him.

Tara also provides a lifeline while a parent is in prison. She is a 42-year-old, married, Native American woman living in the midwest who works at several jobs, including as a nutritionist and a piano teacher, that total 40 hours a week. She raised her own children as a single mom and many of her seven children are currently raising her eight grandchildren also as single parents. At the moment, two of the youngest grandchildren are living with her because their mother died due to a drug overdose and their father is in jail because of DUI charges. Tara's house burned down several years ago and currently Tara and her husband and the two granddaughters live in a garage. Another granddaughter is there for a month or so while her broken ankle heals. Tara is a temporary custodian for a few more months. What will happen when her son-in law is released from jail?

> We would love for their dad to care for the two girls but he is in jail and no one thinks he will be able to do it. We will take custody of the girls; I will want them to live nearby. I don't like having any of the kids move away.

Grandchild-Centered Families

At least for some, grandmothering has intensified. For most of the women I interviewed, grandmothering is now about much more than sleepovers and puzzles. For many US grandmothers, being on duty is performing virtually all of the tasks required to raise a child including chauffeuring, dealing with baths and meals, helping with homework, and providing medical care. These grandmothers do a lot of mothering. There is no question that if the US welfare state guaranteed a minimum amount of paid time off to the mothers and fathers—for vacation days, sick leaves, and parental leaves—or assured universal health care, high-quality, low-cost daycare, or universal preschool, grandmothers would not need to provide so much intensive care. In the absence of supports provided by the states, we see tremendous amounts of support being provided by working grandmothers.

For some it is constructed as a matter of choice. Indeed, many talk of making the choice. But despite the rhetoric of choice, it is a choice made in a certain social and historical context. Many are trying to live up to a family tradition of hands-on grandmothering. Some do not trust babysitters with their progeny. And some feel pressured as women to provide this carework even when it directly conflicts with their paid work. Aside from these social pressures, there are economic pressures. Many of the adult sons and daughters cannot afford paid daycare and grandmothers as a rule provide high-quality care for free. Moreover grandmothers are responsive in a way that paid daycare providers cannot be. Children cannot be brought to group daycare settings if they are ill or school is canceled for any reason. But they can almost always be brought to Grandma's. The bottom line is that for many of these grandmothers, the care feels somewhat obligatory. If they did not care for the grandchildren, their adult children would not be able to keep their jobs, work enough to support the family, complete their degree, or buy first homes.[9] There are few other sources of such high-quality, low-cost daycare.

For many of the grandmothers there is a sense of duty or obligation. Some feel a real sense of responsibility; families care for each other, particularly when times are tough. Family traditions and family legacies are on the line. When the situation is particularly difficult, such as when grandchildren have special needs or the parents are providing inadequate care, grandmothers may intervene to provide a lifeline to a safe environment for their grandchildren. They may be enormously frustrated with their adult children, but they do not want their grandchildren to feel the burden of their parents' shortcomings.

These interviews suggest that just as mothering has intensified, so has grandmothering in the United States. All but four of the 48 women I interviewed were doing more hands-on care than their own mothers did, and more than they intended to, especially given that they were working as well. Most of them are happy to be providing this intensive care, though many feel physically exhausted and a few feel financially depleted.

4

Juggling Work and Grandchildren

Many grandmothers juggle work and caring for grandchildren. One-half of Americans are grandparents by age 50; 70 percent of those in their early 50s, and nearly 65 percent of those in their late 50s, are still employed.[1] Studies show that working grandparents are just as likely to provide care as those who are retired, and one-third change their work schedules to accommodate grandchild care.[2] Like younger American women, grandmothers often struggle to balance work and child care in part because the United States does not guarantee paid time off for sickness, vacation, or parental leave, nor does it ensure universal health insurance, high-quality low-cost child care, or universal access to pre-school.[3] The absence of these federal policies simultaneously makes it more likely that American grandmothers will provide grandchild care, and it makes it more difficult to balance work and grandchild care.[4]

During the past few decades, some employers have introduced family-friendly forms of flexibility into the workplace to help families accommodate work and family lives. As methods of communication have multiplied, including email and smartphones, so have methods of conducting business. Flexible scheduling includes compressed work weeks such as working four 10-hour days, later arrivals, earlier departures, or working from home on some days. Employees often have to pursue such flexibility through their own initiative, and some find that it hampers career advancement. But those with children or grandchildren or frail older relatives in need of care may find the flexibility worth it.[5]

The trouble is, flexible schedules are not available to all; those in manufacturing and service sectors are often excluded. Employees who are black or Hispanic, have less education, or earn lower wages are less likely to be in positions that are offered, or allowed, to arrange flexible scheduling. Indeed, middle and higher earners are significantly more likely than lower earners to be able to set their start and end times through traditional or daily flex-time benefits.[6] But those that can get them appreciate flexible schedules. The National Study of the Changing Workforce indicates that employees who have more control over their schedule or access to flexible schedules typically report greater involvement in their workplace, higher commitment to their jobs, and better well-being.[7]

Much has been said about the difficulties young mothers face as they attempt to juggle work and children, but little has been said about how grandmothers do the same.[8] All of the 48 grandmothers I interviewed are working and caring for grandkids. These are the two conditions to be in my sample. They are working for a range of hours and caring for their grandchildren for an additional wide range of hours. Some of them are balancing these responsibilities seamlessly. Indeed a few women juggle work and grandchildren without changing their work schedules or using sick and vacation time. As with other studies, grandmothers commonly reported that they rearranged their schedules frequently. Some use nearly all of their paid sick and vacation time to care for the grandchildren. Some are willingly, or out of necessity, downsizing or changing jobs.[9]

The ease with which they rearrange work schedules varies considerably. Some are in highly autonomous positions and control their own schedules. Those who are managers, business owners, consultants, or per diem workers tend to have a fair amount of control over their scheduling. Others are in lower-income work that typically does not allow much flexibility. Nonetheless, as in other studies, many of the grandmothers I interviewed work in lower-waged jobs in offices with responsive employers who readily accommodate changing schedules, often by bending, breaking, or disregarding workplace policies.[10] Studies have found that women whose jobs provide flexible hours, unpaid family leave, and paid sick leave are likely to remain employed, improving financial security for their own old age.[11] Many of the grandmothers interviewed in this book have these lower-waged but fairly flexible positions.

Others have changed jobs or schedules specifically to accommodate grandchild care, often giving up paid sick days, paid vacation
days, health insurance, private pensions, and other employee benefits
in the process. Still others work in settings with strict scheduling policies or administrators and therefore find it much more difficult to rearrange their schedules to respond to the needs of their grandchildren.
They face limits to flexibility and, if they are not careful, they may face
repercussions.

Underlying many of the grandmothers' comments is that, given
their ages and levels of experience in the job market, they often have
more flexibility and job security than they did when they were young
mothers, and more than their daughters do now. A lifecourse perspective highlights the shifting sands upon which women balance work
and child care differently during different stages of their lives. When
the grandmothers were younger, many were either new to their jobs or
busy trying to establish careers and found it difficult to take time off
to accommodate their kids' needs. Today, many of their daughters and
sons are relatively new to the job market; have recently changed jobs
due to layoffs, moves, or divorces; or are just completing their education
and looking for new positions. Many adult children have yet to accumulate sick leave, vacation days, or job security. Additionally, the US
economy has been weak and many workers are vulnerable in the face
of high unemployment and layoff rates.[12] According to the grandmas I
interviewed, when someone has to leave work to care for the children,
it is often the grandma. Many are happy to do so but some find it difficult to endure the financial ramifications, the physical exhaustion, or
the gendered expectations. Whatever their situations, all of these working grandmothers juggle paid work and unpaid carework.

Balancing Work Hours and Grandchild Care Hours

One question that arises in examining working grandmothers is
whether they decide to reduce hours to provide more grandchild care
or whether they decide to provide less grandchild care to work more
hours for pay. During the in-depth interviews, many grandmothers
commented on this sort of rebalancing. But that sample is not randomly
selected and is not nationally representative. I analyzed the Health and

Retirement Survey (HRS) data set from 2010 to determine whether this sort of reallocation of hours is occurring on the national level.[13]

Table A.5, which appears in the appendix, shows the results of a regression equation predicting the number of hours of grandchild care grandmothers provided. HRS respondents were asked how many hours they provided during the preceding two years.[14] When we explored what shaped how many hours of care grandmothers provided, we found that those with more education, those who lived within 10 miles of a grandchild, those who lived in multigenerational family households, those who were white, black or Hispanic, and those who were married or divorced, and those who are light drinkers, were all significantly more likely to report more grandchild care hours. What did not matter, however, was how many hours of paid work the grandmothers were reporting. Hours of paid work was not related to hours of grandchild care when we controlled for other factors. In other words, these findings support earlier findings that suggest that grandparents working a lot of hours tend to provide as much grandchild care as grandparents working fewer, or no, hours.[15]

Conversely, table A.6, which also appears in the appendix, shows that when we examined the number of working hours grandmothers reported, the number of hours spent on grandchild care was not significantly related. Women who were black worked significantly more hours, and women who were married, or doing more physical exercise, worked fewer hours. But increasing hours of grandchild care did not reduce hours of paid work or vice versa.

Flexible and Inflexible Workplaces

The vast majority of women I interviewed indicated that their workplaces were quite flexible, making it fairly easy for them to rearrange their work schedules to accommodate ever-changing grandchild care schedules. Had I interviewed working grandmothers who were not caring for their grandchildren, I may have found much less job flexibility. Marta, for example, works full-time as an administrative assistant and though she only has a little flexibility in her work schedule, she rearranges it fairly often to care for her two grandsons. Her own mother did not provide help to her when her three daughters were young and had even told her that if Marta chose to work she should not count on her mother to babysit. Marta does not want her daughter to have to hire help; she wants to provide as much care as she can. She often takes days off work to care for the boys, uses at least one of her four weeks of vacation each year to care for them, and works through lunch so that she can leave a half hour early to see the boys. Marta is one of many grandmothers who has been at her job for decades and has a great deal of job security. She says her coworkers are happy to cover for her. After all, she often covers for them. Her job is flexible enough to accommodate her as a working grandmother.

Similarly, Vanna is a 53-year-old, white, married mother of three and grandmother of two who works part-time at a very flexible job. But she only watches her grandchildren after work and on weekends. Even if her grandchildren are sick or there is a snow day, she is not called for duty because the parents work opposite shifts so that one of them can always watch the kids. Nonetheless, she appreciates how flexible her work at the Catholic Church is; she sometimes rearranges her schedule to attend the grandchildren's events.

> We job share, so I can ask my coworker to switch days with me, so that I can go to the Halloween parade or some other thing they have at school. I never need to leave early. If the kids are sick, one of their parents can get the day off. The job doesn't get in the way. I am able to switch, and she is very accommodating—and I am with her. There is a day coming up when the kids have things at school and I could take the day off but really don't need to. I like to keep my schedule as it is.

Occasionally she has work to finish but needs to head out to collect the grandchildren. In those instances, she takes work home and the grandchildren help her get it done. Her boss, the priest at the church, accommodates these and other requests readily. In fact, Vanna's husband is about to retire and wants to spend at least a month each winter in Florida. Vanna is confident she will be able to rearrange her church schedule to take a full month off.

> There are times when I bring work home to get it done. I will sometimes bring home work the grandkids can help me with; the job doesn't get in the

way. And if my husband wants to go to Florida for a month, I think that my coworker would switch schedules with me and then I could take off with him. And I think they would all say fine. The Father is so flexible.

Many of the grandmothers are free to rearrange their schedules fairly often. Janelle often rearranges her work schedule to come in late, leave early, or take paid sick and vacation days to care for her two grandchildren.

> I do take a day off now and then. I took one day off a few weeks ago because he had a fever and I stayed home and took care of him. I took half a day when she had the babies. I took him to daycare and then went to see her in the hospital. . . I could take a vacation day, but they said that I can use my sick leave for that, too. I have plenty of days off. I have come in late or left early, but not often, just a little here and there to go pick him up or take him to daycare.

Her boss and her coworkers do not mind when she gets a phone call asking for her help or changes her schedule. They all enjoy the same benefits with their jobs.

> I do get a call at work now and then to plan things, but it just takes two minutes. My coworker doesn't mind at all. Absolutely not. My coworker is always going to be there. I factor that in. My job is flexible; that makes this easier. I feel I can offer whenever. My boss is completely okay with me helping out.

Like several grandmothers I interviewed, Janelle does not say no very often. Newly divorced, she wants to spend as much time as she can with her grandchildren.

> I want to be the go-to person. I sometimes get jealous if I feel he is spending too much time with his other grandparents.

Janelle would like to keep working until she is 70. She likes the work and the balance of work and grandchild care. The role diversity suits her well. In any case, she needs the income after she and her husband divorced after 35 years.

Work doesn't really get in the way of the grandchildren. There are only a few days that I could not miss work; otherwise there isn't anything that can't be worked around. . . . I would like to work until I am 70. After that it depends on how I am feeling. I may work longer. I feel that working keeps you younger. I was afraid if I stayed home I might just sleep. I am a little worried financially. Especially with my husband not around now, for these three years since he left, I am more worried about finances.

Janelle can readily reschedule work hours to care for her grandkids, but she limits grandchild care because she has both financial and physical constraints.

I would like to keep working and caring for the grandkids, for a few more years, absolutely. . . . I enjoy work. I don't want to quit either; I could not take care of grandkids full-time, physically. Also I would want more. I like the balance, the juggling. It isn't disruptive to my life.

Natalie's schedule is also fairly flexible and she frequently rearranges it to care for the grandchildren. Natalie works full-time but has arranged her schedule so that she has one full day off a week. She spends that day, all of her evenings, most of her weekends, and most of her paid vacation and sick leave time caring for the grandchildren. She rearranges her work schedule frequently to care for the kids when they are sick or there is a snow day.

I see my grandchildren every day. It is rare not to see them. . . . I use my vacation days often to help out with the kids, especially before they started to go to daycare. I rearrange my day, come in late, or leave early. I will use my day off every other week on the days she needs me in a pinch. I have some flexibility about scheduling those days off and I will schedule what she needs most. We do talk while I am at work, with her and with my husband, to set up the schedules. "Can you pick them up, or take care of one that is sick?"

But there are limits to her flexibility and when Natalie's job responsibilities do not permit her to take time off for the grandchildren, she calls her mother who, at 70, is very fit.

My mom will still go help if the kids are sick. She is young for 70 and she will take care of them. It is my time; no one at work cares. I don't take time that I don't have. It never becomes a problem. Yes, there have been many times when I had to work and really wanted to be able to take care of them. I love having them. There are times when they need me, and I would love to be home and do it, but I have to call my mom and ask her to do it.

Similarly, Sharon can rearrange her schedule fairly easily. She is a 61-year-old, full-time employee and cancer survivor. She uses nearly all of her four weeks of paid vacation each year to care for her grandsons. She also watches them many days after work and most weekends. Her son and daughter-in-law appreciate the help. Without it, their paychecks would go to paying for daycare and they would never save enough money to buy their first home.

I use my vacation time to care for the kids all the time. I have to help out my son; babysitting is so expensive. I use two weeks every summer, and sometimes the whole month, and take care of the kids all day during the summer. I watch the kids on weekends during the school year and she works on weekends. Then in the summer I watch them two to four weeks and she works extra during that time so they can get caught up on their bills. Babysitters would take their whole paycheck. I have to help them a lot.

She is the only person in her office and so, she teases, there is no drama. Nonetheless her workplace is flexible and workers from other offices will cover for her when she changes her schedule.

I have left early when the kids need me to take the kids. And I use my vacation and personal days. I get phone calls all the time at work asking if I can take the kids. . . . No one at work cares if I take off time for the grandkids. I have the time off to do it. I use my paid time off to care for them. The job never really gets in the way. My kids don't bug me about leaving work to care for the kids. It is rare that I need to leave work to go get the boys. But if I have to, another lady will take over my job and help me out.

Although she is trying to get her partner to retire due to his health, Sharon has no plans to retire any time soon. She loves her job. She is feeling better from the cancer, she loves taking care of the boys, and perhaps most important, she wants to provide this free child care so her son can save for his first house.

> We want them to buy a house. We want them to save the money. Some-times my son will leave money, hidden for me. I find it after he has gone home with the boys. Sometimes they say they are worried I am doing too much, that they will get someone else to babysit. But I say, "No, I will take them." But I am doing good. I was sick with cancer and that was a hard time for all of us. But now I am doing good. The doctor says I am good.

Janet's workplace is also rather flexible and she rearranges work often to care for her grandkids. She would really like to reduce work because the job itself is just too stressful. Janet is a full-time employee who cares for her grandchildren some evenings and most weekends. She occasionally uses vacation days, especially when there is an emergency.

> I use vacation days rarely to care for the kids, but not a sick day. I may take a few hours off in the morning or leave work early to go care for them. When my granddaughter broke her leg, and they could not reach her parents, my work was very understanding, I had to go pick her up and take her home so they could take her to the doctor. No one at work minds. But I am very careful not to let it interfere, unless there are emergencies.

Many of the grandmothers work with other grandmothers and they cover for each other readily. For example, many of Lee's coworkers are grandmothers and she says that they are all making use of job flexibility to care for grandchildren. Lee, a 60-year-old, white, married woman with two children and two grandchildren, works full-time at the court house, provides care for a neighbor, and watches her grandchildren about four times a week. Even though her daughter is not currently working, Lee rearranges her schedule frequently to care for the grandchildren, coming in late, leaving early, bringing the children to her workplace, and taking vacation or sick days to be with the children.

> My boss at work is very flexible and I keep track of my own hours. I can take my neighbor-lady to the doctor and just make up the work later in

the week. The eight years before, when I worked at the high school, it wasn't as nice. My boss is very flexible with my leaving for a half hour or an hour. I make it up another day, go in an hour early or so, and I keep track of it all. A lot of places wouldn't do that. When the grandkids come to visit me early, before I get off work, they are there usually for just half an hour. . . . And if I'm doing security I have to be sure I lock all the doors if she's there. She likes to come see Gramma at work and she likes having lunch with Gramma and we eat in the lunch room.

Lee is not alone in changing her work schedule to accommodate grandchild care or in having the grandkids at the courthouse. In fact, so many fellow employees bring their children or grandchildren that they host special events for the kids at the courthouse.

Some of the other people there, my coworkers, bring their grandkids or even their kids. We have a Halloween walkaround and everything during that time of year. My grandkids came to it this year and got candy. I see quite a few coming to say hi or visit, so we do see them. Quite a few of us became grandparents these last three years, so we share gramma stories.

Grandmothers in higher-ranking professional jobs tend to be able to modify schedules fairly readily. Estelle has a high-profile professional job that allows her to come and go, but it also requires her to meet many strict deadlines. Though they often ask for her help, Estelle has decided that she will only rarely miss work to care for any of her grandchildren. Until recently, just as her own mother did not help her much when her children were young, Estelle did not provide much care for any of her earlier grandchildren. That changed when her youngest daughter, unmarried, had a son and they both came to live with her. Estelle's job allows her quite a bit of flexibility, so she can take time to watch him or take him to the doctor, though she rarely chooses to do so.

There have been a few times that I have left work to take him to the doctor, or leave work to take care of him. . . . It was easy to leave for a bit because of the job I have. I am salaried, a special assistant. I have some flexibility. No one would tell me I can't go. It is that I am so driven by the deadlines of my job.

Currently, Estelle works more than eight hours a day and then heads to the gym. She recently lost a significant amount of weight and is committed to keeping her exercise regimen. She then goes home to make dinner and take care of her grandson. She feeds him, plays with him, and puts him to bed most nights. Her daughter, who sometimes has a job and sometimes does not, either takes care of the boy all day or takes him to daycare. Then Estelle takes over in the evenings and on weekends to give her daughter a break. Estelle likes spending some time with her grandson. Though she provided very little care to the older grandchildren, she enjoys her time caring for this new grandson.

Some grandmothers have flexible jobs because they are their own bosses. Toni is a 48-year-old, white, married mother of four and grandmother of four who is working part-time as a retail manager, caring for her grandchildren during most of her free hours, and caring for her mother who is dying of cancer. Because she is the manager she can schedule her work hours to coincide with when she is needed to watch her grandchildren, whom she calls her grannies.

> My job is really nothing because I work my schedule around the grannies, because I am the manager. Yeah, it's easy for me to do it. If I wasn't in a manager position it would be a lot more difficult for me as far as my schedule and seeing them and time off if I ever needed it. I haven't had to do any leaving, or missing work, or anything like that. There aren't really any distractions, not really.

Toni rarely has to change her schedule or leave work to care for the grandchildren, but she receives frequent calls from them asking whether she can help them or whether they may stay with her. Though she has a lot of flexibility in scheduling her hours, once she is at work she really cannot leave. So at times she says no to the grandkids' requests.

> Yes, sometimes the kids call me at work and stuff, they do. It all depends, sometimes their moms step in and sometimes I handle it. Yeah, actually let me see, last week or the week before, on Friday I think, my granddaughter called me from school. She was having a hard time; she was at school and she wanted me to leave work and come get her. I couldn't leave so I called her mom and we made her stick it out at school because it was no big deal. She

really wanted to leave over nothing. The grandkids call me first; if they could stay with me, they would. The 8- and 13-year-old like staying up here with me.

Having such a flexible schedule leaves Toni readily available to care for the grandkids, and she takes them with her on walks, to church, to care for her mother, and all sorts of other activities. She knows her children appreciate her help but caring for the grandchildren is a bit of a mixed blessing.

Sometimes you have to have that alone time and they never seem to want to give you that. I tell them, my grannies, that I'm retired as a mom, my kids are grown. But then they're just like, "But, Gramma, Nana, we love you so you can't get rid of us." Sometimes it might raise my blood pressure, so, no, it doesn't make me feel healthier, really, no. It's stressful sometimes. But I do feel fulfilled. I guess, I like doing it. It makes me feel fulfilled. I love my grandkids.

Maryann is one of many grandmothers who puts the grandkids before her work. She runs her own business and that gives her quite a bit of flexibility. She takes advantage of that to care for her son's children as much as she is able.

There is a set schedule of me taking care of the kids, but there are lots of phone calls. They call, "Mom, could you?" I say, "Sure, no problem." I turn right around and get the kids. Those grandkids take precedence over everything. They still do. My granddaughter will call and say, "I missed the bus." I will get her and drive her to school. They come first, the job is always second. My job has lately gotten in the way of my time with grandkids. We moved our business and it got more difficult during the move. We had my grandson for the week of his spring break and I could not take him to do things he wanted because we were moving the store that week. I had to tell him to come with me. Normally though, it doesn't because I can rearrange the job to fit the kids. I own my business and that makes it really easy to rearrange my work and appointments to fit the grandkids' schedule.

Some grandmothers have changed jobs so that they would have more flexible schedules. Diane did. When her granddaughter was born, Diane switched to part-time work so that she would have more flexibility. She gave up paid vacations and paid sick days, but she gained control over her schedule.

> I rearrange my work schedule all the time. My daughter and her husband have very demanding jobs and schedules. If they have something they have to do, I will just not go in to work that day. Baby comes first. I don't get paid vacations, since I went to part-time. I am on straight commission. I went to part-time right when she was born; I wanted to be available. I wanted to be able to organize my work schedule so that I could be with the baby. I work four days a week. Every weekend I work. So I often have Tuesday, Wednesday, and Thursday off and that is great because my daughter often needs me during the week.

Diane has a BA and works on commission as an interior designer. She only gets paid on the basis of what she sells. She has a lot of loyal customers and earns more than $50,000 a year. Some of her colleagues complain when she comes and goes on a part-time schedule, but she gave up paid vacations and paid sick days for this flexibility.

> There are people at work who mind that I don't go in some days. They are working more hours but they are getting paid vacation. I gave up three weeks of paid vacation to have the option to not come in. There are people who are jealous that I leave early. But it is commission. So I only get paid when I make sales. I have a lot of return clientele. Some are jealous that I can come to work less often. I will keep working forever, but maybe eventually go to three days a week. I love what I do. I need the challenge of being creative.

She says she has her life arranged just the way she wants it; a creative job and a loving granddaughter fill her days and nights. She has rearranged her job so that her schedule is completely flexible. Now she is always available to help with her granddaughter.

> I never say no. When they want me to take the baby, I do it. I can always help out. I can always make my schedule work. If I have to not go to work to do it, I will not go to work.

Other grandmothers have changed careers, and even places of residence, to be able to help care for their grandkids. Marsha did just that when her grandsons were diagnosed with disabilities. She is 64 years old, married, and the mother of one and grandmother of two. She has an MA in secondary education but switched to real estate, and she moved five hours closer to her twin grandsons, when one was diagnosed with Down syndrome and the other with moderate autism. Like several of the grandmas I interviewed, she gave up paid vacation and sick leave but wanted the flexible schedule more.

> I am a real estate agent. I work about 15–40 hours a week. It changes quite a bit from week to week. I am doing this instead of higher education because of the boys and their schedules. So that I can take care. I needed something very flexible so I could help at various times of the day and week. I just can't do a Monday through Friday job. I gave up paid vacation and paid sick leave when I went into real estate. I needed to be available to help with the kids, especially because they have special needs.

Marsha's son and daughter-in-law work full-time in what she describes as demanding and stressful jobs. The boys have a lot of doctor appointments, therapies, sick days, holidays, and snow days. Marsha covers nearly all of them. She says, "If there is an emergency, bad traffic, someone is sick, I am on call. I drop everything and go." She also watches them every Wednesday during the day, often during the evenings, most weekends, and occasionally for entire weeks while the parents travel.

> I change my work schedule constantly so that I have flexibility to take the boys. That is exactly why I went into real estate, so that I could be available for the boys. I am on call all the time. I can work early, late, weekends. If I am in the middle of a deal, I might not be at their beck and call for a day or two. But the rest of the time I can reschedule, or even take the kids with me to show houses. They love it. I look at properties with the boys all the time. We call and text all the time to set up times. So far they have never needed me when I was in the middle of a deal. So far every time they have needed us either I or my husband was there.

Self-employed grandmothers may choose to only take clients that will allow them to be available for their grandkids. That is precisely what Jamica does. In fact, she has always put the children before her job. She is a 49-year-old black woman. Twice divorced, she has four children and three grandchildren, one of whom has autism. Though she has a BA, she has never gotten to use it. When she was young she took care of her children and now that she is older she takes care of her grandchildren. She supports herself by cleaning houses. She only takes clients who understand that the grandchildren come first. Sometimes she does not get the house cleaned; other times she does so only by bringing the grandkids with her.

> I have cleaned houses off and on for 25 years. Right now I work every day; I work about eight hours a day. I can help out with my grandkids because the people I clean for let me be on my own schedule. If I have to go get the grandchildren, I may clean a customer later, at 7 that night, or even the next day. I explain to my customers right away that I have grandchildren and that I may not get to them at the time they want. I only take customers that will allow me that flexibility. I also do other work for some of the customers. They pay me to garden, or nurse them after surgery. I only take these jobs when I am not taking care of the grandkids, though.

Jamica is a housecleaner because it provides maximum flexibility. She rearranged her schedule for her own children and now she does so for her grandchildren. Her children frequently ask for her help and she readily reschedules a housecleaning or takes the grandkids with her to work.

> There are lots of phone calls. I am constantly changing schedules. I change my work schedule to fit the kids'. If I can't fit in the cleaning job, I just don't go that day. People mind, of course, I am sure they do, but they have been lenient. I am blessed. Many of these customers I have had for a long time. This is why I have this job. Being a cleaning lady was flexible when I raised my own kids. And now it is flexible with my grandkids. My husbands were never any help. I needed a job that would pay me so that I could take care of the children, and that was flexible if there was an emergency. And it seems there was always an emergency. I often take the grandkids with me when I clean. I took my own kids and now I take my grandkids.

Once the grandkids are at the job, they find a variety of things to do. Sometimes they even help her clean.

> They will bring backpacks full of books and toys, watch TV, color, they stay busy. I have put a couple to work, vacuuming, helping me get the work done. They like helping Grandma. The older grandson likes to vacuum; he is good at it. And he wants to get a $1 for doing it, to save money for a new Transformer. My schedule is my own.

Jamica has lost customers who grew weary of having their house-cleaning postponed. And at times the crunch of needing to complete a house and get to the daycare center before it closes is stressful and tiring.

> At times I feel stressed. Mainly the stress comes in when there is just 15 minutes running late, but have to be at the daycare center at a certain time before they close, but I need 15 more minutes to finish cleaning. That can be very stressful. Other than those hard deadlines, that is the main stress. Somedays I absolutely have to get the person cleaned that day; there is no other way. But I need to be there for the kids. Sometimes I just have to clean as fast as I can, and that does make me tired.

Patty also only takes clients who will allow her to be flexible. A 63-year-old white woman who cares for her husband, her mother, and her four grandchildren, Patty constantly rearranges her work as a housecleaner to accommodate her grandchildren's needs and schedules. Her husband, who has Alzheimer's disease and cancer, and some of her grandchildren often accompany her to the housecleaning jobs.

> Sometimes, when I have to work, the other grandma likes to have the kids. I take them early and get them ready and drop them off at her house. But she was just diagnosed with Alzheimer's disease so I am not sure how much longer she can take them. I balance cleaning jobs like this. I take my husband and my granddaughter to the job with me. When the baby will be napping, my husband will watch the baby and I clean during the nap. If it is a four-hour job, I break it into two days, so I can clean during the two naps.

If she has a lot of houses to clean and wants to get them done quickly she sometimes puts the grandchildren in a nearby daycare for a few hours. But often she just reduces the number of clients she takes so that she can take the grandkids with her to work.

> I have a daycare home near my house and sometimes I would drop the babies there and do all my cleaning on those days. My daughter paid the $25 a day. I don't do nearly as much cleaning now. I used to have 13 customers, but now I do less and only have three customers. I clean two small apartments in just two hours each, during the baby's nap. . . . My older grandchildren will watch TV while I clean. The people don't mind, they are not home.

She has lost customers who grew tired of their houses not being cleaned on time. But she finds new customers who are flexible. Then, as always, she rearranges her schedule, takes grandchildren with her, and steps out to take calls from her daughter.

> When I am taking care of the kids, especially if they are sick or something comes up, I have had to call and cancel a cleaning job, delay it for another day. For the most part, people don't care; they say we don't care when you come as long as you come. But sometimes, a few people minded; they wanted me to come at a certain time. Sometimes I get phone calls. My daughter and I text each other incessantly and some places don't have coverage, so I have to go outside to see the messages.

Taking care of so many people on such ever-changing schedules can be difficult. Patty is constantly balancing her cleaning schedule, the kids' school schedule and sick days and snow days, and her husband's and mother's medical appointments. Sometimes she makes scheduling mistakes.

> Yes, I have had trouble keeping it all straight. If I don't keep track of days off, then all of the sudden the kids have the day off school and I did not realize. In September there was a day when we ended up with all the kids at my daughter's house and I had arranged to clean a house and had to call and cancel the cleaning. Usually I look at the schedule at least a week in

advance to cover all the contingencies, so that my work time doesn't impact on taking care of the kids.

Some grandmothers have tremendous flexibility at certain times of the year and then absolutely no flexibility at other times. Susan is 62 and even though her husband is partially retired, she expects to continue working until at least age 65, in part so she can continue to help her son pay for law school. She works full-time and rearranges her schedule frequently to care for the grandkids. She often uses vacation and sick time to care for them as well. Her workplace is flexible, but there are limits during certain busy times of the year.

> Yes, the job gets in the way. . . . Recently I wanted to leave work for one of their competitions, but it was a busy time. Should I lie, say the kids are sick, so I can go to their competitions? But I told the truth and my manager said it was fine if I missed work, and I did take a week off for the competitions. But I have told my daughter there are certain times I can't take the week off, when I can't miss work. She has to make other arrangements.

Many grandmothers have quite a bit of flexibility but their desires to care for their grandchildren are thwarted by adult children who fail to give them enough advance notice. Like many grandmothers, Reagan would like to help as much as possible but her adult children often ask for help at the last second. Last-second help is rarely possible. A 60-year-old, white, married woman with one stepson and three grandsons, Reagan routinely rearranges her schedule to care for her grandchildren. She is CEO of her company and she allows the other grandmothers to do the same.

> I take time off a lot to be with them. When the youngest was born, we helped out extra days every week. I took time off from work. It doesn't really get in the way at work. I can rearrange my schedule and so can my daughter-in-law. So we can make it work. I just wish I had 48 hours in every day. Then I could do as much as I want of everything. We text a lot at work to set things up or have an email exchange. We might get a phone call if they are in dire straits. There are many other women in the company who also take time off to care for grandkids. As CEO, I let them. Not an issue.

But if she has clients or meetings scheduled, which she is in charge of running, then Reagan cannot care for the kids. She needs some notice. Often, to her great frustration, she does not get it.

> We always want more access than we get. My daughter-in-law knows that; we tell her all the time. But she does things at the last minute. She will call at three to see if I can take care of them that night. But I will probably have a meeting I am running. I can't just go on a dime. It isn't that work is in the way. It is more that my kids do things at the last minute. They will ask at the last moment if I can watch them for three days, but I can't change everything at the last minute. If they plan ahead, I can always rearrange. But in an emergency I have taken time at the last minute to help out.

Grandmothers whose jobs include appointments with clients or customers are much less likely to be able to rearrange work schedules, particularly on a moment's notice. Lucinda is a 53-year-old, white, married physician's assistant. Her job is quite flexible if there is enough advanced notice. In fact, when her grandchild was born, Lucinda rearranged her schedule so that she has every Wednesday off to spend with her granddaughter. She also takes vacation days to care for her granddaughter. She is using an entire week of vacation to care for her granddaughter while her parents take a trip. But once she schedules appointments with clients, Lucinda is not able to change her work schedule. Her daughter knows that and saves her calls for emergency help for the weekends.

> I never get emergency calls from my daughter for help. She understands that I have a full patient load and that I can't just leave 12 people in need of appointments. She understands my career, what I do. So she knows that I can't just leave work or miss a day to help her out. I have never rearranged my work schedule for her, other than taking every Wednesday off. But on a Saturday she will ask for emergency help, maybe three or four times, when they both have to work and I go help.

There are times when many grandmothers simply cannot leave work. For the last four years, Corey, a 57-year-old white, divorced, mother of three and grandmother of four, has rearranged her work schedule as a substance abuse counselor almost constantly to provide care for her daughter's three children. Her daughter does not work but is unable to go pick up the kids or take them to the doctor herself because she does not drive. One of the grandchildren has autism, and Corey misses a great deal of work picking him up from school or taking him to the doctor. A few years ago her daughter and the grandchildren lived with her. At that time it was easier to rearrange work to care for the grandchildren because her job was more flexible. It is more difficult now because with her new position Corey has client meetings and sometimes cannot leave work.

> During the years they lived with me I would get phone calls, have to leave early, and come late, take days off, to take care of the kids. At that time I was on the detox unit at the hospital and I could be more flexible. Now I am in the meth clinic and I have client appointments, so I cannot just skip work because they would all have to reschedule. I try not to miss work now. But when they lived with me I would get calls to go to school and I would have to take my grandson when he had a meltdown. My daughter doesn't drive so she can't take them to the doctor unless her boyfriend has the day off. To this day if anyone has to miss work, it is still me.

Corey would retire if she could afford to do so, but at age 57 she estimates that she has at least 10 years to go. She gets exhausted trying to balance work and the grandchildren but says she has no savings because she has paid for rent, groceries, clothes, medical expenses, camps, gifts, and other expenses for her daughter and grandchildren. As a result, she plans to work until she is age 67 to receive full Social Security benefits.

Miriam is one of many grandmothers who only have workplace flexibility if they get sufficient advanced notice from their adult children. At 67 and approaching retirement, she has worked as a secretary full-time and has juggled work and grandchild care for nearly two decades. She uses nearly all of her vacation and sick days to care for grandchildren. But her job is a busy one and there are limits to how much she can help. Sometimes she has to say no. Unless there is an emergency.

> I get 30 vacation days paid per year. I often don't get to use them all, so I lose them. Sometimes we are simply too busy to be able to use them. I use almost all of them to be with my grandchildren, to take care of them, to go see them.

In the earlier years, she rearranged her schedule and took all of her vacation days to care for each grandchild as they arrived. Miriam also kept the kids on weekends and took a half day off every Wednesday to provide care.

When my first granddaughter was born, I used all my vacation taking care of her. Also, I would miss half a day of work every Wednesdays to care for her. I would take a week of vacation to babysit her. I would keep her Saturday and Sunday over night. I did all this for the oldest two. By the time the third child came, they lived in a house adjoining her parents and they did most of the care. So I do less now. They would bring the kids to me to keep them for the night so they could sleep. I used my vacation in those days to babysit. I had the two oldest ones a lot. We took them to our camp. I was doing everything. I fed them, did their laundry. My daughter-in-law had odd hours. I was forever picking them up and taking them home and taking care of them.

Sometimes she works from home and answers the work phones from there. The kids call her often at work to ask for her help in covering child care. Still, Miriam has told the kids that there are certain busy times at work during which she cannot leave. In an emergency, however, they still call and she still goes to help them.

At times I was working and had the phones transferred to their house so I could still answer them. I was doing a lot of care. I enjoyed it. I loved it. If my kids call me at work and it is busy, I hang up if there is anything going on at work. . . . I try to take my vacation time when they have a day off school so we can do things together. They will sleep at our house. But I never let it get in the way of work. My two sons will call and ask if I can do this or that, drive here, pick up this one, take care of that one. They need me. They know they can call me. But I ask for some warning, so I can rearrange my schedule. They know they can't call during my busy times; certain times of the year, they know not to call. They would only call then for emergencies and a few times I have had to go help them out. I never say no. . . . But they don't ask that much. Unless they need me.

Miriam says that her coworkers are all taking care of their grandchildren as well and they often cover the phones for each other. The most important thing is to uphold the tradition of hands-on grandmothering.

I do have to make arrangements to leave work for a play or a game, and that is harder sometimes. My coworkers don't mind. We all take our turn; we are all taking care of our grandkids. My children grew up with grandparents always part of the picture and now their kids are growing up that way, too. Both sets of grandparents are around all the time, taking care of them.

Miriam wishes she could have afforded to retire years ago, as her husband has done. But they needed the money so she is staying on the job until she turns 68. She never expected to be working to this late age. She did expect to be caring for grandchildren.

This isn't what I imagined. I did not think I would be working. I thought I would be home with my kids and home with my grandkids. But we could not afford for me to stay home. I would quit work. I retire in July; it is all set. I will be 68 and it is time. My job isn't that flexible, I have to be here 8–5 every single day, and sometimes weekends. I often don't get my lunch hour. My job is demanding; I am eager to be done. I would like to work less, have more flexibility. If they would let me go part-time, I would do it. But they will not do it, there is no way. My job can't be part-time.

Similarly Bennie can get off work with plenty of notice but has little flexibility once her shifts are scheduled. Bennie is a 53-year-old, white, married mother of three and grandmother of three. Her goal is to spend as much time with the grandkids as possible but occasionally her job makes that impossible. She completed high school and works full-time as a lab technician. Her husband has been out of work due to a bad back for three years. Last year he finally became eligible for disability benefits through Social Security. Bennie said the two years when she provided the only source of income were very difficult for them. Recently he had a heart attack and was diagnosed as diabetic. She takes care of the grandchildren after work and on weekends. She readily rearranges her work schedule and uses sick days and vacation days to care for the grandchildren.

If they need me to watch the kids, if they are stumped, I will take work off so I can take one to the doctor. I leave work early to pick the kids up. I use

my sick days and vacation days to stay home with the grandkids. If they are
sick and can't go to daycare, I will take my sick day and stay home to take
care of them. Normally I don't take phone calls during work. Usually I will
do phone calls only during my break and lunch. But if the kids are sick or
something I will leave my phone on and take the calls during work. I tell
them if you get stuck, call me and I will see what I can do to watch the kids.

Even though her husband, friends, and coworkers tell her that she is
devoting too much energy to the grandchildren and not enough on herself, Bennie is always trying to maximize her time caring for the grandkids.

I want to spend as much time with them as possible and I tell my kids
that. The more the better. Other people I work with are also taking time to
watch their grandkids. Nobody ever minds; they all know how I am with
my kids and grandkids. It isn't a secret. They are my life. I don't do enough
for me. They say that to me all the time. So does my husband. It is true. I
don't. But they are my life.

Bennie recently had a knee replacement and missed three months of
work, but she only took one month off from grandchild care.

Three months ago I had a second knee replacement on the same knee—
took three months to recover, so I was out of work. I had built up disability
time and so we got paid. My husband was able to take care of me during
that time. After the first month, we did still take the kids; if they needed us
we took them. They came to visit a lot. That is my best medicine. Helped
me recover. Kept me really motivated to recover.

There are times when she cannot get off work and that distresses her
quite a bit. Bennie loves her job and would like to work until she is 65.
She would reduce to part-time to permit more time with the grandchildren if she was financially able to do so. But her husband's disability
precludes employment, and her youngest daughter still lives at home.
She is the only breadwinner and must continue with full-time work.

Sometimes I can't get off work to care for the kids and that makes me feel
very bad. I can't get someone to cover my shift and so I can't get off and I

just feel terrible. I always try. I want to work until I am 65 and would like to retire then. I love my job and I love the patients. The job is stressful because of the coworkers. But I love the patients. I would like to keep this job till I retire. My dream job would be to move to labor and delivery. . . . They have a part-time opening now but I need full-time work. My husband doesn't work; my daughter lives here for free. I have to have income, a full-time job.

Some grandmothers do not have a lot of flexibility but manage to rearrange their schedules anyway. Cherry still works full-time and cares for the grandchildren before and after work and on weekends. Cherry said she does not, and in fact has been told by her boss that she may not, rearrange her work schedule very often for the grandkids. Nonetheless during the interview she mentioned several times that she had in fact left early or taken a day off to care for the grandchildren.

Never have taken time off work to care for the grandkids. . . . I sometimes leave a bit early. A job is a job. If someone was sick I might take a vacation day to stay home with them. Rare that it interfered with work. I have my cell phone, and before that my daughter would call here at work.

Her job is not flexible and her manager and coworkers have told her she may not rearrange her schedule or take phone calls about the grandchildren. Nonetheless, she continues to do both. For her it is just a job and caring for the grandchildren is much more important.

Similarly, Paula is not really able to rearrange her work schedule to accommodate grandchild care. She works three nights a week, for 12-hour shifts, and then takes care of grandchildren during the days. She frequently uses her paid vacation and sick time to stay home and take care of the children. Additionally, she brings them to work at times, though she has been told not to by some of her coworkers. She feels she has little choice because two of the grandchildren have special health concerns.

I will take days off if they had health problems. One has peanut allergies and one has sickle cell. Not many daycare people will take kids with these serious issues. And so I will use my vacation days to take a day home with them. And for snow days, I would take a vacation day. I get three to four weeks of paid vacation a year. I will use at least half of my vacation days to be home with the grandkids. I get paid sick days and I did use some of them to be home with the grandkids, especially if they were in the hospital. Then I would take the day home with them. I did not have to start a shift late or leave early but sometimes I would take them with me to the job.

Though some of her coworkers object to the grandchildren being in the workplace now and then, her boss never voices any objections.

I had people working with me and they would say you can't have your kids here. But really my grandkids would only be there a few minutes then one of my kids would pick them up. My bosses never said anything about my time with grandkids. They really did not know. I never went into detail about why I needed the day off.

Grandmothers who work nights and weekends found that their jobs were maximally flexible when the grandchildren were young but less so once they were older. Renee owns her own real estate agency and therefore has tremendous flexibility. She readily rearranges her daytime schedule to care for her granddaughter who lives nearby.

When she was little, because she was right here, she was part of my life almost every day. Her mom would go to work and then I would run, pick her up from daycare and bring her back here. . . . We would keep her over- night when she was little so her parents could go out or if they went away. Once she lived with us for two weeks, she was just 2 years old, so we did everything. We ran her to the doctor, took care of everything. By then I owned my own real estate business and I had an assistant, so I would work at home a lot. Or my husband would take her and I could go to work. Or I would take her to work with me. I was showing homes and just put her in the car seat and she would go with me. I would work from home and juggle things. Real estate lets you do that. If she was in trouble or sick, or on a snow day, they would just drop her here on their way to work and I would keep her for the day. And I would work from home, and then we would go show houses; she just rolled with it.

But now her granddaughter is in high school and wants her grandmother to be at her volleyball games and other evening activities. The job feels much less flexible now because most people want to be shown houses on evenings and weekends, precisely when her granddaughter is free from school.

> My job was great for flexibility when she was young, but now that she is older it is the worst job because everyone wants me to show houses nights and weekends. I have a window of just four years to spend time with her, before she goes to college, and this time is critical. I need to shape her to remember, for traditions, and family, and where her roots are.

Renee would retire from real estate and spend more time with her granddaughter if she could afford to do so. In fact she had planned to retire at a much younger age. But she loaned her nest egg to her son for a business venture that failed. He is unable to repay that loan. So Renee keeps working to accumulate a new nest egg.

A few grandmothers were warned by their bosses that they were missing too much work while caring for their grandchildren. At 48, Annie is a black part-time worker, divorced mother of five, and grandmother of five. A few years ago, she worked for the county full-time and also looked after her grandkids before school each morning. Often, she found it difficult to care for the grandchildren and get to work on time, and her boss was not happy when she was late for work.

> There was a time, maybe four or five years ago, I worked for the county for about 14 years, and my grandchildren would come over in the mornings because I would get them ready and they would wait at my apartment in the morning for the bus to go to school. So sometimes the bus wouldn't come get them on time, and because they were late, I was late for work. So I would get in trouble at work from my boss when I got there. And some days I would have to call someone, and then wait for someone to come and get them and take them to school, because I didn't always have a car.

Similarly, Tara was warned that her job was at risk. Tara is a 42-year-old Native American mother of seven and grandmother of eight. Two granddaughters live with her at the moment because their mother died of a drug overdose and their father is in jail. Tara juggles several jobs that amount to 40 hours a week.

> I do have to change my schedule for work all the time to take care of the girls, but they told me to make sure I have a backup child-care plan, so that the kids will have somewhere to go if I can't leave work. I teach a lot and the schedule is set a year in advance, and so I can't just reschedule if the girls need me. I will get calls during the day to go pick up the girls because they are sick or something, and if I can go that day I will go pick them up. But if I have classes scheduled that day I can't leave work. If they can't reach me they call my husband or the other grandmother.

Her husband helps with the girls as much as he can, but his health is not good. As a result, Tara is constantly rearranging her work schedule to care for various grandchildren. Her boss has made it clear that her job is at risk.

> My husband has had several heart attacks. He is 12 years older than me, 55 years old. . . . If I have to I will lose my job if I have to take care of my family. They have said a few times that the girls are interfering with my job, that I am taking care of too many people and it interferes with my job.

A few months after the interview, I happened to bump into Tara and learned that she did indeed lose her job because she missed too much work because of caring for her grandchildren.

A few grandmothers actively resisted taking time away from work to care for the grandchildren. Christine's workplace is plenty flexible but she is not interested in, or willing to, curtail her career to care for the grandkids on a constant basis. She is a semi-retired PhD who works on public policy. She travels the country speaking at conferences and panels and protests. She loves the work but does not want to limit it to care for the grandchildren, even though she loves them, too. She struggles to find the right balance.

> I have changed my schedule many times to help out with the girls. I was taking my granddaughter to swimming. She is a star. I was taking her several times a week and waiting for her and during that time I would rearrange my

schedule and turn down meetings or trips so that I can be there. Then I pick up dinner and we all go eat at their house. For any emergency, if the parents get hurt on the job, I have had to change my schedule, cancel my trip, postpone my meeting. My daughter would say I am not much of a caregiver, that I don't do much for the girls. She says I don't do enough. And I don't do that much. But I do take care of them many times each year.

Christine is devoted to work but under constant pressure from her daughter to do more for the grandchildren. She joined a support group aimed at helping her achieve a balance that might satisfy all.

My work is very important. I have prepared for this lobbying work my entire life and I must do it. I have been in conflict. I am addicted to work, and that does take me away from the girls. I go to a support group . . . to help me with balancing the work and the grandkids, the things my daughter wants from me. The goal is to help me find a different balance. There are people there working on their child-parent relations. Other families have problems with drugs, setting boundaries. But my problem is that my work gets in the way of what my daughter thinks I should be doing with her children. I need to set my own boundaries, try to do less work, and be more available for her and her family.

Christine is one of only a handful of grandmothers that I interviewed who balked at traditional gender roles and carework. She is frustrated that women, and not men, are expected to give up meaningful work to care for grandchildren. She finds the pressures even more troublesome now as a grandmother than she did when she was a mother. When her daughter was young, Christine had a live-in nanny who cared for her daughter around the clock. For any kind of emergency or last-minute scheduling matters, Christine turned to the nanny for child care. But now as a grandmother, she does not have a nanny. There is no one to back her up now when there is a schedule change for her or for the grandchildren. Nonetheless she is trying to find a new balance to meet her daughter's expectations.

I am afraid of losing myself. If I was at their disposal, if I did as much for them as she wants, I might lose myself. I would lose my work. When she was young, I was at her disposal but I had a 24-hour support system. Who is there to help grandmothers? There is this agenda that women should have to do this, give up everything for the family. I just don't want to do that.

Job Security

Many of the grandmothers have been at their jobs for decades. They felt they had quite a bit of job security and could risk arriving late, departing early, skipping lunch, or using sick or personal days to miss work and care for the grandchildren. But they felt that many of their adult daughters and sons did not enjoy the same job security. The economy has been fragile and in the face of high unemployment and layoff rates, workers generally, and newer workers in particular, are vulnerable if they try to take time off for family concerns.[16] Many of the adult children were relatively new to their jobs, having just completed degrees, or left marriages, or returned from unpaid family leaves. Many grandmothers said that their adult children did not feel secure taking time off, or asking for late arrivals or early departures, to accommodate their kids' schedules and needs. So they turned to Grandma for help, with much less concern that her job would be at risk.

Calista is one of many grandmothers who says she has more job flexibility and security than her daughter. She rearranges her schedule frequently to care for her grandkids while their mother is at school or at work. She gets her grandsons off the bus five afternoons a week and watches them until their mother gets home from work at 11 pm. When needed, she also takes sick days or vacation days to care for the boys. Sometimes she has to go to work late to put them on the bus or leave work in the middle of the day if their mother is not able to leave work. Her daughter is less secure in her job and therefore has less flexibility in her scheduling.

> I watch them while she works. Actually so she can go to work. She wouldn't be able to go to work without me. I've been at my job long enough that it's okay for me to change my hours so that I can accommodate her schedule.

Betty does not have much flexibility, but she has more flexibility than her daughter. At 59, Betty is a black divorced mother of four and a grandmother of 14, whom she cares for often. She traded her career for per diem work and while she gave up health care, private pension, paid sick leave, and paid vacation benefits, she gained flexible scheduling. She frequently rearranges her work schedule. Betty's daughter is relatively new to her job and cannot risk missing work, while Betty has been with her company for decades. She often gets calls from her children while at work, asking her to pick up a sick grandchild. She sometimes leaves work early or brings a grandchild to work during the shift. Betty says the people at work know she has these responsibilities and they accommodate her need to be with the grandchildren. In fact, she said that many of the nurses have similar responsibilities and they all pitch in for each other to make sure the grandchildren are cared for properly.

> If I have to go from work, I just have to go. One day they were short and
> I had to go get my grandson [who has Down syndrome] off the bus and
> then I went back to work. Sometimes I take him to work with me. We have
> a room that we eat in; he sits there and he likes to draw. He gets to see
> people. People cater to him and he likes that. If I was full-time it would be
> bad. But because I am per diem, it isn't bad. I can get off work when the
> kids need me. I don't have to leave that often but when I do they accept it.
> They have no problem with it. No, they have kids and they have to leave
> sometime, too. I cover for them and they cover for me.

Similarly, Blake could rearrange her schedule more readily than her daughter. Blake is a 68-year-old white mother of one and grandmother of two boys who live with their parents in the bottom half of the house. Blake is a lesbian who is married to her partner and together they provide some financial help and a great deal of grandchild care for Blake's daughter and her husband. Though her daughter is rarely able to rearrange her schedule, Blake does so often. As the years go by, the financial help is needed less, and the grandchild care schedule changes constantly. But that is not a problem for Blake, who runs her own business, takes Thursdays off for grandmothering, and brings work home when needed.

> I own my own business and I shuffle work for the kids frequently. Last
> week when I took him to chorus I had to go back after chorus and do some
> work in the evening. At times I cover when they are sick and I have to

juggle parts of the day for work and parts for them when they are home or sick. I can work while they are here. It is a balance. I am often juggling or shifting my time between work and the kids. . . . I have had to reschedule or shift meetings if there is illness. It is easier for me to shift a meeting than it is my daughter. We assess who can shuffle and it is often me. All of my clients know I can't schedule things on Thursdays. I would say Thursday is my grandma day and I can't meet.

Blake and her wife often rearrange their social schedules as well, foregoing evening plans so that they can care for the boys. They have no complaints; they feel there is a short period of time in which their services will be needed and wanted. They share a unique living arrangement and they enjoy their time with the boys. They are very glad to be getting along so well with Blake's daughter and her husband.

My daughter and her husband are very respectful; they don't ever make assumptions. They ask and if I can't help, they are respectful of that. My daughter and her husband make it easy by appreciating having us around. And the boys are terrific and I enjoy having them.

Grandmothers who work in management often have more autonomy and flexibility than their daughters who do not. Meryl became a grandmother at age 46 when one of her three children became a single mother at age 18. Her daughter continued to live at home with her and her husband and they helped raise the grandson for the first five years. They covered all of the expenses for their daughter and grandson, including tuition for college and graduate school. Meryl, a white grandmother of one who lives in the northeast, works full-time as a registered nurse but is in management and rearranges her schedule often to take care of her grandson. Even now that her grandson is 8 and her daughter is raising him independently, Meryl said she has a lot more flexibility, autonomy, and security in her own career than her daughter does in hers.

I have often left early in the day or early because he was ill and it was easier for me to leave my job than my daughter. Because I am management and I have more autonomy. I am often aware of my coworkers dealing with issues with their children at work, or taking a day off, or leaving early. I leave sometimes early to go to his school performances, or I often take the day off when he has a half day, then I babysit when he gets out of school. They live about a five-minute drive from me. So I will go pick him up at school and always come back to my house; I can be productive in my own home.

Especially during the first five years when her daughter and grandson lived with her, Meryl would rearrange her work schedule to take care of the boy. As management, she was better able to respond to his schedule than was his mother, given her college class schedule and her lower-income entry-level job.

They lived with us until he was about 5, and that is when I did more of the babysitting. Being in management I could take a day off to watch him during the day. I am fortunate I can take a day at a moment's notice if he is ill. How did I juggle it, I don't know. Family is there for family. She went to school in evenings or work in evenings so that most of the babysitting I did was in the evening after my daytime job. My husband babysits, too, but it's usually not him alone, usually us together. Babysitting for my grandson was always a pleasure. There were times I was tired but more so from my job. My job comes home with me at times, so it is hard to juggle both responsibilities.

Flexible Schedules and Flexible Grandmothers

Though many scholars focus on how younger women juggle work and child-care responsibilities, this chapter demonstrates that many middle-aged women also routinely juggle work and grandchild care. Whether their multiple responsibilities lead to role enhancements or role stress hinges to a large extent on whether they have flexible scheduling in the workplace and sufficient resources. For the most part, the grandmothers I interviewed had quite a bit of job flexibility and were routinely able to rearrange their schedules to care for grandchildren. This is due, in part, to the fact that I only interviewed working women who were indeed providing some care for their grandchildren. Had I interviewed grandmothers who were not providing care for their grandchildren I may have talked with women in much less flexible workplaces.

Indeed, all of the women worked in at least partially flexible situations that permitted them to at least occasionally come in late, leave early, skip lunch, or use paid sick and vacation days to care for grandchildren. Many of the grandmothers had changed jobs or clients precisely so they would be readily available for grandchild care. Several had traded jobs with pension plans, health insurance coverage, and paid vacation and sick days for jobs with more flexible scheduling but many fewer employee benefits. Others had worked their way up the corporate ladder to positions that afforded them more flexibility. Many of their colleagues were also often rearranging their schedules to care for grandchildren and they readily took turns covering for each other. Even those with less flexible positions and workplaces were still able to rearrange their schedules fairly often. Several were frustrated that their adult children did not give them more advance notice so that they could care for the grandchildren even more. There were limits to workplace flexibility, however, either due to the workloads or the workplace policies, which adult children nearly always respected. Only a few of the grandmothers faced any sort of warnings about taking time away from work for grandchildren.

Most of the grandmothers indicated that they had more flexibility now than they had in their younger years or than their adult children currently have. The absence of federal guarantees for paid time off for vacation days, sick days, family leaves, job flexibility, or health insurance coverage, coupled with a paucity of affordable daycare, lack of universal preschool, and relatively high unemployment rates, makes it difficult for many young parents to rearrange work schedules to accommodate their kids' needs. Even the best of daycare arrangements are thwarted by sickness, school holidays, and snow days. At those times, grandmas may be more readily able to rearrange work schedules because they generally have more tenure on the job and that makes them valued employees whose managers, and coworkers, may be more likely to allow substantial flexibility.

5

Financial Ebbs and Flows

Intensive grandmothering can be quite expensive. Many grandmothers who care for their grandchildren report less money coming in and more money going out. Some grandmothers reduce earnings because they reduce paid work hours to increase unpaid carework hours. Some also change jobs, in an effort to have maximum scheduling flexibility, and in the process they give up some of their pay, hours, and benefits, notably paid sick time, paid vacation time, health insurance, and private pensions. Decisions that prioritize the care of grandchildren over earnings and benefits may adversely impact current and long term income, investments, savings, and private and public pensions.[1]

Many grandmothers also spend their earnings covering a multitude of their adult children's and grandchildren's expenses.[2] Providing assistance, particularly financial assistance, to the younger generations can be both rewarding and costly. A lifecourse perspective highlights the cumulative effects of various choices, opportunities, policies, and programs at different stages of life.[3] It also allows us to analyze the sort of financial juggling that women undertake across the lifecourse.[4] Trying to raise a young family and launch a new career may work very differently in periods of economic growth than it does in periods of recession, when it can be much riskier to take time from work for a sick child.[5]

Each stage of the lifecourse may present different challenges and consequences. Young mothers, who may have low earnings and little savings, face different sets of issues than grandmothers, who may have higher earnings and established investments but may be willing to forfeit some of the economic security to improve the economic security of their adult children and grandchildren. The costs incurred at any one stage may not seem like much, but the cumulative impact of providing so much financial assistance may lead to reduced savings, investments, and pensions in old age.[6] The impact of expenditures on younger generations may be particularly problematic during and following the Great Recession of 2007–2009. The percent of families with retirement accounts declined, and the value of those accounts declined as well. Between 2007 and 2010, families headed by a person ages 35–44 lost 20 percent, and families headed by persons ages 45–54 lost 10 percent, of the median value of their retirement accounts.[7] Many middle aged people lost substantial portions of their old age investments and have little time left in the labor force to attempt to recover those losses. As a result many are delaying planned switches from full- to part-time work while others are delaying retirement altogether. My interviews suggest that while many working grandmothers are readily able to absorb the impact of their financial contributions, others struggle to find enough dollars to cover their own needs and the needs of the younger generations.

Natalie is one of many grandmothers who spends money not just on gifts and splurges for her kids and grandkids, but also on daily necessities. She and her husband provide a great deal of financial help to all three of their children. Natalie works full-time, earning about $70,000 a year. She would like to retire in about eight years but it is not clear that she will be able to if they keep up this level of support. For their adult children, she and her husband help pay for education, cell phones, clothes, travel, sports, workouts, and much more.

> We still financially help our children. For our oldest daughter, we helped her a lot. We paid for college but she paid for her master's degree. I would buy her clothes. For our other daughter, we pay her cell phone, half of her college education. I buy her clothes, things for her house. She would ask for money, for help. Our son got college paid for but it was still expensive for room and board. And then we support him in the summer as he trains for hockey. We would give him a lot of money for his workout program, buy his clothes, and pay for his travel. He was totally dependent on us. We also

spend a lot of money traveling for the hockey games. It takes us the rest of the year to pay off those expenses. I would fly him home a lot, too. We went through a lot of money for hockey.

In addition to paying for a great deal of her adult children's expenses, Natalie pays for many of her grandchildren's expenses. There are not just gifts, but also daily expenses like diapers and clothes. "I buy the grandkids a lot of things. I buy diapers, formula, clothes. I do not help with rent." Like most of the grandmothers I interviewed, Natalie has rearranged her work schedule to provide grandchild care on evenings and weekends, and she spends a sizable portion of her paycheck on expenses for her adult children and her grandchildren.

Paid to Grandmother?

Natalie is not paid to provide grandchild care, nor were any of the 48 grandmothers I interviewed. In fact, most found the question itself offensive. Betty said her daughter, who makes more than she does, sometimes gives her money to cover gas or food for the kids. But she has never received money for the carework itself, and like the other women, she would not accept it if it was offered. Nationally, however, studies report that about 29 percent of grandparents providing child care receive pay.[8]

Grandmas do not receive pay for several reasons. Most were not offered any pay. Those who were offered it declined. Being paid contradicts the underlying rationale for why grandmothers provided care for the grandchildren. They were doing it because they loved time with the grandchildren. They were providing high-quality care so that their grandchildren were raised in the best possible way. They were providing care at no cost so that they could contribute financially to their adult children. By providing care for free, they offset what would otherwise be a substantial monthly bill. Finally, they refused to take money for their services because they wanted to be grandmothers and not employees. They did not want their adult children to have control over them, or their actions, while they were with the grandchildren.

Mariam, who has been caring for her grandchildren for nearly two decades and has provided a great deal of financial assistance, explained that she would never accept money for taking care of her grandchildren.

They have offered to pay me to babysit, but I refuse. I tell them I am not a babysitter, I am a grandma. Do not tell me what to do when I have them. But they will give us really generous gifts. Things we need, to show their appreciation. But I tell them the real reward is to do for their own kids when they are grown up.

Financial Contributions

Studies show that in the United States and abroad, parents give their adult children, and grandchildren, tremendous amounts of financial support, ranging from modest gifts to lavish splurges to daily and monthly expenditures for necessities.[9] Virtually all grandmothers I interviewed gave frequent, and sometimes quite expensive, gifts to their children and grandchildren. A few of the very low-income grandmothers receive money from their children to help with expenses now and then, particularly gas or grocery money. Some grandmothers provide a little financial assistance now and then, in the form of groceries or gas money or summer-camp tuition. But many grandmothers provide an astonishing amount of financial assistance. Some let their adult children and grandchildren live in the house rent-free and pay for virtually all of their day-to-day expenses. Others pay the down payment or mortgage or rent so that the younger families have an independent place to live. Some can easily afford the financial aid while others use their entire nest egg, or even go into debt, to provide so much assistance.

Nearly all of the grandmothers said that their own parents provided little financial assistance when they were young parents. A few of the grandmothers were keeping with that tradition and told me they expected their children to raise their grandchildren independently. In these families, Grandma buys gifts, but little else. But the majority of the women I interviewed were breaking with tradition. Given that most of the respondents mentioned that their own parents provided little if any financial assistance, why are so many of these grandmas giving their adult children and grandchildren so much money? The answers to this question are numerous. It appears that grandmothering is becoming more intensive with respect to both care and financial help. The economy has hit some of these families particularly hard. In some of my interviews, the adult children appeared to be in particularly difficult financial situations due to layoffs, divorces, illnesses, prison sentences, or attempts to complete college degrees, and the grandmas pitched in even while saying that their own parents never would have. These grandmas appeared to be providing a much-needed, temporary helping hand.

But some of the grandmothers appear to be helicopter grandmas who may be overly, even adversely, involved in their children's household economies. These grandmas worry, and are being constantly reminded, that they are providing too much assistance and enabling their children to be irresponsible adults. Some grandmothers even reported that their adult children have asked them to stop spending so much on the grand-kids. Whatever prompts the financial contributions, it is clear that many of the grandmothers, when they make these financial contributions, are paying for more than just electricity or diapers. They are paying for peace of mind. Though they are generally fine with their adult children doing without, or learning at the school of hard knocks, they do not want their grandchildren to do so. They do not want their grandchildren to suffer more than necessary the consequences of tough times.

Betty is one of few grandmothers who provide very little financial support. For example, Betty never gives her daughter any money. She is also one of only a few who in fact receive a little money from their adult children. Betty receives a private pension, as well as income from her current job, generating an annual income of just under $40,000. She lives in a well-maintained home in a very run-down part of a north-eastern city. Betty spends some money on the grandchildren because she often picks up the kids and drives them around, using mostly her own car and gas. She also feeds the grandchildren dinner most week-nights. But Betty's daughter, who lives with her four children in a house she owns less than a block away, holds a nursing job that pays relatively well. She never pays her mom to provide care, but she sometimes gives Betty cash for the car or groceries.

> I never help her with money. She makes more than I do anyway. Some-times she pays me, like if I go pick them up and she gives me gas money.

In lower-income families, money often flows in all directions. Paula is never paid for providing care but describes a constant stream of cash between all the adults in her family. Sometimes she gives, sometimes she receives. Her annual income is below $20,000 and she is providing temporary custody to one grandson and caring for the others almost daily.

> We have ups and downs but we are very family oriented. People can be across town and we will all take care of them. We are tight. We give each other rides, everything. Everyone keeps coming to my house. If someone doesn't have money, we pitch in, give money to the one who needs it. I take my son packages in prison every month. And I am paying for everything for his son.

When cash is tight, families concentrate their financial help toward whoever needs it most at that time.

> I will help my married daughter with money but she helps me with money sometimes, too, for gas with the car, or for food, or whatever I need. My daughter who has the 7-year-old doesn't need my money. She works, but I babysit a lot for her daughter. She helps me with money sometimes.

Some grandmothers say that they do not provide financial support but in fact they do. Lucinda says that she and her husband provide quite a bit of grandchild care for their only granddaughter but do not provide financial assistance. Lucinda said her daughter and son-in-law, a cashier and a construction worker, respectively, have enough money. When her daughter's family was house hunting, they moved in for six months. But it was not rent-free.

> I never buy them things, in fact, when they lived with us for that six months, while they looked for a house to buy, I charged them rent. Is that terrible? I made them pay rent. I did not want them to think they could just live with us. Of course we put that rent in an account and later used that money to help with things they needed, like the washer and dryer we bought for their new house.

Lucinda was the only grandmother I interviewed who charged her adult child and grandchild rent. Even though Lucinda says they never buy things for the kids or grandkids, in fact they do. During the interview, she gave several examples of gifts they had purchased, in addition to the washer and dryer.

Most grandmothers provide quite a bit of cash assistance and some keep their jobs primarily so that they can continue to provide such support. Diane had always hoped to be a hands-on grandma and is very grateful that her daughter moved nearby when her only grandchild turned one. Diane loves caring for her granddaughter, something she does at least three or four times a week. She also loves her job. When her granddaughter was born she shifted from full-time to part-time work. She gave up paid vacations and paid sick days but gained a flexible schedule. And now that the job fits well with her grandchild care demands, Diane intends to keep her 30-hour-a week job as an interior designer as long as possible. She loves the creative challenges it poses, and the income allows her to buy more for her children and grandchild.

> I do not ever want to stop working. I love my job. It is a creative outlet for me. I sell furniture; the company loves having me because I make them money. I may go three days a week. Another lady worked there till she was 75. That is what I would like to do. I need stimulation. Besides, I like to be able to help my kids financially. My son is a gifted artist and he will never have a lot of money. And I like to work to help them financially. I want to be able to help my children. I have started a college fund for my granddaughter. I contribute $50 a month to that. And I buy her lots of pretty clothes and love her to death. My children are so not selfish; they never ask me for anything. Ever. . . . That makes you want to give even more.

When grandmothers see the bills piling up, they often intervene to assist with finances. Marsha is 64 and would have liked to retire already but cannot afford to do so. She has a personal income of about $30,000 and together she and her husband have a household income just over $100,000. But they have paid quite a bit for therapies for their twin grandsons, who are diagnosed with autism and Down syndrome, respectively.

> I would have retired if I could have but financially we could not. We needed more money and we wanted to be able to help the kids with

financial strain. It was a big financial strain on the kids to have two sons
with special needs. While my son stayed home for two years with the boys,
we paid about $500 a month for therapy for the boys. Now that he is back
at work we really do not help financially anymore. They can afford the
therapy the boys need. The speech therapy for my grandson with autism
worked really well, worth every penny. I would gladly pay it again twice
over.

Their financial situation is not what they planned because when
the twins were diagnosed they moved to a new city to be close to the
boys. Marsha and her husband both changed careers, and invested in
additional education, in their early 50s. Additionally they have already
helped with some of the boys' expenses and plan to continue to do so
as they reach adulthood. As a result, their incomes, and their nest eggs,
are all much smaller than they expected. They both expect to work for
another 10 years, until Marsha is 74.

I plan to work for a long time, and so will my husband because he is a lot
younger. We both went back to school and started second careers. We lived
off our savings for years, and so we do not have much put aside for retirement. I think I will probably work another 10—and will he. I would plan to
still be helping the boys; I will probably always be pretty involved in their
everyday lives.

Some are giving more financial assistance than they can readily
afford. Janelle is a 67-year-old white mother of two and grandmother
of two. She plans to continue working full-time until she is 70, in part
because three years ago her husband of 35 years left her for another
woman. Money has been tight but she still buys a lot of gifts for the
grandchildren.

They do not want me spending so much money. They say I should not buy
all that stuff. I buy the grandkids clothes, toys, magazines, everything. It is
terrible. I spend a lot, and they will say I did not have to. I am cognizant
that I should not spoil them. It is me. I want to buy the clothes, the toys. It
is about me. Yes, I do spend too much on them sometimes, and every now
and then I worry about my own future, my own finances.

Because the divorce settlement is not yet complete, she really is not sure of her financial situation. She earns less than $40,000 a year and has spent quite a bit of her nest egg on the grandchildren. She tries to put these worries out of her mind.

> I am going to get some money from the divorce that will go into my retirement account. But I am still waiting to get it to see what my account will look like. I am not good with this stuff. I am not really sure. I guess I am all right. It is the fear of the unknown. I don't know what it will cost, what I will have. I have not put a lot into my retirement account. So I guess I am just not focusing on it. A little out of sight, out of mind.

Several of the grandmothers pay for daycare, house payments, and other monthly expenses. Janet and her husband provide a lot of financial support to both of their adult daughters but provide quite a bit more to the daughter who has children. At 61, Janet works full-time for a little over $30,000 a year. She and her husband provide substantial financial assistance to that daughter and grandchildren, including monthly house payments, food, and child care.

> We pay for our granddaughter's after school daycare, about $250 a month. Until she was in first grade, we paid for her daycare. That was quite a lot more. My granddaughter could go home with her dad after school, but her little brother is there, so she would rather go to daycare. We have helped a lot financially. We have covered several mortgage payments, groceries, clothes. But now my daughter has a different job, so they are handling it more themselves.

Many grandparents cover all expenses whenever they are with the grandchildren. Blake and her wife bought a house together with Blake's daughter and her husband so the grandsons could live downstairs with their parents and Blake and her wife could live upstairs. This way each owns a portion of the house and is building up equity. Blake can take the boys to school, pick them up from school, provide rides, and take the boys out to dinner or for cookies and ice cream. Blake does not help with any living expenses, but she pays for a lot of splurges like dinners out or fun toys. Whenever they are with the boys, which is about three or four times a week, Blake pays for all of the expenses.

I do a fair amount of evening care. Sometimes dinner and to bed. Sometimes I monitor them, since I live just upstairs. My daughter will put them
to bed and turn on the monitor and the boys just yell into the monitor if
they need me and I run downstairs. I have taken them on trips to visit family and friends for a weekend. Sometimes keep them here for the weekend.
I cover frequently for the before and after school shift if their parents can't
get to them on time. I care for them at least three or four times a week.

Blake had hoped to be a very involved grandmother but she did not
imagine she would still be working, at least not this much. In two years,
she hopes to reduce paid work and rely on retirement income. She has
no desire to reduce time with her grandsons, however. She expects to
continue to care for them, providing financial boosts and child care, as
much as possible.

I will probably turn the business over and reduce paid work quite a bit in a
year or two, when I am 70. Already most of my income comes from Social
Security and my retirement plan. I will have more downtime, time to read.
And keep caring for the boys. About every other year we take the boys on a
trip and I pay for all of that. And I would like to do that more often. We are
aware that now is the time to spend with the boys; as they get older they
will be less interested in spending time with the grandmas. The boys have
time for us now.

Some are giving more than they feel they should. When Amelia and
her husband's 17-year-old daughter had a baby while still in high school
they did what many new grandparents would do. They moved their
new grandson in to their home and provided a tremendous amount of
grandchild care and financial support. As the years have passed, and her
daughter and grandson have moved out, they are still providing substantial financial assistance. She and her husband sometimes disagree
about how much help they should be providing, particularly when it
comes to money.

We will occasionally disagree. I will want to give more help than he does.
He feels sometimes I do too much, not worried about the time but the
money. We help her financially. We gave her the car. She lived with us. We

helped with her tuition. She is on my insurance. We give her credit cards to pay for her groceries. I don't want to know how much we help her. I buy a lot of our grandson's clothes. My husband worries that we need to make sure she is standing on her own two feet. He is more worried that my grandson will not get what he needs—will she be able to help pay for his sports, etc. We will help if she can't afford those things.

Even though their own parents did not help them, some grandmothers are providing much more financial assistance than they want to be providing. Sarah, 67, and her husband have paid for nearly everything for their grandson, who is now 17. They paid for the down payment on their son's first house, nearly every article of clothing their grandson has ever owned, and activities like tennis lessons and trips. Starting next year: college. Increasingly they are paying for more things for their daughter and her family as well. Their daughter's marriage is on the rocks and in the past few years, Sarah and her husband have cleared out all of their credit card debt twice, added their granddaughter to their cell phone plan, and much more. Sarah never expected to provide so much financial assistance; her own parents certainly never did. She keeps trying, and failing, to set limits.

With our son, he is always in financial trouble. We always say this is the end. Then there is a crisis and we give him more money. We give him money constantly. Then my daughter and her husband separated for five months this summer and so I helped her then. Two different times we have helped her by clearing out a huge credit card debt. I feel that it is endless. . . . Our parents did not help us with anything, but we will be helping our kids forever.

Sarah and her husband try to limit the financial help, and the child care, they provide. But both seem to keep escalating. As she looks ahead, she has decided she would rather pay more money than let them move back home.

I imagine us keeping up this level of caring for the grandkids but I am not willing to do more. . . . It is a scary thought, what if my daughter gets divorced. The worse thing would be if she moved into my house. I would rather give them money than have her move in. Both of my kids would love to move into my house and have me take care of things. I would not do that. . . . I know I could not. That would wreck my life. I like peaceful time. I like privacy. I like them over for two hours then, okay, go home. I would rather buy her house than have her live in my house. I would give them money to stay where they are. That is the limit, what I could not do, have them live with me.

Her husband is already retired and Sarah may join him within a few years. After years of taking care of her own disabled mother, her ill father, her disabled son, and now all three grandchildren, she feels the time has come to refocus her energies on her marriage and her husband. To do that, she must effectively limit how much financial and grandchild care she will provide—and keep the kids from moving back into the house.

I feel I need to put our marriage first now. My husband has always been pretty far down on the list. I feel that I put so much time in my career. That had to come first for a long time. And he came last, after the career and the kids. And for 13 years I took care of my mom, and then my dad, before he died, lived right by us. So I have been taking care of a high-pressure job and kids and grandkids and parents all at the same time and my husband was last priority for a lot of the time. Now I feel that has to reverse. He has never said it, but I know he felt it.

Depleted Nest Eggs and Debt

Some grandmothers are readily able to provide financial assistance, whether large or small, to their children and grandchildren. But others have given so much that their own nest eggs are diminished or depleted. As middle-aged women, they are at the stage of life where they should be saving for their own old age and, instead, many have no retirement savings whatsoever and some are actually accumulating debt. They should be diverting as much money as possible into pension plans and investments so that they have enough resources for retirement and any rainy days that await. But most of the grandmothers I interviewed are not putting much aside. Most are spending money on the kids and grandkids, some are taking money out of pension investment accounts, and some are taking out new loans to provide financial assistance to the younger generations. With resources running out, many older grand-mothers have to revise their plans about age of retirement, place of resi-dence, and dreams of travel.

Several of the grandmothers have provided so much financial assis-tance that their dreams of moving or traveling have all but evaporated. Bennie and her husband have struggled with disabilities and an insa-tiable urge to spoil their grandchildren. As a result, their finances are in trouble. Bennie works full-time, despite her recent knee replacement. Her husband is out of work due to a disability and now receives Social Security benefits. They have no savings, no nest egg built up, but Bennie says she spends a lot of money on the grandchildren. It is not that they need her financial help. In fact, they have told her to stop. It is that she wants to give it.

> Our total income is just $40,000 a year but I spend a lot of money on the grandkids, for backpacks, school supplies, clothes, electronics, four-wheel-ers, Kindles. . . . I buy all sorts of things for the grandkids. Remote-control cars. I do not help my kids with rent or mortgage, but I will pay for gas, groceries, school things, clothes. And my youngest daughter lives here with me now and she pays nothing for food or rent. I would be happy to have all my kids and grandkids living with me here.

The combination of having low-paying jobs, health problems at fairly young ages, and her husband out of work due to disability has left Ben-nie and her husband with fewer resources than they ever imagined. But the paucity of income has not prevented her from showering her grand-children with gifts. She is worried about having enough money for their old age, and her husband is even more worried.

> But I never imagined we would be this disabled this young, me with the second knee replacement and him with the bad back and now the heart attack. He is 47, and disabled, and out of work. So the money is much less than we thought it would be, and much less than we need to buy things we want. I thought we would be working, traveling, spending on the grand-kids, not struggling with health and money. But I love to spoil the kids

now, and I love to spoil the grandkids. My kids are always telling me I buy too much for the grandkids. That I spend too much money. I do; I am very worried we will not have enough. My husband is worried, too.

The money is in short supply. Bennie keeps spending on the kids and grandkids. In exchange, she is watching her retirement plan slip away. She and her husband had hoped to move to a quieter neighborhood and to travel. That plan is becoming increasingly unlikely.

We do not have enough. We are young and we have so much disability already. We want to move but we need more money to do that. We need to move to a quieter neighborhood. This one is loud, busy, crazy, not as safe as I would like. He worries about the money, especially now that he is disabled. He worries we might run out. He feels we should do more for ourselves. He would like us to travel more. And move to a better neighborhood.

Similarly, Janet has neither the money nor the time to travel. She is too busy helping her grandkids. Janet and her husband had hoped to retire around age 60 and travel, as her parents had done. But now they are providing a great deal of care to their grandchildren and financial assistance to their daughter and her husband. The economy has not been good and the stock market took a tumble. They will now have to work at least until age 65, maybe longer, forfeiting their dreams of retirement excursions.

I am not sure we had a plan, but probably not this. In my ideal, my parents retired when they were 60 and traveled a lot. That would have been our plan, to retire and travel. But we can't afford to retire with the economy like this. And we don't travel much because we are helping with the grandchildren. But I am glad that I am working. . . . When we retire at 65, I hope we will travel. It depends on the stock market. It has been stressful watching our retirement accounts dwindle.

Grandmothers who assist with the daily expenses of their adult children and grandchildren often divert that money from their own nest eggs and as a result are postponing dreams of retirement. Jamica, a

49-year-old divorced mother of four and grandmother of three, works full-time as a housecleaner so that she can control her schedule. Her annual income is less than $30,000 a year and she has no health or dental insurance. At times, she has paid for nearly everything for her grandchildren.

> I help my kids a lot financially. When my oldest daughter had her baby, and they lived with us, I paid for nearly everything. And I was a single mom, raising four children on my own. When my second daughter had her baby, she did not want much help, and even now when I help her and the two boys financially, she tries to pay it back. But my oldest girl, she still wants help. She is 30, married, and her husband is about 90 percent disabled, can't work. So she got way behind on the rent, and I paid some of it. Some other bills, too. My two sons are in college. The oldest is at community college and the tuition is covered but I have to help with his apartment and food. My youngest son got a full scholarship. Very lucky. I have no money saved up at all for when I am old. I have no health insurance and have not been to the doctor in eight years. No dental insurance.

Thanks to an intervention by one of her clients, she is now contributing to Social Security, but that is all she will have. As a result, there is no hope of retiring.

> The kids are worried that I do not have money saved, but then they ask for money. For a long time, I was not paying into Social Security and Medicare. Then one of my customers, a professor, sat me down and told me I had to. So he sent the papers to all of my customers and they all filled in the forms. Now I have been paying into both for 12 years, so I will be eligible when I am older.

Some grandmothers provide so much financial assistance that they can no longer cover their own living expenses and are worried about falling below the poverty line in old age. When there is not enough money for a new heater, there is not enough money for travel or other leisure pursuits that were supposed to accompany retirement. Corey, a 57-year-old white woman, has helped her daughter and three grandchildren by paying for virtually everything for more than four years. Corey and her lesbian partner bought a house for them to live in rent-free. Though Corey's daughter, who is recovering from substance abuse, has no job or money, her boyfriend sometimes now pays some expenses. Nonetheless, Corey and her partner have paid for the house, food, clothes, medical expenses, gifts, summer camps for the grandson with autism, and much more. Despite working 40–60 hours a week, Corey has no nest egg, no savings of any kind, and growing debt. Increasingly she is struggling to make ends meet. She needs a new heater but has no resources with which to make the purchase.

> My daughter has recently slowed down what she asks for. But before last summer, she would ask me for things till I was dry. Ask for every single thing she can. But since last summer she has taken pride in raising her own family. And so she tries to ask for less. I sometimes really struggle to pay my bills. I have only recently told her that I am struggling financially. I had to get a new furnace, and I did not have the money for it. I do not make enough to cover. I probably should have told her years ago that I am struggling.

Corey's partner disapproves of the constant flow of time and cash and is struggling to set limits on the supports that go to the daughter and grandchildren. They fight about it all the time. Corey said the relationship is over and she would end the relationship today if she could afford to do so. But she plans to stay with her until the grandchildren are in college and then leave her partner.

> My partner is opposed to all the time and money that I spend with my daughter. I would leave my partner today if I had the money. I recently nearly left her. I am so tired of living with her complaining that I am spending time and money on my grandkids and daughter. I can't stand my partner anymore. She will not see the kids at all. When they come over she stays in the bedroom. She will not go to their house at all. I have to get so that I can live independently, then I will leave my partner. I will hang in for eight years, and then the grandkids will be in college and I will sell the house in eight years.

Though she would like to retire now, Corey will work until she is 67 and eligible for full Social Security benefits. She is very worried that even so she will not have enough money for the basics like housing, much less retirement dreams of travel.

> Very concerned. Very concerned about poverty when I retire. I do not allow myself to think about it. To change that, I have to stop supporting my daughter and I will not change that. So I am just going to keep supporting her even though it isn't wise. I am scared to death of being really poor.

Grandmothers who have spent all of their retirement savings and taken on new debt in their efforts to assist their children and grand-children have to give up all dreams of retiring or traveling. Estelle has given financially until it hurts. Estelle had been enjoying her empty nest but then her adult daughter asked if she could live back at home for three months. During that time she became pregnant. Over the years, Estelle has provided a great deal of financial support for her three chil-dren and six grandchildren, but now much of the money goes toward the youngest daughter and her 7-month-old son, who live in Estelle's home. Estelle's daughter does not have a job right now and is not paying for her own or her son's expenses.

> She is putting me in the poor house. I have always put a lot of money into my daughters and their kids. I will pay a phone bill or bring gifts or buy school supplies. I have always been in debt because I have chosen to support my kids and grandkids financially. But this last year with my daughter living with me has sunk me. I am now in serious financial prob-lems. . . . Her daycare is $200 a week. She has no health insurance, but at least my grandson does. She is looking for jobs but can't find one she can keep. She has applied for unemployment and other things, but she has not gotten anything yet. She doesn't have a dollar—I just paid her car insur-ance. She gets food stamps.

Providing so much support for her daughter and all of her grandchil-dren has taken a tremendous toll on Estelle's financial situation.

> I have taken most of my retirement account over the years, so it is nearly empty. I have a total of eight existing loans against my retirement account. My entire end-of-the-month paycheck pays that loan back. I have closed

my credit card accounts because they were maxed out. I know where the money went. I know I was not gambling. I have been caring for my kids and grandkids. But I still have shame. I make a decent salary, but I have used it all. I have shame over this debt.

Estelle will never be able to retire or travel. She told me she will likely have to die at her desk.

My daughter especially doesn't see that my money is gone. She thinks I am a never-ending fountain of money. She wants independence, and I want it for her. But she doesn't have it and I do not see it any time soon. But I am 63, and I should be traveling and getting ready for retirement, but I am not even close. But I love going home to my grandson. He is the most precious child in the world. I am paying for nearly everything for him.

Even the wealthiest grandmothers sometimes give more to the kids than they have and then delay retirement and travel plans as they try to rebuild their nest eggs. Renee and her husband have provided tremendous amounts of money to their children and grandchildren. Renee raised her own three children and her niece from age 4 and up. When that niece was 18 she was in a car accident that left her a paraplegic. Renee covered all of the expenses. Even after the court case was settled, all of the money went to pay for the future care of her niece; none went to repaying Renee. She has paid for college and down payments for each child.

We help our kids financially all the time. We helped them each with a down payment of $25,000 and $50,000 for a down payment for the first house. I put them all through college.

Renee also helped her daughter after she was in a serious car accident, missing a lot of work to provide direct care and covering a lot of her expenses.

Also our daughter got in an accident with an uninsured driver and she was out of work for over a year. So I helped her. I paid her house mortgage, and bought her a new roof on her house, and new car after the accident. I have helped my kids so much. After the accident I stayed with her for two weeks and cared for her. I had to dress and bathe and toilet her. Then I brought her here for a while, for a few weeks, to care for her after the accident. . . . And then when she came here I worked from home as much as I could but then I had to take her to all these doctor appointments. It took over a month. But I owned the business and had all my employees take over everything.

But by far the largest financial payout involved helping her son who lives nearby. He asked her to pay $500,000 for a business venture that she knew would not be successful. After endless badgering she gutted her retirement account. He then lost all of the money and she is now repaying that $500,000 loan to her retirement account. This debt is the only thing that prevents her from retiring.

I have helped one with a business, gave them $500,000 for his business. That is why I am still working. The business failed and closed. He has massive debt. He owned a printing business but then it went bankrupt, and I am paying off the $500,000 loan I gave him. Otherwise I would be retired. I took that $500,000 out of my retirement account. Financially, I have helped my kids with over $1 million.

Once the business venture failed, Renee's son began to ask for help with many more daily expenses for her granddaughter, including summer camps, clothes, and school supplies. She clearly articulates why she provides so much assistance. She does not want her granddaughter to suffer.

My granddaughter called one day and said we do not have power and my son had not been able to pay the power bill, and so I have jumped back in to be in my granddaughter's life. I am trying to let them figure it out without opening my checkbook. I have no problem letting my son suffer to figure this out. But I do not want my granddaughter to suffer. So I get her clothes, her Ugg boots, her volleyball camp, her trip to Florida to see Grandma. She doesn't even know I am paying for all of this. She thinks her parents are. I bought the calculator for her school, $125, her parents could not afford.

Though her household income is well over $200,000 a year she cannot afford to retire because the nest egg is gone. She is feeling her age and finds work more tiring because she works full-time. She has very little time to spend with her granddaughter. She would like to reverse the arrangement and work less and spend more time with her granddaughter. She would also like to spend three months in Florida every winter with her husband, who retired years ago. But none of this is possible because she gave the nest egg to her son.

> I never imagined we would be helping our kids this much. Never. Not financially. But when these things happen you just jump in and you do it. So then now I have to work longer. But then I have less time with the grandkids. I am older now. I can't work as hard and fast as I used to, so now since 65 I have not been able to run as fast. So it takes longer to get things done. Some days you just do. I have hoped to retire for years now, but I think I have to work at least another two years. The stock market crash made me lose a lot, and then giving the kids so much money, my portfolio took a double whammy. The things you thought you had, you just did not have. You can't be mad. I do not have time to be mad. I have to feel blessed that I had it to give to them.

Some grandmothers give enormous amounts of money to reduce the amount of child care they are expected to provide. But then they delay retirement to pay off the debts. Christine's salary, even in semiretirement, is over $150,000 a year and she dedicates a significant proportion of it to her daughter, son-in-law, and two granddaughters. At first they lived with her and she paid for everything. She took loans to help them buy their first businesses. Then they moved out after Christine took additional loans to cover much of the costs of their new home. Even though Christine's parents never helped her financially, she pays for her daughter's housekeeper, and her granddaughters' sports teams, private school tuition, tutors, camps, clothes, and much more.

> I have bought a good part of their house, which they now live in. I have since given them all but 5 percent of that house, so that we can keep the loan. I still help them. I give them $400 a month of their monthly $1,400 mortgage; I have done that for 10 years. This was not expected. I had not expected to do it,

and they do not expect me to do it. My parents did not support me. They did not ask me, but I wanted to help them. I took out loans; I took out a $75,000 loan for the first business, and then $150,000 on the second business. I have been giving them more and more of the ownership. I pay $300 a month for their housekeeper. I pay $100 a month for their sports club for them.

It seems a bit like guilt money. When I gently asked her if it was, she nodded and shed more tears. She said her daughter complains that she is not a hands-on grandmother and so Christine pays for more of her expenses. Unwilling to part with her professional career, she parts with her money instead.

I have insisted on helping them with these things. I felt that if they were going to come live near me, that is how my daughter presents it, that they are here for me, then I wanted them to be in a good place where they would want to stay. It was important to see them thrive and enjoy where they are. I have also helped pay for my granddaughter's tutors, $400 a month for reading. And I pay for camps, lessons, and $2,000 for each child into a 529 each year for their college. And I spend a lot on toys, costumes, clothes, for the kids. I have bought most of their clothes.

Despite her high income, Christine has debts to repay. She says she has to stop spending on her daughter and granddaughter, but she gives them money because she is not giving them the time they want.

I have debt now, too, because I have helped them so much. They do not ask, I insist. It is one way I can help them. I help them financially because I am not giving them the time they want—I give them the money but not the time. But that isn't enough for my daughter. The first two years of my granddaughter, I paid $2,000 a month for her daycare. I can't continue to pay all of this though . . . some of this spending has to stop.

Fewer Dollars In and More Dollars Out

Of the grandmothers I interviewed, not one is being paid to care for her grandchildren. They want to be grandmas, not paid employees.

By providing free child care they are helping the younger generation save money for first homes, degrees, trips, and other expenses. Many have fewer dollars coming in because they are reducing their paid work hours, or even changing jobs, to be readily available to provide grandchild care. Nearly all have more dollars going out because they are helping financially. Some are helping in modest ways with occasional expenditures for gas, food, clothes, and gifts. But many are also helping with major monthly expenses such as electric, rent, or daycare bills. This creates a real conflict for middle-aged women who are at a stage in the lifecourse where they should be saving resources for their own old age. Some have high-enough earnings to take these expenditures in stride, but for many it creates financial hardship. Indeed, many are deflecting contributions from retirement accounts to their children and grandchildren. Some are spending their own retirement savings and a few are incurring new debt. The net effect is that many are reducing their own expenditures for travel, downsizing their dreams, and delaying their retirement so that they can continue to earn money. Most worrisome, many will enter old age with little to no accumulated savings to cover the years of retirement that lay ahead.

The financial contributions of grandmothers are clearly intensifying for many. Though they are quick to say their own parents did not help them much, or at all, they are also quick to open their wallets for the younger generations. Many are responding to periods of great need caused by layoffs, divorces, illnesses, prison, or other challenging events. Some appear to be helicoptering, providing more assistance than their adult children want or more than their partners and friends think advisable. Those with more meager resources make these contributions at their own financial peril. They know what they are doing, and they agree with their critics that they should stop. But they do not. They love their grandkids and do not want them to suffer. Some would rather that they, and not their grandkids, do without. Grandmothering appears to be growing more intensive in hours and dollars.

6

Containing Carework

Though grandmothers may love their grandchildren, and many may want to provide almost limitless care and support, some want to set limits. For some grandmothers, enough is enough. These grandmothers limit grandchild care to protect their time, health, finances, jobs, social lives, or retirement plans. Some limit the care they provide by simply saying no or refusing to change their plans to accommodate requests from their adult children. Others limit the care they provide by working more hours, or years, than they need to so that they are not as readily available to provide care.

Others find themselves limiting grandchild care in part because their partner does not want to participate. Some grandmas told me that their partners have little interest in spending time with or caring for grandchildren. Some told me that their partners resent that long-laid plans for leisure, travel, and retirement have been replaced by the commitment to provide hours, and dollars, to the grandchildren. Having such different views on the role of grandparents, and on the best ways to enjoy middle age and empty nests, sometimes generates conflict.

Finally, others limit grandchild care because they are also providing care to frail older parents. All of the 48 women I interviewed are already working and caring for grandchildren; 38 percent are also caring for a frail older relative. Caught in a new kind of sandwich generation, these grandmothers are caring for grandkids, adult kids, and aging parents, and some have simply run out of hours, or dollars, in the day.

Limits to Grandchild Care

Many of the grandmothers have no need to set limits. Their children do not ask too much of them and they feel free to say no to requests whenever they are busy or tired. Other grandmothers have no desire to set limits. They want to spend as much time as possible with the grandchildren. In fact they try hard not to ever say no because they want to continue to receive that call asking them to babysit. But some of the grandmothers do feel the need to set limits to protect their time, health, finances, employment, social activities, or plans for retirement. Some just say no. Others, apparently unable to say no, discreetly use the demands of their paid jobs to limit just how much unpaid grandchild care they can provide.

Estelle is a grandmother who feels the need to set limits. She actively resists the gendered expectation that she will provide grandchild care. For a while her efforts were successful. She has been careful to define what she is willing, and unwilling, to do. She rarely readjusts her work schedule and frequently tells her children no.

> I said it from the beginning, and they were not young moms. It was always known. I am not a babysitter. Don't come to me. . . . I was enjoying being single. Life began for me at 39 when I separated from my husband. I enjoyed every bit of it. . . . I did not want 24/7 care of the kids. . . . I told them right away that I was not their babysitter. I tell them I don't like kids, and I certainly don't like misbehaved kids. I struggle with what a grandmother's role is.

Estelle's husband was abusive and once they divorced, she went through a 12-step Al-Anon program, worked full-time, and took several part-time jobs as well. She wanted to be busy and she needed to earn money. She also did not want to be available to care for the grandchildren on a moment's notice. This strategy worked for a while.

> My life was structured. I would go a long time without seeing my daughters or grandkids. This is what I had chosen; it is what I wanted. I had devoted my life to my kids and an abusive, alcoholic husband. Now I was free, doing what I wanted to be doing.

But then her youngest daughter, who had never married, moved in with her and became pregnant. Then her daughter and newly born grandson stayed on to live with Estelle. Despite her efforts to set boundaries, Estelle's life has become one of full-time work during the day and grandchild care during the evenings and the weekends.

Several grandmothers use work as a defense mechanism; when they are expected at the office they cannot be expected to care for the grandkids. Karen's husband does not help with the grandchildren, but she cares for them after work and on many weekend days. She also takes care of them when their parents are out of town. But given that the older one has mild autism and the younger two are 2-year-old twins, she feels that the carework is very difficult. One way she sets limits is to mostly stay at their house. Another is to ask that her daughter be there with her as much as possible.

> I watch the kids without my daughter there, but it is hard. The twins are always going in opposite directions. If they don't want to do something they drop and become a dead weight. You have to drag them up. It is easier to have more than one person with them. I don't feel that comfortable with the twins on my own. I get nervous. I take them sometimes, but I would rather have my daughter there. I am fine at their house, where they are contained. That is fine. But it is taking them out to places, negotiation getting them into the car, into the shopping cart, that is so hard. Sometimes it is totally exhausting. Yesterday was exhausting. . . . The oldest child has a disability, an autism, a mild case, and he can be challenging, too. And then the twins. I am always yelling at the oldest one, but he has a hard time with the twins always following him around.

It is easier to watch them at their own home because their things are there and then Karen comes home to her own clean house. Her preference is to relax once they are in bed, but sometimes she has to clean her daughter's house.

> They never come to my house. I always go to theirs. Everything is there at their house and they are so close. I help with dinner, bathing, laundry, cleaning if I have to. When I am there I am very busy. I get them to bed and, if I am lucky, Mom and Dad get home soon after and I will relax until I leave.

Another way that Karen sets limits is to refuse to take time off from work to watch them when their parents travel. That way, the kids spend the day with a sitter and she is only on duty for the evenings and weekends.

> I know they are more active and I don't always want to watch them. I don't always have the energy to run around with them. They wanted to go away for their anniversary and I said yes, but I said that I will not take time off from work. I want the babysitter to cover while I am at work and while I am swimming. I want the babysitter to do as much as she can. I put some boundaries up on what I will do. They will be gone three days, and I know I would be totally exhausted if I did not put boundaries up. I am used to feeding them and playing with them. My daughter agreed with this plan, that mainly I spend the nights and the babysitter does the days. I have had them many times for this long, three days, but it is harder now with the twins at age 2. They are the sweetest things; they are all over though.

Karen has also set limits by retaining her paid job. Though she does not need the money, and had planned to retire so that she could provide more grandchild care, she has instead decided to keep working. She does not want to be readily available to care for the kids. She is waiting to retire until the kids are in school and will need less care and be easier to care for.

> Sometimes I feel overwhelmed, because the job and the grandkids take most of my time. It is easier to work full-time than it is to take care of kids. I imagined I would quit my job and watch the kids, but I never did that. It crossed my mind, and I really did not need the money. But I realized that I am not the mother. I don't have to quit my job to be part of their life. I can spend time and still have my job. Still have the mental stimulation of my job. Also work provides a boundary. I could not watch kids full-time. Work gives me a place to be so I am not available all of the time.

Once the grandkids are in school and she retires, Karen plans to watch them after school and on weekends, but she wants to reserve weekdays to take care of her own things like appointments and housecleaning.

I would like to retire in a few years and be there when the kids get home from school. But the rest of the day would be for me, not all for them. I spend all day Saturday and Sunday with them, so it is hard to get things done.

At the end of the interview, Karen reflected on the hour we had just spent talking. As with many of the grandmothers, their days of work and grandchildren are so busy that they do not have much time to reflect on what they are, and are not, doing.

This interview gave me the chance to think of things I had not thought about. Makes me feel good that my priorities are good and that I know what I can and can't do. I have boundaries. And good communication with my daughter. She respects what I can and can't do. It was good to review this.

Work also provides Janet with an excuse to limit care of grandkids. At age 61, Janet would like to reduce from full-time to part-time work, but she does not want to spend more time with the grandkids. She would like to reduce work so that she could be away from the stresses of a workplace that is constantly changing. She already takes care of the grandkids some evenings and most weekends and cares for her frail older parents at times as well. She is concerned that if she worked less she would be asked to care for the grandchildren even more.

I would not want to reduce work hours for the grandkids. I am not trying to spend more time with them. But sometimes I would want to reduce the work because of the work. It gets me down sometimes; constant changes like this are stressful. I carry the benefits and we need the benefits through my job. I would not want to work less to be with the grandkids. I already get to see them a lot on weekends.

Similarly, Cherry would like to reduce her work hours to part-time but is not interested in leaving work altogether. She likes the structure of work and is well aware that it limits how much time she can spend caring for the grandkids. Her adult children asked her to be the full-time daycare provider but she declined. She wants to be a grandmother.

I did not want to be a full-time nanny. I wanted to be their grandmother. I might have become the full-time nanny, but they can afford nursery school fees, and I wanted to be a grandmother rather than a nanny. I don't want to be the disciplinarian, the second parent. I don't miss a thing; I am either there by phone or there. I am a full-time grandparent.

Though some grandmothers readily make their whole lives about their grandkids, some actively resist. Maggie is a 67-year-old mother of three and grandmother of eight. She works part-time and helps with the kids lots of evenings and most weekends. She has set limits on her availability. Partly, her job is not very flexible and changing her schedule is often not possible.

Sometimes I can't move work. My kids joke, if you want to book Mom, get her three months ahead. Please let me know ahead. I say that all the time. I say no to the kids all the time. My oldest son is the most slighted when I say no. I take care of my closer son's kids the most and my oldest son minds that. My oldest son will call last-minute and sometimes I have plans and I have to say no. My daughter has high expectations of me when she gets here, for me to take care of the kids so she can go out and do things. But if I say no, she understands.

After her husband died, and she was very lonely, Maggie set another limit. When her son asked her to be the full-time nanny of his children, she said no. She wanted to build a richer, more diverse life and have time for herself.

At one point my son asked me to be a nanny but I said no. It was after my husband died. I was tempted. But I need to go on with my life and I can't make my whole life about these grandkids. They will be grown before I know it and what will I have done? After my husband died, I needed to rework my life. I needed a fuller life. It would have been so easy to fall in as their nanny. But I needed to grow and have my own life.

Some grandmothers with health concerns limit carework to preserve their health. Annie is perpetually trying to limit the amount of grandchild care she provides. Her income is below $20,000 a year and she is receiving Medicaid. She expected to help with the grandchildren, her own mother helped her, but she never expected to help so much. So she is trying to limit her involvement. In the earlier years of grandmothering, she worked full-time and took care of the grandchildren most evenings and weekends. Then, for the last few years, she was on disability and stayed home to watch the grandkids nearly all the time. Recently she went back to school and then back to work part-time. She rearranged her schedule to wean the kids off grandma care, encouraging her kids to rely less on her and more on a babysitter. She now typically watches the grandkids when their parents want to go out. And she does so reluctantly because they tend to take advantage.

> So most of the time, I babysit when they want to go out or something, which I don't do that often because they don't know how to come back. So once a week, four hours or so, I'm watching them. They sometimes ask me, "Can you take them so that we can go to the mall?" But that's something they can take the kids with them for. It's only because they want to go out afterwards that they do that. But I'm kind of hip to that, you know.

Annie did not always set firm boundaries and she paid dearly for it in terms of her health. Annie used to have children and grandchildren living with her on and off, and she provided grandchild care nearly around the clock. She would get very tired after a full day of work and then a full evening of grandchild care.

> There was a time when it was very tiring, which is why I stopped doing it. My daughter lived with me and was going to school to become an LPN. So she was going to school and working. . . . Then when she'd get home, I'd wind up still running behind the kids, because she was doing her homework or whatever. It was really to the point where it was getting on my nerves. But I knew that at some point that would pass, that it was only a temporary situation. When she moved I was so happy.

Annie wanted her daughter to complete her LPN training and have a good job, so she wanted to help with the grandchildren. But it was proving to be too much. As a result, Annie was always finding babysitters who could care for the kids more so she could do less, but her daughter balked. Ultimately Annie feels she must set limits to protect her own time, health, and interests.

> She just liked the convenience of having them with me. She felt like the kids should be with their grandmother. But I had things I wanted to do for myself that I couldn't do and babysit at the same time. . . . And on Fridays even now, I don't babysit. I tell my daughters, "I'll come by to see you but don't ask me to sit because I have to take time for myself." I've never had a problem saying, "Hey, time out." I guess that's a selfish quality I have, just to have them back off out of my space. I know at one point I was on overload and I can't let that happen again. I got very comfortable saying this is what I can, and can't, do.

Annie does not worry about saying no because she has explained her reasons to her children and she knows that they can and will find others to help care for the kids if she steps back.

> They know that if I don't want to do something I'll say so; I won't put my needs on the backburner for them. We've had that whole "well, you didn't come and get the kids today," and I tell them, "I'm not supposed to, it's not my job," conversation. They expect me to do certain things. But if I wasn't around they would just find somebody else to watch their kids, which they do sometimes, because they want to go out or something.

Partners Who Limit Care

Many of the grandmother's husbands or partners help and are happy to do so. But not all. Some are unable to because of work or their own poor health. Others are unwilling to, because of lack of interest or resentment that she is providing too much care and financial assistance. These disagreements can add to the stress levels that already busy grandmothers endure.

Some partners are too ill to be able to pitch in. Patty loves caring for her grandchildren and would do much more of it if she was not also balancing care for her husband. Patty's husband is 80 and in addition to having cancer he has Alzheimer's disease. He loves having the kids around but is unable to care for himself and is certainly not able to help much with the grandchildren. During the interview, he was in the other room watching TV. When the granddaughter woke from her nap, Patty went up to get her out of the crib and change her diaper, then brought the baby to her husband. He sat in the chair and fed her a bottle while he continued to watch TV. But that is the extent of the help he is able to provide. Patty cleans houses part-time and sometimes she takes her husband and some of the grandchildren with her. Often he watches over the youngest grandchild as she naps while Patty cleans the house. More often, though, Patty leaves him home alone while she spends the day at the grandkids' house caring for them.

> I take care of my husband; I do his meds. I get most of his meals, and when I am gone he is okay. But he is lonely if I am gone everyday all day. I need to call him while I am gone. Every day I write on a piece of paper my schedule for the day for him to keep—and a list of things for him to do so he is focused on something. I have a special pad that tells him where I am and another special pad that tells him things to do. I never write anything else on those pads. If I don't keep him busy, he will call all the time asking when I will be home. He does all the gardening. He keeps everything in order and schmoozes with the neighbors. I am not sure how much longer it will last that he can be alone. I am concerned about my husband.

Patty is hoping that he can continue to be left home alone for four more years because that is when her youngest granddaughter will go to kindergarten. While this is her plan, she did not seem to believe it would work because his cognitive decline appears to be gaining speed. As she looks ahead, she expects to be doing less for her grandchildren and more for her husband and her mother.

> I will keep taking care of the grandkids till they go to school, four more years. I hope that my husband and mother will stay healthy enough till then. Then I imagine becoming a caregiver for these two old people: my husband and my mother. My husband's cancer has come back and his Alzheimer's is getting worse.

Some partners do not want to spend time caring for the grandkids. Karen's husband does not seem to mind how much time she spends caring for the grandchildren, but Karen minds that he will not come along and help. They could provide a lot more support and care if they joined forces. She provides a great deal of child care on evenings and weekends, but not financial help. She loves her job and is not eager to leave it, in part because it limits how available she is to help with the grandkids. Her husband does not help with the grandchildren. He stays busy with work and projects.

> My husband never comes to help with the grandkids. I don't know why, but he does not. He does not mind how much I do. He is a workaholic, and he is busy, has projects, has several jobs. So he is working most of the time late at night. So I am freed up to go be with the kids. I would like more time with him but right now it does not work that way. I get satisfaction being with the kids.

She wishes her husband would join her with the grandchildren but he does not. She has asked him. They all have. He will not.

> I wish he was more involved. I think he just does not feel comfortable with them, especially little babies, and he prefers to work. I think he is missing a lot. And my husband does not say he minds. I don't get the feeling he minds that I am with the kids. I told him I would be over there next weekend while they go away for their anniversary. He does not care. He is welcome to come over and be with us but he has not come over in the past. He will not. That is his choice.

Some partners squabble with the grandmothers about how much is too much. Candi's fiancé disapproves of how much she helps the grandkids and they bicker about it frequently. She always wants to provide more; he always wants her to provide much less. Candi is a black woman with three children and three grandchildren whom she watches each evening and weekend after her shift as a nurse. At 43, she is recently divorced and engaged to marry again. Her fiancé is unemployed and does not help with the children or grandchildren. She said he minds very much how much money and time she devotes to her children and grandchildren.

> My fiancé being out of work puts even more stress on me. He thinks I do too much and we're at odds all the time. But what I do is what I do. Those

are my kids and my grandkids. And no one can tell me what I can or can't do for my kids. That's how you have generations. You have to keep the family together.

The Sandwich Generation

Providing care for multiple generations can also limit grandchild care. Since the early 1980s, aging scholars have noted the emergence of women in the middle, or the sandwich generation. Initially, it was conceived of as middle-aged adults who were simultaneously still rearing children and caring for frail older relatives.[1] Empirical research revealed that to be a relatively rare situation, with the more common sandwich between adult but still dependent children and frail older parents. Scholars have analyzed data in the United States and Great Britain and found that for women ages 55–69, about one-third were caring for an adult but still dependent child and a frail older parent, and one-fifth were caring for neither.[2] Similarly, Charles Pierret used the National Longitudinal Study to study the sandwich generation and found that one-third of women ages 45–56 were providing either care or money simultaneously to adult children and older parents.[3] Scholars predict an ongoing rise in the number of women in the middle because of several demographic changes, including longer life expectancies, adult children returning to the nest, and increasing employment rates among women.[4] Generally, women in the middle of caregiving for multiple generations report more negative health and financial effects.[5]

My analysis of grandmas at work points to another form of sandwich generation: working grandmothers who are in the middle of caring for their grandchildren *and* adult children *and* frail older parents. It is a virtual club sandwich of carework responsibilities. Nationally, according to the Health and Retirement Survey (HRS) 2010, of the working grandmothers who provide care to their grandchildren, at any one point in time 7 percent were also providing care to their parents and 93 percent were not.[6]

In my in-depth interviews, 38 percent of the working grandmothers who provided care for their grandchildren were currently also caring for a frail older relative. Many others had already provided such care or could see it upon the horizon. Some grandmothers are young enough that their parents are still relatively young and healthy and do not need any assistance. Other grandmothers are old enough that they have already provided care for their parents and now their parents are deceased. Somewhere in the middle, several of the grandmothers I interviewed are currently providing regular care for their aging parents. Balancing paid work, care for grandchildren, and care for frail older parents is tricky. And tiring. It can adversely affect financial, emotional, social, and physical health. Women in this club sandwich generation are constantly trying to redefine what they are doing for whom, balancing one generation's needs against another.

Betty is one of many grandmothers who helps out three generations at once. She helps her sister look after their mother after work, often with the grandchildren in tow. Betty is a widowed black woman who retired from her nursing job so that she could work per diem and schedule more time caring for her grandchildren and her mother. Though she gave up her paid sick leave and vacation and private pension, she felt she had to because she is caring for her grandchildren and her failing mother. Most evenings, Betty drives three miles to her sister's house, while her sister is at work, and helps her mother. Some nights she takes the grandchildren with her and other nights she leaves them at her house with the 13-year-old in charge. On the nights she does not have her grandchildren, she does more for her mother, including bathing her, doing laundry, and cleaning. On the nights she has the grandchildren, Betty makes a shorter trip, just getting her mother dinner and to the bathroom.

> My mom lives with my sister and she isn't doing too well. Not eating. My sister works evenings, and I work days. So if I don't have the grandkids, when I get off work, around 5 or 6, I take my mom something to eat and take her to the bathroom. Last night I gave her a bath, made sure she eats, gave her Tylenol for the pain, washed the clothes, and cleaned up her room. She lives about three miles from here. She walks slowly. Still getting around, but not very well. I will go tonight after I pick the kids up from school. . . . Tonight I just need to make sure she eats and take her to the bathroom. . . . In the future, I will probably be doing more for my mom. She isn't doing too good.

Meryl is not doing a lot for her parents yet, but she can see it on the horizon. Meryl, a married mother of three and grandmother of one, just completed a five-year turn of intensive grandmothering. Her daughter became a single young mother at the end of high school and she and her son lived with Meryl and her husband for the first five years while she completed high school and college. Now her daughter and grandson are living independently and Meryl and her husband are working full-time and babysitting on evenings and weekends. But Meryl's thoughts are already turning to her parents.

> I do help my parents out with household tasks like cleaning the bathroom. Maybe once a month, and we will pop over and do some things. Being the nurse in the family, I keep an eye on their medications. And because I live close to them I anticipate the day when I will be going more. . . . I think I will work until at least 62 or 65, as long as I am physically able. Until I can make it financially without working but I don't see that happening. I would like to quit when I think I can afford to. But I wonder if I will have to quit early to care for a parent. I want to not have them in a nursing home. If I could care for them without quitting my job I would like to do that.

As an only child, Carol sees a lot of caring for frail older relatives in her future. What she did not see coming, however, was her in-laws living with them nearly two months each fall and spring. Carol is a married, 48-year-old black woman with two daughters and one grandson living in her home. Currently, she works full-time and cares for her grandson, who lives with her on evenings and weekends. Carol and her husband had planned to retire from their full-time jobs and sip coffee at an outdoor café, but she suspects they will be caring for their parents instead. To date, the parents do not need care. But a few years ago one set of parents needed financial help and Carol and her husband agreed to buy their house. To their surprise, the parents expected to continue living in the house part-time. These snowbirds spend most of the year living down south where it is warm. Then each spring and fall they move back into Carol's house so that they can spend some time in the northeast.

> My in-laws live with us for five weeks each spring and two months each fall. They don't need care. They live with us because we bought their house, so mainly for economic reasons. We bought their house thinking they

were leaving, but they did not leave. We bought their house and we bought them. My parents are both remarried. They are retired; they don't need help. But in the years to come, they are all going to need help and I am an only child. I will be helping them all. I expect to be doing a lot more as time goes by.

Scheduling care for parents and grandchildren keeps Marsha busy. Marsha, age 64, and her husband work nearly full-time, care for their twin grandsons who have disabilities, and care for his parents who live 10 hours away. They make the drive one weekend a month to care for his parents. During that weekend they fit in as much work as they can to tide them over for the month. That is the only weekend of the month they do not care for their grandsons. Marsha and her husband expect to work for another 10 years and would really like his parents to move close by so they could care for them more easily. So far they have not agreed to such a move.

> My husband's parents will stay in Oregon. We have asked them to move up here, but they want to stay in their home as long as they can. But it is too much for them to take care of it. My mother-in-law likes to garden; that is her escape. But my father-in-law is now no longer driving. We are worried she will wear out taking care of his Alzheimer's disease. We have not convinced them that moving here is the answer but that is what we would love.

Several grandmothers knew the expression "sandwich generation" all too well. At age 61, Janet works full-time in a fairly stressful job. She also cares for her grandchildren most weekends and some evenings after work. Increasingly she is being asked to help her parents with home maintenance, chores, and medical issues. But they live five hours away and so it is difficult to get there. For now her parents are able to help each other much of the time, but eventually that will no longer be enough.

> I am the only child. I mainly just listen on the phone, visit as much as I can. I get there as much as I can. They don't drive on the highway anymore. We go get them and bring them back up here to see us. They live in their own home and they are able to take care of arranging their own care themselves. They assist each other, and they are able to do most of it themselves. I hate

to think about what will happen over time. My mom would move up here in a minute, would love to be close to the great-grandkids. But my dad says he will die in the house they are living in now, across the street from where they were born. I will be able to care for my mom more easily than my dad. My husband says we will deal with it when it happens. My father is very frail but stubborn; it will be hard to care for him.

Janet finds it difficult to balance the demands of work, grandchildren, and parents, even with the constant support of her husband.

Sometimes I feel pulled in too many directions—my parents, my kids, my grandkids, two sons-in-law. For this Thanksgiving I feel I need to go be with my parents but I feel I should be here with my kids. So I will go to my parents and they will go to their husbands' family or be with friends. I used to pooh-pooh the sandwich generation but now I am living it. I have a lot of guilt that I can't be there more for my parents. I am lucky to have my husband. He is my friend, too, and he really helps with all of this. I have taken time off work to care for my parents, more than for my grandkids.

Women in the middle sometimes do it all with very little sleep. Diane is 55 and works 30 hours a week as an interior designer, cares for her granddaughter for three or four days and evenings a week, and visits her mother, who just recently entered a nursing home. She makes this all work and even has time for trips to the gym and lunch with her friends, because she rarely sleeps. She says she is awake from 6 am to 1 am every day, so she can fit it all in.

My mother has advanced Parkinson's. For the last 14 years, my brother, sister, and I worked together to help keep her at her home. But in March she fell and is in a nursing home now. My sister and brothers and I go see her all the time. Take her out for the holidays. When she was at her home, we all went over to help her all the time. But now instead we go visit her at the nursing home.

Diane does what she can, but her mother wishes she visited her more often. Though she only sleeps five hours a night, she says she is still not doing enough for all of the people who rely on her.

She wishes I could see her more. She has many illnesses, and she was born in Italy. Her kids were everything, and she wishes she was with us more. She has a lot of fears.

Some grandmothers are caring for their own mothers in part because no one else has stepped up to do the work. Toni is frustrated that her sibling brothers do not help with their mother, but she is grateful that her own children do. Toni is a 48-year-old, white, married mother of four and grandmother of four. She works part-time in retail sales and cares for her grandchildren during nearly all of her free time. She is also caring for her mother, who is dying of cancer. Toni is the youngest of five siblings in her family and cannot understand why the others do not come to help with, or even visit, their dying mother. Her siblings are brothers and she is frustrated by the gendered expectation that she, and not they, should be providing all of the care.

And I'm the baby, so with my mom being sick it's not like they have offered to help much. And the only time that they come and spend time with her is when I call and say, "Hey, why don't you guys come see Mom," or when it's specifically suggested. I'm having a hard time dealing with that and I'm like, "How can you do this? This is your mom." There's a big age difference. Between me and my brothers there's 20 some years difference and I don't know if the way they act is just because it's old school—or because they're guys.

Between her job, her children, and her grandchildren, Toni is already pulled in many directions. But caring for her mother has become yet another of her jobs. She is grateful that her husband helps, but the work is difficult.

My mom has cancer and right now it's basically just get her to eat, bathe her, change her, and that's about it. I just have to take care of her. My husband is my support buddy, I guess. . . . With my mom, I have a hard time. . . . I feel bad because she's not eating for me. . . . First of all I'm blessed to even have her, she's 91. They didn't think she'd make it through surgery last time but she made it with flying colors. Sometimes she has trouble going to the bathroom and she has a hard time with other stuff. But I push her because I know she's strong. She's a strong person.

Toni has been caring for both the younger and older generations for some time now. She cared for her father and her mother-in-law, and now she is caring for her mother. She is older and wiser this time, and she wants to assist the woman who helped her so much when her own children were young and she was trying to juggle work and kids. But the work is fairly high skilled and she is not confident about her actions. She relies on hospice workers. And, in addition to her husband helping her, her oldest daughter has begun to help with morphine administration.

> I've already been down this road before, with hospice, when my dad had cancer and then my mother-in-law. Because taking care of my dad and mom-in-law I pretty much didn't know how it worked. But hospice came in and they kind of took over and were feeding my dad meds. . . . I know certain things are going to be hard to do and I need to have another person in my house who is able to give medicine and stuff. So I have to pick somebody else to do that for me. So my oldest daughter said, "Mom, don't worry about it, I think I can do it." So they're helping out already. They do what they can.

Some are more comfortable taking care of their own parents than their partners' parents. Madeline already provided almost constant care to her parents before they died, and now her in-laws have moved in. But she finds herself drawing limits this time, before the real carework even begins. Madeline works part-time and watches her only grandson five mornings a week from 7 to 11. For years, her parents lived in an in-law apartment at her house. She provided a great deal of care to her parents before they died. Initially she helped by cooking extended family meals, buying groceries, doing laundry, and performing other chores. But as their health worsened, her care became more medical.

> We took care of each of my parents around the clock before they died. . . . My dad came here at-home hospice; he knew he would die. My daughters were in high school and they helped some. And my mom and I took care of him till he died. Then the girls helped a lot with my mother, and she needed a lot of care until she died. We did at-home hospice with her as well.

The in-law apartment did not remain vacant for long. Her husband's parents moved in. Madeline is not providing much care at this time, nor does she expect to in the future. She expects her sisters-in-law to provide the care. She does not expect her husband to do so. Challenging traditional gender stereotypes does not appear to be on her radar.

> My husband's parents moved in shortly thereafter. . . . They moved in one year ago. They are very independent; they do their own meals. We usually eat together, and we each do some of the cooking in our own kitchens. I think when they start to need care, his sisters will have to do something. I always wanted to do whatever I could for my own parents, but I cannot see me taking care of his parents. They are so private. I would not be comfortable. . . . His own sisters would have to do it if they need care.

Some women in the middle are doing so much carework, and under so much stress, that they are putting their own lives at risk. Maggie works about 16 hours a week and has no paid vacation and no paid sick leave. She is able to rearrange her schedule if given enough notice. She cares for the eight grandkids some evenings and most weekends. She also cares for them for weeks at a time if their parents are traveling. For several years she also cared for her mother. Three years ago her mother died, but she remarked many times during the interview about those stressful years.

> When I was taking care of my mom, and working full-time, and taking care of the grandkids, that time was horrible. The doctor said to me if we did not get her placed somewhere I would be dead. But now I do have time for my own things, for volunteering and friends. If you had called me three years ago, when I was working full-time, caring for my mom, and helping with the grandkids on the weekend, we would have had a very different interview. I was stressed. Frustrated. It was a horrible time. My mom died three years ago and I helped her for years before she died. That was very frustrating. I helped her constantly. She would fall twice a week. She was living in her own home, and in and out of rehab, and would fall. There were times when I slept with my clothes on because I was called to help her so much. That was a very difficult time. When she was in the hospital and rehab I would go daily. For much of that time I

was working full-time. I would still have the grandkids for the weekend and they would come with me to help take care of Grammy.

Often she would bring her daughter or her grandchildren with her when she went to care for her mother. She was grateful for their help.

They would help me take care of her. They would get things for her and it helped me a lot. Back then I thought I was going to break. I was stressed to the limit. My daughter, who is completely nonviolent, said she considered poisoning Grammy. That is how bad it got when my mom was frail. My daughter, my doctor, both feared I would literally not live through it.

Some grandmothers just want to be done providing care. Though she owns her own real estate business, Renee has provided a great deal of hands-on care in the last few decades. She would like to be done. Her niece, whom she raised, was in a car accident that left her a paraplegic. Renee paid for much of the care and provided the remainder of it herself. Her daughter was in a car accident and Renee cared for her almost around the clock for a month. Her own mother needed years of care before she died. And her mother-in-law lived with them and needed personal care for a few years before she died. At one point, Renee exclaimed, she had two wheelchairs in her house at once.

I don't want my kids to have to do for me what I had to do for my mother-in-law and my mom at the end. I had to clean my mom after she used the toilet and I did that for my niece, too. I did all the personal care that one would not normally do. I cleaned up after the incontinence. Yet I felt that I did not do enough. I put my mother in the nursing home for the last one and a half years, and I feel I failed her. But I could not do it all, run my own business, help my son with his business, take care of my niece in her wheelchair, and help my daughter after her car accident. How could I do even this?

After so many years of caring for others, she is eager for some time to live her own life. It is not clear that she will get it any time soon.

But I did all that work and now I want life. I want time. It is not about money it is about time. I have had so many tough things happen along the

way. There were so many health problems with his parents, my parents, my
niece, my daughter. There have been so many people and I have provided
the direct nursing care to every one of them. I have done all this work. I
am exhausted. And I helped them all with money. I still do all the time.
But I am trying to stop. I am so tired of caring for everyone. I loved them; I
wanted to help them. But now I am older. I choose life. I want time to live. I
just accepted it all, life rolled, but now I am done. I want a break from it all.

Containing Carework

Grandmothering in the United States is driven by both a joyful desire
to be with the grandchildren and a sense of responsibility to assist with
the unmet needs of the younger generation. But carework is work and
not all grandmothers want to, or are able to, do it. Some grandmas limit
care either to protect their own time and health, because their partner
is unable or unwilling to pitch in, or because their time and energies are
also focused on the welfare of their frail older parents.

In a society where there are few supports for families with working
parents, and a rising number of single parents, it often takes multiple
generations to provide sufficient care for the grandchildren. Many of
the grandmothers provide almost limitless time and resources to the
grandchildren. Others set limits, attempting to restrict just how much
care they will provide to protect either their leisure time or their health.
One common way to set limits is to let the structure of paid work
make them less available when their kids or grandkids call asking for
Grandma.

Most partners pitch in and help Grandma with the grandkids, but
some are either unable or unwilling to help. The additional duties of
caring for a husband or partner in poor health, or of arguing with a
husband or partner who disapproves of the level of help, create additional stresses for women who are already feeling quite overwhelmed.

Unless their own parents are deceased, spry, or living quite far away,
many grandmothers are balancing paid work, grandchild care, and
parent care. Their days are long and often filled with care for others
in multiple generations: driving, feeding, bathing, cleaning, launder-
ing, shopping, and more. They balance paid work and carework, and
they balance joy and exhaustion. Some juggle it all fairly seamlessly but

others become too weary, suffer health problems, and worry that they cannot continue this level of care. Some are a new kind of sandwich generation, a club sandwich, of working grandmothers who are caring for their grandchildren, adult children, and their frail older relatives.

7

Emotional Ups and Downs

The emotional impacts of working, and caring for grandkids, are mixed. For some the combination of roles generates a tremendous emotional high, but for others it generates somewhat more negative sensations. Many working grandmothers enjoy terrific emotional rewards of providing high-quality, and much-appreciated, grandchild care. Most, but certainly not all, of the grandmothers feel very appreciated. For those who are perpetually thanked, the emotional rewards of helping their adult children by caring for their grandchildren are remarkable. Verbal expressions of gratitude are most frequent and most desired. Many adult children also give gifts and find ways to repay in kind by helping the grandmothers with chores or errands. At 54, Marta feels her daughters are very grateful for all of the care she provides. "Yes, they appreciate it, my daughter definitely appreciates it. She always thanks us and she appreciates the fact that I try to make myself available."

However, some are not so sure their children are appreciative. Some grandmothers said they receive little in the way of thanks and at times feel the need to remind their adult kids just how much care they are providing. Others struggle with emotional questions about whether they are enabling their adult children to be irresponsible. I did not ask any questions about whether grandmas felt they were doing too much, or enabling, but that topic arose in 17 of 48, or roughly one-third, of the interviews I conducted. This is not a nationally representative sample, so that percentage is not generalizable. And two-thirds of the grandmothers I interviewed felt that they were providing appropriate amounts of support and that their adult children were responsible parents. But about one-third of the grandmas I spoke with mentioned that they felt they might be doing too much and were at risk of enabling their adult children to then do too little. A much smaller proportion of the sample, in fact only a few, grandmas mentioned that they were concerned that their carework was not fairly distributed. These grandmas were worried that they might spark conflicts between siblings who feel that some receive too much, and others too little, support.

Appreciation

Expressions of gratitude are the norm. Cally's daughter, who is 31 and lives at home with Cally, makes it clear that she is very grateful to be working together with her mom to raise her son. She never meant to rely so heavily on her mother, and she expresses her appreciation readily and frequently.

> She will do favors for me, help me out, bring something I need to me, or take something home. She will just help out. We are pretty easygoing; we just help each other. She is very appreciative, and we both are weepy, cry easily. She will thank me and well up with tears. She really appreciates how much I am helping her. And we have fun together. We get together with other families, have a lot of fun. . . . She has thanked me so much and we both cry happy tears. . . . We have a good balance. She is always aware when I am doing extra. She always said she never wanted me to have to do that much. But I always tell her I am fine.

Lynn is one of many grandmothers who feel very appreciated, not just because she provides care but she gets the entire family to provide care. Her husband helps, her mother helps, her other children help. "It's a family thing, we all do it," she exclaimed. Her children are really grateful for her help. Her daughter, who works from home, is very thankful that her mom watches the kids each Friday and does not hesitate to express this.

> Sometimes she'll say, "Mom, I'm taking you to lunch" or "I'm filling up your gas tank." But I don't ever ask for things like that. It's a fun day for me.

They do that when they come over. She'll bring dinner home or do something else nice for us. It's always a treat to know that you're gonna give me a gas card or fill up my tank or buy me lunch when I'm off. It's nice. Oh, they definitely appreciate it.

Lynn's adult children wish she would stop working and provide full-time child care. She is not about to become a full-time nanny, but she agrees to their requests as often as she possibly can.

Oh yeah, they wish I could do it full-time because they know they're in good hands. They would manage without me, ask someone else in the family such as her father-in-law. I've never turned them down unless it was absolutely necessary.

Many grandmothers feel their efforts are generously repaid in kind. In addition to working full-time, Molly provides 40–50 hours of grandchild care a week for her five grandchildren. She also provides a constant stream of cash to cover babysitters, prescriptions, clothes, school supplies, food, and the gas bill. Molly says her children are thankful for all that she does for them and one way she knows it is the constant gifts they are bringing to her.

Gifts! All the time! Clothes, lotions, just little things. She's like, "Here, Mom, I saw this and thought you might like it." If she sees something when she's shopping, she grabs it for me. When she realized my gas wasn't on, she brought me two electric burners so I could fry an egg or whatever I wanted.

Like many of the grandmothers, Molly does not expect or need these expressions of gratitude. But they do make her feel appreciated. This excerpt begs the question: Why are Molly's kids paying for gifts for her instead of paying their own gas bill? Perhaps most troublingly, why do Molly's kids have gas when she does not? When I asked, Molly explained that her children's incomes fluctuate and while some months they do not have enough for the basics, other months they have enough for gifts. There is a constant stream of giving and taking, of both care and money, between the generations. She said she is part of a family and this is what families do for each other.

So the whole family is kind of doing it. But they're all supportive in terms of how much support we give the kids. The rule in our family with kids is you love them, and then you love them, and then you love them some more. Regardless of the circumstances.

Heartfelt thanks revive the energies of weary grandmothers. Madeline's daughter and son-in-law are grateful for how much she helps them by watching her grandson every morning from 7 to 11.

She is very appreciative. She always says we would not be able to raise him without you. She always does something special for us on holidays. For our anniversary she gave us five restaurant certificates. She sends nice things to us because she does not pay us. She does ask me at least once a month, "Are you sure this isn't too much?" And whether it is or not, I always say it is fine.

Madeline and her husband have a household income of over $110,000 a year and plan to retire in five years. Madeline already reduced her paid work hours from 20 to 12 per week so that she could provide more grandchild care. Her job may be terminated in a few months and the family is discussing what to do. Should they rely even more on the other grandma, who already babysits five days a week from 11 am to 5 pm, even though she is becoming more frail? Or should they pay Madeline to babysit full-time? Madeline does not want to be paid to babysit but said she needs an income until she is 58.

The other grandma is 10 years older than I am, so sometimes my daughter worries that caring for my grandson is too much for that grandma. She sometimes wishes I could do more for him so that the other grandma does not have to. My daughter is glad I am working. They all feel badly that the job may end in June. If I could not help her, I think they would be looking at daycare near her work. The other grandma could not take all the work.

Madeline is touched that her family is so appreciative. She is also touched that they are all so concerned about her well-being once her job ends. They want what is best for her and, for that, she is grateful.

Sarah is one of several grandmothers who are a little less sure how much their efforts are appreciated. Sarah and her husband have provided a great deal of care and cash for their son's son, and a more moderate amount for their daughter's two children. Because he is less mature and has so many financial problems, it is more difficult for their son to show his appreciation. But he finds ways to reciprocate.

> I think they do appreciate our help. But with my son, it is almost like he is jealous that we like being with our grandson instead of asking him for dinner. He wishes we would invite him for dinner all the time, too. He is a little jealous that we take care of our grandson but are not as excited to take care of him. They never pay for child care; they never give us money. But my son will buy us a gift card to thank us as a present. . . . He will want to take everyone out for dinner, and he will, but then I think I will end up paying for this in one way or another. . . . He does a lot of stuff around our house; he has helped remodel the house. He is really handy. He can do painting floors, air conditioning, electrical work. . . . That is a wonderful way that he reciprocates and we really appreciate it.

During the interview, her son called her cell phone. He said he would be home Thursday and wondered if she could invite the whole family over to her house for a big dinner. She said she was going to be at a conference on Thursday. She told him she would host the big dinner on Saturday. Her daughter, who will no doubt be at the dinner with her children and husband, has a more stable income and is more readily able to express her thanks.

> But with my daughter, she is really appreciative. She really likes that I do these special things with her children. She will buy lunch sometimes if we go out for lunch.

Natalie is one of several grandmothers who feel that their children do not discuss their appreciation often enough. Natalie and her husband balance full-time work and caring for their grandchildren every evening and many weekends. They love it but they get tired. Her daughter is thankful for what she does, most of the time.

> I think they do. Every once in a while she has to be reminded of how much we do. It just becomes second nature to call us because we are here. We

have to remind her that she should not expect the help. But she does appreciate it. She sees our sacrifice, the time we give. Don't think she wishes we were doing more. We give her nearly everything she asks for. She nearly always gets at least one of us.

Occasionally her daughter will see that she has asked too much of Natalie and will get a substitute to give her an hour off. Natalie says often that hour is all she needs.

> Sometimes she will see that I am very tired and worry a bit. She will say, "Mom, you are exhausted, go home." Or she will have someone else come for an hour so I can relax for an hour between work and taking care of the children. Sometimes I just need that hour to rest, read, watch TV, just get a little break. And I will go home and relax, when I am really tired. But then come right back after an hour or so to take care, to play with the children, feed them dinner, bathe them, tuck them in, pick up the house.

Regardless how much appreciation is being expressed, sometimes differences in parenting philosophies generate a lot of emotional friction. Maggie loves caring for her eight grandchildren. Juggling part-time work and frequent carework makes her tired. But the differences in parenting philosophies raise some emotional challenges for her. One challenge was that she and her beloved husband shared only the first grandchild. He had died by the time any of the others were born and she has provided care on her own ever since. Another challenge is that the first grandchild's parents were very busy with jobs and internships and did not have a lot of time to focus on this first grandchild.

> My happiest memories are about how happy we were to have her, our first grandchild. My husband just loved her; we rejoiced in her. It was great to see, had no idea it would be so short-lived. I loved that we shared her. It was hard to give her back. Her own mother was at that time very immature, very wrapped in medical school. . . . She was just in the background of their lives. Both parents busy with jobs and internships. Her mother was not focused on her. In the end my son quit his job and stayed home to take care of their first child so his wife could establish herself as a doctor. It was very trying.

With the next set of grandchildren a different set of emotional challenges emerged for Maggie. Differences in parenting styles can lead to conflict or, at a minimum, exhaustion. These younger grandchildren are what she calls free-range kids. When Maggie is grandchild sitting, TV and computers are not allowed and creativity is to be encouraged. Maggie wants to follow their rules and respect their parenting decisions, but by the end of the day, she gets very tired.

> These are free-range kids. It is different than the way I raised my kids. They are encouraged to be creative, and I respect that parenting. But these kids are not sure of what they can and can't touch, or do. My kids knew that there were limits. And these kids are great kids, but I need to remove everything before they come in. No TV is permitted in the house for these grandkids. I am not to be on the computer when they are there. Those three kids don't use computers at all. These kids are sleeping in a family bed at home, and so they want to sleep with me. Free-range kids. I respect their parents' parenting. I respect their wishes. But it isn't easy. And I am exhausted.

Maggie's commitment to helping her children raise these free-range children is driven by the desire not to repeat her own mother's patterns. Her mother did not help her much when the kids were little and thought that her brand of parenting was the only correct brand. Maggie is determined to respect her children's parenting wishes, no matter how tired she gets. And she knows her kids are grateful for her efforts.

> My mother did not help me. My mother expected me to help her, even when I had little children. She expected me to have her for dinner. She did not help me much at all. Occasionally she would have one overnight and that was great. But she was short-tempered with them and they all knew it. And my mother thought her way of parenting was right. I did not use physical punishment or yell at them. She did. But now I respect how my kids raise their children. And I do what they do. I respect my kids' parenting because my mother did not respect mine. I don't want to make that mistake. I don't want to act like my way is right. I want to help them and not expect them to help me the way my own mother expected me to help her.

When the gratitude is insufficient, some grandmothers feel frustrated. Janelle is one of a few grandmothers who have to read between the lines to find any gratitude. She is 67 and divorced. In addition to full-time work she provides a lot of grandchild care evenings and weekends. She says her daughter is thankful for the help, but even though Janelle is demonstrative, her daughter is not.

> I feel my family appreciates how much I take care of them. I don't always feel appreciated. I am demonstrative but my kids are not. Not that affectionate, not a lot of hugs. I have to wait for a card for them to say anything. How could I have raised kids who are not affectionate? How could I always be waiting for that card to hear anything at all?

A few words of gratitude, a hug, or a little surprise gift would go a long way toward helping Janelle feel that they are grateful for all that she is doing for them. But such expressions are few and far between.

Enabling

Many experts suggest that mothering has become more intensive in the United States, with families centered in an unprecedented way around the cultivation of children. My research suggests that grandmothering has become more intensive as well. One of the most adverse aspects of intensive mothering,[1] and grandmothering, may be the ways that it becomes too intensive in some cases. It had not occurred to me to ask questions about enabling, but the topic arose in the responses of one-third of the grandmas I interviewed. Most who shared these concerns were actively trying to establish boundaries but they, and their adult children, crossed them often. The topic was the source of a great deal of emotional stress. Some of these grandmothers had tremendous anguish that the amount of help they were providing was enabling their children to shirk parental duties. Often these grandmothers argued with husbands, partners, coworkers, and friends who told them they were doing too much. For the most part these grandmothers agreed that they were providing too much care, but they were unwilling or unable to set firm boundaries. No matter how much damage their excessive giving was creating in the lives of their adult children, they did not want their grandchildren to do without or to suffer the consequences of incompetent parenting.

Several of the grandmothers I interviewed feel their kids rely on them for much too much but do not set boundaries that stick. Sarah is a 67-year-old white mother of two and grandmother of three. She works full-time in a very high-paying, high-stress occupation in the southeast. She and her husband provide a tremendous amount of care and money to all three of their grandchildren. But Sarah grows weary of her children taking advantage of their help and failing to act like adults. More than the almost perpetual financial help they request, Sarah minds the chaos of children and grandchildren who do not behave well, the lack of reciprocity in dinner invitations, and the thought that her adult children might try to move back into her house.

> But it is like chaos. When her brother is there, my granddaughter degenerates. She is jealous that he gets attention. . . . We don't offer to take both kids at the same time; it deteriorates fast. The 1-year-old is always a lot of work and his sister gets so jealous when they are both here together. My daughter likes to come over and hang out at our house with the kids. But then she will sit and read a magazine, which means one of us will have to chase them around the house. When they leave we think, thank God they are gone.

Sarah and her husband are concerned that they are doing too much for their children and grandchildren, enabling their adult son and daughter to behave irresponsibly. They try to set limits but they do not seem to stick. After a full day at the office, and an evening of grandchild care and providing dinner to the entire family, Sarah often just wishes they would all go home.

> I have been trying to set more boundaries. . . . She wants to come to our house with the kids and she relaxes while the kids run crazy. I don't have the same patience for that perpetual motion. We don't go to their houses very often. We almost always have the kids at our house. I would like it if they would have us over for dinner. My son likes to have people over but his dogs have fleas. Not as eager to go there. But I would like to go to my daughter's more, have her do dinner. But they all like to come to our house.

We have a hard time getting them all out. My husband will go shower and brush his teeth and come back and we will all still be saying goodbye at the door. They will not go home.

Even as they continue to provide it, many grandmothers realize that the amount of care they are providing may be too much, too enabling. Natalie and her husband work full-time and watch the grandkids on their one day off per week, every evening after work, many weekends, and most vacation and sick days. They are only 50 but feeling pretty tired. As Natalie looks ahead she worries about whether they can keep this up. Currently only one daughter has children. What if the other two children also have children? How can they maintain this level of support for them all?

This is going to get harder if they marry and have children. Because there will be more grandkids, and we will be getting older. I hope we can do the same for them but it probably will not be quite the same. But hopefully they will have more regular hours. It is unusual that both our daughter and her husband both work till 7 or 8 so many nights. If they did not have us, one of them would have to have a different job, or not coach soccer.

Natalie and her husband are aware that their willingness to watch the kids every evening after work enables their parents to schedule long days away from their own children. Coaching soccer seems optional to Natalie yet she enables her adult children to do it by babysitting. Their friends have been telling them they are doing too much, enabling their children to do too little, for the grandchildren.

We are making it possible for them to have these schedules, for them to go out and take trips. If they did not have us to watch the children every night after work, they would have to rearrange their schedules. I have had many people say to me, "You do a lot. I would never do what you do." One friend told me, "I like my own time. I am not willing to give up all of my time for my grandchildren."

Several grandmothers spoke of enabling. Janet and her husband both fear they are enabling their children by providing too much support.

They provide a lot of financial help and take care of the grandchildren, often on weekends. They rarely say no to requests for help. Their son-in-law became a stay-at-home dad and now spends the weekends doing things he enjoys such as hunting. They take the kids on weekends when their daughter is either working or wants a break from them. Janet is worried they are enabling a certain level of irresponsibility.

> We are so readily accessible. . . . I sometimes worry that we are interfering. By helping them financially, are we enabling them? Are we enabling them? By helping, are we allowing my son-in-law to not work? Is that how it should be? During the hard times, we would help pay for their mortgage. They said they would pay it back but we have never seen it and we haven't made an issue. I guess it is a gift. I am cautious to make sure we are not there too much. We don't just drop in. We let them know we are coming. I don't want to be their interfering mother-in-law. I don't want to help unless I am asked.

While she loves seeing the grandchildren on weekends, she finds it hard to juggle work, her own housework, and care for the children. She is not certain it should be this way. Should she be watching the children while their father hunts and their mother rests?

> So this last weekend we had the kids a lot. Sometimes my daughter can't deal with them on weekends. But it was not the best weekend. We had not done laundry. The kids are easy, no trouble, and I did get my laundry done eventually. But I was exhausted, completely exhausted afterward. My son-in-law hunts and we watch the kids. Not sure that is how it should be. Normally we would clean, grocery shop, do laundry on weekends, and my husband helps with all that. But if we have the kids then it is hard to fit it all in.

Many grandmothers wish their adult children would act more adult, even as they continue to provide support that may in fact be helping them to resist adulthood. Pauline said that she and her husband both feel they are probably enabling their kids. They want their adult children to raise their own children, as they did years ago, but then they provide almost continuous support that allows their adult children to shirk parental duties. At 61, they both work full-time and provide many hours of grandchild care per week for their eight grandchildren. Her friends tell her, and her very helpful husband, that they are doing too much for the kids. At times Pauline agrees. She says her husband likes spending time with the grandchildren but he is better at setting boundaries. There are times when he says she is doing too much for them or when he says he wishes Pauline would spend more time with him.

> The only people who make comments are saying things like, "Oh, you're the perpetual parent," and that I'm just so giving and loving, you know. Occasionally somebody will say, "You should tell them no, take care of their own kids." But mostly they're pretty accepting and they know my family comes first. My husband, he feels the same way I do. Occasionally he'll say, "Tell them no, we've got plans." But mostly he's as willing as I am to work something out when they need it. He's more willing, we're both more willing to help out, if it's work-related than if they want to go out or go away for the weekend. Then we're not as accommodating. We tend to bend over backwards for job interviews and such, for things like that.

Her sister also tells Pauline that she is doing too much for the kids and grandkids, but Pauline says that is like the pot calling the kettle black.

> My sister has said to me, "You shouldn't do so much!" But then she goes and does the same for her own kids. She complains more than I do but does the same thing, even more!

No matter how much they give, some grandmothers are always being asked for more. Estelle struggles to get along with her adult children. She feels taken for granted and knows full well she is enabling. Estelle is a divorced white woman who works full-time and has, until recently, minimized her grandmother role. But Estelle's daughter and her 7-month-old grandson live with her now and Estelle feels her daughter asks for too much and is neither appreciative nor helpful. Estelle says she examines that relationship and worries that she is enabling, but she says this is just how she is. She likes people and she likes to give.

> She definitely wishes I would do more for her, pay for everything. She would sit and let me pay for everything. She never worries about me. There

is no concern for me. It hurts sometimes. She acts like I am the enemy. She just asks for more. She is snotty, not friendly. Her sisters get mad at her for some of the things she says to me. . . . My daughter does not help at all with laundry, cleaning up after the baby. I get really angry at her and I need her to pick up. She leaves his toys out and I could trip on them. I told her to clean up the space, but she does not. She does not take out trash. She has no gas. She isn't out shopping or doing errands, not doing laundry, does not help out at all.

Some grandmothers resent doing without while their kids ask for more from them. Candi is doing without basic necessities to provide them for her grandchildren. She is at the end of her patience with her adult children behaving so poorly. Candi is a 43-year-old, black high school graduate who works 50 hours a week as a licensed practical nurse. She is the mother of three and the grandmother of three. Her youngest daughter is living at home with her in Section 8 housing. Her older son and daughter are both single parents with little income. They ask her to care for the kids when they work and also when they party. Candi tries to say no but they often just drop off the child and drive away. They also tend to divert some of their money to beer and cigarettes and leave Candi to buy necessities for the grandchildren, including diapers, clothing, and milk. She cares for grandchildren nearly every day after work. She is exhausted from so much work and feels her children only rarely appreciate her efforts. More often, they simply expect more from her. She feels she is doing without even the simplest of luxuries, such as new underwear, movies, ice cream, or having friends over, because all of her resources are spent on the grandchildren.

I have cable but I don't even watch it. So what am I paying for? Then, as soon as I think I might be able to save, they throw another baby at me. Then nobody had a good job. I haven't bought myself new underwear, but I'm buying Pampers and milk. Seems like that's what I work for now and I'm getting disgusted with it. . . . And not because I want to. But I get calls at 2 am: "The baby doesn't have enough Pampers," or "We can't go back to the daycare center because of this or that." So I come up with the money for it. It's not like, oh, I think I'll buy my grandson a bike or take them out. It's milk and things he needs day to day.

Candi said she is increasingly resentful that her oldest son and daughter expect her to do without and to pay for the grandchildren while they continue to party. She spends all of her time and money on necessities and has little energy or resources left for fun with the grandchildren.

> I come home so tired I can't even shower. But then there are days like this.
> I actually get to see him play and not just be grumpy or have resentments.
> I can't go to movies because I have to buy Pampers. And I'm watching my son struggling to find work when his education level isn't as it should be. And it kills me to watch him hitting all those dead ends. Some people don't care as long as they're comfortable but my son isn't like that. Or maybe I need to step back and let him find his own way.

She wonders if she is making the problem worse, enabling her son to remain unemployed and enabling her son and daughter to buy drugs for themselves instead of milk for their kids. She feels she is constantly trying to teach her adult children to behave more like adults.

> When I want time with my two older kids I find myself being more of a lecturer than talking or spending time. I just end up tired, and trying to see what they can do to get some of the stress off of me. You know, you get your money and you do what you want. But I have to buy diapers to see my grandson because his mom drops him off with nothing. So out of my $20 I'm taking $11 to buy Pampers, praying I don't run out of gas on the way to work. And I have to buy him a decent outfit, because his mom drops him off with nothing, no clothes. I can't entertain now because I use what I want to use to have fun to take care of them. . . . I think it's a big shock to all at once have three babies, innocent babies, looking at you and knowing your kids aren't equipped to raise them. And I have to make sacrifices. I have resentments toward not the grandkids, but my children. Like how easy it is to go buy weed, but not hand me money for anything nice, ice cream or anything.

Candi feels she is still working to raise her children to be good parents, but her efforts sometimes appear to be in vain.

> I want them to be good citizens. . . . I'm trying to instill in them to invest in their kids, and if that means instead of going to the bar staying up late and

helping with their homework then that's what you do. The stuff you can get and possess has nothing to do with what's important. It's a respectable quality of life.

But when she tries to be firm and refuse to care for the grandchildren, they often have fights and conflicts. That had happened recently when she tried to be firm with her daughter.

> My daughter, she's not here right now because we had a fight because she asked me to babysit. After all that I do. I come home after 50 hours at work and she wants me to babysit so that she can go out with her friends. I told her no and after all I do, she got mad and left. She took the baby with her. I think she went to her aunt's or something. I don't know. This is really the first time I haven't known at all and haven't called to check but she went off. I said I'm not babysitting while you party. And I haven't seen her since I told her no.

Candi tried hard to raise her kids to wait and have children after they were educated and married. She waited, and she expected her children to wait, too. She lectured them about it, gave them condoms, and made appointments with social services. But they had children young and on their own. She now hopes she can get the grandchildren to wait to have children until after they have completed their educations and have decent jobs and marriages.

> But I hope they raise their kids in a way they don't have kids until they can afford them. I did it. I could afford them. Well, I had a husband who worked so we could afford them. And then maybe I shouldn't have had the third that wasn't by him. That was after we weren't together anymore. But I did and I struggled. If you can't buy the damn Pampers don't make the damn baby. Don't do it. And it's more being ready mentally, and morally, than financially. If you're not together how can you raise a child? If you don't even know who you are, you know? But it is too late for my two. They're gonna have to raise kids while they work. They put themselves in a position right now where they have no choice but to work. They know.

Candi feels her children expect her to do too much for them and the grandchildren and worries that they really do not care much about her, only that she continues to do more for them.

> Don't need me like that. How do I know if you care about me for me or if you care about me because of what I'm doing for you? How about, "Hi, how are you doing?" Instead of, "Hi, I need this."

Candi is exasperated by how unfair the situation has become. She is so busy taking care of the necessities, things the parents should be taking care of, that she does not get to enjoy the luxuries that she feels a grandmother should be enjoying. Instead of paying for diapers, she would like to be buying her grandkids new bikes.

> I just don't like feeling like I'm being misused or people think I'm supposed to take care of the grandkids. And that's not my job. . . . I don't think it's fair I should be the only one doing anything for people. I took money I had planned for an oil change for my car and bought Pampers, and it's not my job to take care of either of you. And then my kids ask for money, too. But if you didn't have the grandkids I could actually take care of you. But that's not my job either. . . . If you were taking care of their basic needs, I could get them their culture, go to museums, all the fun stuff, buy them bikes, all that.

No matter how much they try to limit the help, some grandmothers continue to provide more help than they want, or are even able, to provide. At 48, Carol is a black married mother of two and grandmother of one who works full-time as an administrative assistant in the northeast. Both of her adult daughters live at home and the oldest daughter, who has attention-deficit disorder (ADD), is a single mother of her only grandson. He, too, has a disability that affects his vision, bones, and joints. Carol's own mother did not help much when her two girls were young. In fact Carol told me that her mother was "not granny material." Her mother was a young mother, and a young grandmother, who always said that when the grandkids were old enough to order in French from the menu they could do lunch. By contrast, Carol and her husband are providing care for her live-in grandson during all but their working hours. She wishes her daughter would either do more to care for her own son or move out of the house and leave the boy for Carol and her husband to raise. After just three years as a grandmother, Carol is coming to resent how much of the work she is doing and is growing increasingly worried that she is enabling her daughter to be less responsible.

> My daughter was a 21-year-old single mom. She lived with us; I was her labor coach. I was a young mom myself. I feel that experience allowed me to say that I knew this was much tougher than she thought it would be. I had to respect what she wanted to do, to keep the baby, but when you are 22 and your friends are bar hopping and you can't go because you are breastfeeding and the baby is colicky. Hard for her to balance being a single mom. She does not pay rent. My husband and I are providing her with home and food. She and her son share a room. I don't let them each have their own room. In my mind I feel she needs to take the steps necessary to make her own home. I am afraid that if they have their own rooms she has no reason to want to step up to the plate.

Carol has agreed to watch her grandson all day on Sundays and then on Mondays after work while her daughter is at work. She has not agreed to watch him when his mom is not at work but at home relaxing. Nonetheless, that is happening more and more often.

> Every day, when I come home from work, I hear, "Nana is here!" When I get home I cook dinner and he tells me about his day. There is always a puzzle he wants to do or a book he wants to read. He will tell me what flowers he has seen that day. They do their own laundry. If they wear it they wash it. . . . She does not have her own initiative to clean around the house, but if I press she will, begrudgingly. She has some chores; since her youth, she takes out the trash, she unloads the dishwasher half of the time. I will take him to the doctor. . . . When younger he had a lot of appointments. He has eye exams under anesthesia every six months. With age he has the potential to have complete or partial visual and hearing loss. . . . He is very mobile. No contact sports, but he can swim. I take him swimming after work.

Working full-time and caring for her grandson much of the rest of the time leaves her rushing to attend to her own personal matters and worrying that she is making this too easy for her daughter.

> It isn't a problem getting my own things done. I have to get them done. But it is having to rush or not being able to spend time on each thing because another thing is looming that needs my attention. . . . Sometimes I am resentful but other times I am glad to be of service. Sometimes I am assumed to be of service and I am the easy out. And I wonder if I am enabling her. I feel rushed, so I have to do everything at once; I may short-change something.

Carol and her husband are doing so much grandchild care that they are increasingly feeling like they are the parents and wondering whether maybe they should just raise him themselves.

> I feel—not that he is my son—but that my husband and I enjoy him so much. It is almost like raising our son. So that he has never yet been a burden. When we went on vacation he thought he could come, too, and we took him with us to Florida. My daughter appreciated having a week to herself but had a car accident in my car. We have taken him on vacation with us before.

Conflicted emotions are linked to conflicted relationships. As the years go by, Carol and her husband do more and their daughter does less. Both sides feel growing resentment.

> My grandson is the prince, and the minute either of us walks in the door he wants our full attention. And my daughter does not divert or distract. She feels when we are there, she is off duty. I feel she should be on duty. But when we walk in the door she is off, doing what she wants to do. She has more free time than I do. I am resentful to find someone in her pajamas asking me what is for dinner. I get annoyed with the term we: "We need a new TV." I get very resentful of the freedom to stay, but the failure to do. She wants us to pay for a new television. I think that if she sees something wrong, she should fix it. My day is much more full than hers. It's not easy sometimes. We often

have words. She says to me that I have no idea what it's like to raise a 3-year-old. My retort is *you* have no idea what it's like to raise a 3-year-old.

Even though Carol and her husband feel they are already doing too much for their grandson, their daughter is constantly asking them to do more. Carol said that she and her husband have no time alone together now and they miss that a lot. And perhaps even more worrisome, they have no nest egg. Their household income is just a bit less than $100,000 per year but they have been buying diapers and everything else for their grandson for these past three years. They have been spending their savings even as they watch their friends, who do not have grandchildren yet, invest for their retirement.

> She absolutely wishes we would do more. She wishes I would be giving him a bath rather than reminding her to do so. I would be in charge of dishing up his meals. She is frustrated that I am at work and not home helping with him. When I walk in the door and she says, "I am so glad you're here, I have to go take a rest." She wishes I would do more. And I am tired and I resent it. . . . My husband loves the grandson as much as me. But we both resent that we do so much and she does not appear to appreciate it. She claims rights and privileges as his mother. She feels we are lucky she lets us take care of him, or take him on trips. I think my daughter and her son will stay living with us. I don't see her mature enough to take the necessary steps. He will be living with us when he graduates from high school. We are both worried our money will run out. We have no nest egg.

A few grandmothers told me that they know full well they are allowing their adult children to behave badly. Belle knows for a fact she is enabling her daughter to be irresponsible. She refuses to marry her partner because she intends to continue providing this level of support. She is a 51-year-old, white, divorced mother of two and grandmother of two. She has a personal income of about $70,000 and a household income of over $100,000. When her daughter became a young single mother, she was still living at home with Belle and her brother. Belle describes the first 10 months as crazy. Belle immediately began rearranging her work schedule as a teacher to help with the first baby, and then later the second baby, before work, after work, and on weekends. She began to pay for nearly everything for her daughter and her new grandchildren.

> It was tiring for me, and I just did it. If I did it now I would really notice the difference. But back then it just was what it was and I just did it. I got very frustrated, going back to the crying baby and how much work it was when I was already working full-time. . . . It was what I did for my free time, took care of the baby and still taking care of my own two adult kids. I don't think I did a very good job; my daughter lives in public housing and for a long time did not have a job. When she moved out, I sort of kicked her out. . . . I have paid her power bill a few times. And she knows that she can spend her money on a new CD because she knows I will pay her power bill. And so I am part of this: I enable her to be irresponsible.

Over time, Belle began a relationship with a man who thought she and her daughter were codependent. He criticized her for enabling her daughter to be irresponsible, moving in and out of the house, in and out of relationships, and in and out of work. They have been together for six years but Belle refuses to marry him because then he will have some control over how much of her money goes to the children and grandchildren.

> I met my partner and he was an outsider pointing out how much I was enabling her. Financially I was paying for everything. Hard to get her out on her own. She would go out and live with friends with the baby and then she would wear out her welcome. Then I would let her come and stay with me again till she found something else. The biggest thing for me has been being torn between my partner who thinks I should not do anything for them and the kids who think I should do everything for them. I always struggle with the money and the time. Should I give it to her? I don't want to lie to him. I avoid his questions. I try not to answer. But if he was not there I would probably still be paying for everything. So he helped me be more objective. The reason I don't want to get married is that I don't want him to be able to tell me how much money I can or can't give for the kids. If we marry it will be his money. I paid her power bill of $600 a few months ago, and I pay both kids' cell phones.

Now that her daughter and grandkids live on their own, Belle still rearranges her work schedule to help with grandchild care, often arriving home so late from work that she cannot go to work out.

All this past semester, and I will again this fall, I would pick my granddaughter up from her daycare and drive her to school at 9 in the morning. So I go in to work late every day. I did not have classes till 10 so it worked alright. It was difficult to stay home and drive her when I wanted to get work done. I can do work from home, too. But students would be looking for me and I would stay later, until 5 or 6, to get my work done. So then I stopped going to Curves on the way home so I worked out a lot less all semester.

Then Belle got cancer and struggled with chemotherapy, work, a critical partner, a demanding daughter, and two grandchildren. She was exhausted.

I was diagnosed with breast cancer about two years ago. And now I am cancer-free. The kids' request for help never really changed, even though I had cancer. They just sort of did not think about it. They still asked me to do everything for them. "I need this, I need that." I worked almost full-time during all that. . . . At the time I did not think it was that hard but now looking back it really was. I would teach my classes and then crash on the weekend. I was not nauseous but really tired. My partner was my saving grace. He was very worried and took very good care of me.

After a while, her partner, who already resented how much she did for the kids and grandkids, now came to resent how much he was doing for her.

But he got tired of it all, and about halfway through stopped going to the doctor with me. He came to resent taking time off from work, using his vacation to go with me for treatment or because I was sick. As time wore on, he just sort of lessened the support. . . . He really resented time I wanted to do things for the kids. He thought I was using my time and energy for the kids. He goes on and on about how irresponsible my kids are. So I just have to shut him down. I don't want to listen to this over and over. We have differences of opinion and he knows it. He tells me daily not to pay their cell phone bills. He thinks I am still codependent. He thinks I want them to be dependent on me for money and help. But I don't want them to hit bottom. I see real progress and so I am pleased with how the kids are doing. . . . I used to spend $1,500 a month on the kids and now I spend about $400 a month on the kids. But he does not see that progress.

Her partner is not the only one who thinks Belle is enabling her daughter to be irresponsible. Belle has heard the same thing from her parents, coworkers, and friends. She agrees and yet does not reduce the help by much. But she minds how much her children ask for and their lack of consideration for her health and her needs.

They don't look out for me; they are not there yet. And they do wish I could do more to help them. More money and more time with the kids. They think I am Wonder Woman, even with the cancer. When I first got cancer we both worried a lot about what she would do if Mom was not there. It would be hard for her to handle her kids without my help. She would really struggle without the backup I provide. And if she got money she would blow it fast, and then be in big trouble. I would have to actually die for her to think I would not back her up. . . . I feel guilty that I don't spend more time with my grandkids. But if I did my partner would be mad. I have to push those limits with him. I thought he might move out over this but now I think he will not. I feel resentful and tired of having to help her out. She always seems to have a legitimate issue, and I do want to pick the kids up and help out as much as I can. And I do like being with the kids, but not a kid person. . . . I pictured them married and raising their own kids.

Belle loves her job and would like to be able to work more, not less. And she would like to have time with the grandchildren as their grand-mother and not as a substitute mother. She is critical of herself, saying that she knows she is enabling but that her daughter really needs her help. This 51-year-old has embraced intensive grandparenting, despite mounting evidence that it may be detrimental to her and to her chil-dren. She is well aware that her parents would never have helped her out the way she helps her children. Though her partner constantly tries to restrain her from doing so, she continues to provide a constant flow of care and cash.

My generation thinks we are responsible for our kids forever. But our parents don't feel that way. What would my parents have done if I had acted like my daughter? My dad would not have allowed much support. They would have expected me to figure it out on your own. They would have kicked me out if I had gotten pregnant and did not have a job. But for me I could not imagine that I would have kicked her out pregnant with no job. If my partner had not come around I would still be doing so much for the kids. I have to answer to him and that makes me do less for them. When I decline to help them they really do find another solution. They really do figure out a way to handle things. Without my help. He was right to a certain degree. . . . My friends often talk about this with me and we all struggle and talk about how much to do for our kids. They all see how much progress we have made.

Belle is not the only grandmother giving too much and yet unable or unwilling to put a stop to it. Corey is a 56-year-old divorcée with a personal income of over $50,000 and a household income of over $100,000. She struggled with alcohol abuse as a teen, and then she and her husband of 13 years struggled with it together. Since her divorce she is clean. She works 40–60 hours a week as a substance abuse counselor and lives with her new partner, a woman. Corey has two children and four grandchildren, but she spends all of her time and money helping her daughter and her three children. Her daughter, and her daughter's boyfriend, also struggle with substance abuse. Corey and her partner bought them a house to live in. Corey's daughter has mostly stayed clean since she had the three children but she does not work, has no money, and will not drive a car. As a result, Corey provides a great deal of care, financial assistance, and transportation for the three grandchildren.

I bought a house for them and her three kids. They are both trying hard to stay clean. She had nowhere else to go. I bought her a house so they would have somewhere to live. My daughter does not have a job. I pay for the house, and they pay rent to me now, but they did not at first. Her boyfriend works and he makes some money. She does not get welfare, but she gets food stamps, Medicaid, and SSI for my grandson because he has autism. . . . I pay part of the house payment, and the power bill, and clothes for the kids. About $400–$500 a month. I buy things like clothes, bikes, birthday presents, all the extra stuff. I don't buy food, but I used to.

This level of care and support has been going on for years. When her daughter and the grandkids lived in her house, the daughter was usually home but Corey did most of the work.

> When they lived in my house, which lasted for nearly four years, and I was working full-time, I helped with baths, cooked meals, cleaned the whole house, laundry for all of us, I did all of the housework. My daughter did not lift a finger. She had just quit using drugs. I would work all day and then come home and do everything. Everything! The only thing I did not do was discipline. . . . She would not let me have any say in discipline. If I said a word to her or the kids it would cause an uproar from her. I picked kids up, drove them places. I did everything.

Corey, who took care of her mother for years until she died of Alzheimer's disease, now provides most of the care for her grandson with autism. While she loves taking care of him the disability presents special challenges. When I first asked Corey to do an interview she said she would not be able to participate because she did not take care of her grandchildren. But when I asked her if she babysat, drove, cooked, or cleaned, she said she did all of that and much more. As she explained, until I asked her to participate in an interview, she had not realized that she was providing care for her grandchildren because their mother was almost always in the house.

> At first I said I did not take care of them. I did not realize that I cared for them. Their mother was there, so I was thinking she was doing it. But now I am thinking that I was doing everything. My grandson has autism and so I did a lot of extra work with him. I took him to doctor appointments. And I still take him to a lot of his doctor appointments. I would do day-to-day work with him. He could not communicate and he would scream. Did not potty-train to age 5. High-end care. So I gave him a lot of extra care. I would take them to the zoo, on outings, to the park. Took them all to the museum. I had to be prepared to leave with him at any moment though. He is doing much better now. He will still have autism and it is still challenging. He goes to a lot of special therapy. He is repeating second grade and is trying to learn to read now. He can talk really well now. He communicates well. He has typical intellect. He is off socially. He notices it

and is sad. He wants friends and he cannot make them. So he gets sad. It is still hard to take him places. I would take him to the grocery store and then have to leave with him, just leave my cart and groceries and take him home.

The amount of help Corey is providing has created tremendous strain between Corey and her partner over the last six years. Early on her partner helped with the grandchildren, both by providing money and care. But over time she felt the need to set boundaries. Corey's partner feels Corey is enabling her daughter to do drugs, remain unemployed, and refuse to drive a car. Corey agrees but is going to continue providing the support in any case.

My partner and I have been together for about six years. We bought the house for my daughter together. I could not afford to do it on my own. So my partner helped pay. This partner, and every partner I have had, hates how much I do for my daughter. And they hate my daughter. My daughter is loving and she is mean. She needs mental health treatment and will not get it. My partner hates how mean she will be—like not letting me see the kids for months after I found pot in her house. The stress between me and my partner is that I do so much for my daughter and she treats me so badly. I am used to it. But everyone minds. I am going to pay for my grandson's summer autism camp and the aide he has to take with him. And I am offering, so he can go. I want him to have this. And my partner really minds. She does not want me to pay for so much for the grandkids. So I have to fight with my partner about the money and also the time I spend with my grandkids, the time I spend helping them. She wants me to spend the weekends with her. It is crazy. It is a lot of stress and pressure.

Despite the conflict it creates between her and her partner, Corey has no intention of curtailing the grandchild care or the financial assistance.

I love helping the grandkids. I love it. Everyone else can go to hell. I will do what I think is right to help these grandkids. I love time with them. I love helping them. I love the hugs and kisses, love every second of it. They are irritating at times; they fight and bicker. I would not do one thing different.

Even when they do manage to stem the outflow of care and money, some grandmothers find that they have to spend years trying to rebuild. At 66, Renee had hoped to be long retired. But, as she says, she is an enabler. Instead, she gave her son $500,000 out of her retirement account for a business venture that failed. Now she cannot retire. She is working full-time to repay the loan from her retirement account. She would like to be taking care of her granddaughter and wintering in Florida with her husband. Instead she is giving her son and his family even more money.

> Now I am trying to be more conservative about money. My granddaughter's parents are going through some tough times; financially they are strapped. I take food to them to be sure they have enough. They both have jobs now so there is income. But now her parents are dependent on me. And for the first time in my life I have said, I have to say, no. Someone just crashed into their car and I nearly bought them a new car. But for the first time I just kept my mouth and my checkbook shut and they are just surviving on one car. I am stepping back or I will never get to retire.

She gives them tremendous amounts of money and they just ask for more. Instead of scaling back their own lifestyle, they ask her to cover costs, including school supplies. This causes her to keep working and to have less time to see her granddaughter.

> I help her parents so much, but then I have to work because I keep giving them money. Then I have to keep working and then I have no time for my granddaughter. What I want is to reduce my hours and spend time with my granddaughter. My son will ask, "Why can't you do this or that?" and I get so upset. I am so frustrated. I am an enabler. I can't do that because I lent you all that money and now it is gone. I have helped all of my kids but the girls have only needed help for a little while. . . . But for my son there is no end; he is always asking for help. My daughters tell me I am enabling him. You have to stop helping him. If they lose the house they lose the house.

They live in a beautiful home on the lake and always have a bottle of wine on the table . . . and I am buying the calculator.

She has helped so much that she feels her son feels entitled and her granddaughter is beginning to as well. She wants to stop enabling but thus far has not.

I am finally deciding to stop being an enabler. I will take my granddaughter to my house and focus on her and stop helping her parents. It paints a bad picture for her to think that Grandma will get everything for her. She is also starting to feel too entitled. Just like my son. They feel entitled to whatever I can buy for them. I keep hoping he will stop asking. And now I see she is starting to ask Grandma for everything. I want to spend time with her but not money on her. I want to be fiscally conservative. It isn't about the dollar. It is about the family.

Renee is embarrassed by how much she has helped her son. She regrets that she is working instead of spending time with her granddaughter and instead of wintering in Florida with her husband.

I almost canceled our interview today. I thought you wanted to hear about what a great grandmother I am, spending time with my granddaughter. But I almost canceled because I feel so guilty. I feel like a failure. I can't spend much time with her because I am always working because I loaned her father too much money. I can't retire and be the grandmother I want to be. I have to work.

Renee's other children, and all of her friends, tell her she is enabling and must stop giving her son and his family so much. She and her husband disagree about how much help they should be providing.

The other three tell me we should not help my son so much, that I am enabling him. And our friends tell us, too. That we do too much for him. They are right. I agree. We have made him dependent on us. I have enabled him to make bad decisions and he is still making them. He has that house on the lake, and gas in his boat, and wine on his table, and I am buying his daughter's calculator and clothes and volleyball camps. My husband and I disagree about how much to help the kids. I am the enabler; he is more likely to say let's not.

Some of these grandmothers may have always provided too much help to their offspring, both as young, and now as adult, children. Maybe they always enabled them. But none of them said they had always enabled. On the contrary, they mainly said that they had no trouble saying no to their kids. The trouble was with saying no to their grandkids. When their adult children asked them to do more for the grandchildren, they found themselves unwilling or unable to decline.

Sibling Rivalry

Some grandmothers worried about whether they provided equal amounts of care and cash to their respective children. Generally the 48 grandmothers I interviewed provide more care for daughters than sons, descendants living nearby, and adult children who are single parents, recently divorced, or completing degrees. Several grandmothers had their own internal balance sheet and worried they were doing too much for one set of grandkids and not enough for the others. In those cases, the adult children did not seem to complain and in fact were happy that the siblings most in need were getting the most help. In other cases, however, grandmothers told me that some of their adult children complained about unfair treatment. Then grandmothers heard an earful about how they were doing too much for one adult child's family and not enough for another's. Indeed, some siblings wanted their fair share. But most often when adult children complained, it was not because they wanted more for themselves. They wanted less for their siblings. They wanted Grandma to stop enabling. Indeed, siblings were critical of the ways that Grandma's help permitted their brothers and sisters to be irresponsible parents.

Sometimes adult children without kids mind that those with kids get all of the attention and support. At 54, Calista has taken care of grandchildren for over a decade, but concentrates her energies on her daughter's two sons, who live nearby. She said that her son who is single and lives four hours away often feels that he does not get his fair share. Even when he comes home to see his mom, she is still in charge of the two grandsons. So he has to help with the boys if he wants time with his mother. Sometimes he even takes the boys so that Calista can have a much-needed break.

With my youngest son being away, sometimes he gives me a break if I have something to do. But he feels his sister gets me all to herself. So he thinks it's all his time when he comes to visit but I still have them. So he helps; then we talk and spend our time together.

Sometimes those who live farther away mind that those who live nearby are receiving more assistance. Janet and her husband have two adult daughters. One lives an hour away and has no children and receives little help. The other lives in town, has two children, and receives a great deal of financial help and grandchild care. Resentments have arisen.

My other daughter sometimes resents that we helped them financially but we have helped her, too. . . . The fact that we live close and she is an hour away is part of it. I have tried to explain that to her. But she also has a big support system where she lives and sometimes we feel we are intruding. We have had some talks about this.

Some adult children mind that their parents are enabling. Maryann provided a lot of care for her daughter's children when they were young, but she provides a lot more for her son's child. In addition to working 40 or more hours a week at her own business, she provides grandchild care 10 to 15 hours a week. Her son had sole custody for the first seven years and now has joint custody. Maryann feels it is important that she provide as much stability for her grandson as she can, but her daughter tells her often that she is doing too much.

I think my daughter feels that I have done too much for my son, helping with my grandson. He was a single dad for a long time and so when my grandson was younger I really helped a lot. Until he was 7 my son had complete custody so I was the only female in his life till he was 7. My daughter thought my son should have taken care of his own son more instead of me doing it. He calls me Mimi because I would not let him call me Mama. Then when he was 7 his mother came back into his life and the judge gave her joint custody.

Similarly, Carol's two adult daughters argue fairly often. The oldest daughter is a single mom who struggles with ADD, lives at home rent-free, works part-time, and counts on Grandma and Grandpa to care for her disabled son after work each evening and all weekend so she can have some time to herself. The younger daughter, who also lives at home rent-free, works full-time as a nurse and is critical of her older sister.

> The other daughter that lives at home does help; she is very blunt. The two sisters argue a lot. She acts as if she is the older daughter, is critical when the other isn't being a good mother. She is focused and disciplined. She babysits him some; she gives him clothes and he is dressed to the nines because of her.

Even though she is also living at home rent-free, Carol's younger daughter is critical of Carol and her husband. She tells them they are being taken advantage of and enabling their daughter to get away with it. Carol agrees but does not like the hard feelings that are emerging. In the end, she feels they have to help their daughter because of her disability.

> There are some hard feelings. My younger daughter and I have a good relationship, and she resents that my oldest daughter is using us. And she resents that we are enabling her. To some extent I agree with that. But my oldest daughter has ADD and did not finish college. She needs help.

Gillian's daughter certainly thinks Grandma is doing too much for other siblings. Gillian unexpectedly took her two grandkids into her home for eight months. Now that they are back with their mother, she and her husband still continue to provide a great deal of care and financial assistance. Their oldest daughter, who lives several hours away and does not have children, thinks they do far too much. Gillian disagrees, but she hears that comment often.

> Much of the family thinks we did way overboard. That we did a lot and spent too much money. I just buy them what they need: clothes, coats, underwear, school supplies. I am taking clothes to them now. I spend a lot on Christmas, more clothes. I never help pay the rent. I do give her money for the kids every month, for food and whatever they need. And when they lived with us we paid for everything. Some people say we are doing too much. She works, she has a job, that we don't need to pay so much.

Gillian's daughter does not mind the helping but she minds that it is allowing her brother and his ex-partner to be irresponsible parents.

Our daughter is a little upset with her brother and that mother, that they are not taking good care of the kids. That it is their responsibility and not Grandma and Grandpa's. She does not mind me helping them but she minds that the parents are not being more responsible.

Emotional Highs and Lows

The emotional impacts for working grandmothers of caring for their grandchildren were decidedly mixed. Many of the grandmothers experience great happiness caring for the grandchildren and feel their babysitting and financial contributions are well appreciated. They are the recipients of innumerable thank-yous, hugs, gifts, surprises, and acts of kindness. For a few, signs that the recipients of their efforts are appreciative are not often forthcoming. While their adult children occasionally express their thanks, sometimes they have to be reminded just how much help Grandma is providing. Though I never asked any questions about enabling, about one-third of the grandmothers I interviewed said they were providing too much help. They said that they are enabling their kids to be irresponsible and they know it. These grandmothers know, and are frequently reminded by their partners, friends, and coworkers, that they are providing too much help and enabling the next generation to be questionable parents. Tensions over enabling generate a great deal of stress and can lead to sibling rivalries about whether some adult children are receiving too much, or too little, support.

The role of grandmothering is being redefined in part because of major demographic and cultural shifts, and in part because of the failure of the US welfare state to respond to these changes. The demographic changes are numerous. More women with young children are working than ever before. More young children are being raised in single-parent families than ever more. And more grandmothers are working than ever before. The cultural shift toward intensive mothering, and now intensive grandmothering, is pervasive but not particularly well understood. The result is that many working grandmothers are doing more mothering. They are providing more help than their own parents did and more help than they expected to provide. Neither the welfare state nor employers have responded with programs that would allow parents to rely less on Grandma. Workers in the United States still do not have national guarantees about paid time off for illness, vacation, or parental leave. They still do not have national health insurance, readily available high-quality. low-cost child care, or universal access to pre-school. In the absence of these national supports for working families, working grandmothers have to help the younger generation balance work and family.

For many grandmas, the work is becoming more intensive. For some, it is much too intensive. At times it reflects the worst form of helicopter parenting, which enables adult children to continue to behave in ways that are irresponsible and at times decidedly unsafe for the grandkids. But given the absence of alternatives, what is a grandmother to do? Many successfully set boundaries regarding the care and money they provide. But others try to set boundaries only to cross them and pro-vide more care and more money because they want their grandchildren to live the highest-quality lives possible. Why do some grandmothers continue to provide care and cash when they know it is not good for them or for their adult children? Why do some grandmothers, whose own parents readily said no and who as parents claim they readily said no, say yes to so many requests concerning support for grandchildren? It is the most vexing question for this book. Their answer is that they do not want their grandchildren to do without or to suffer. For better or for worse, many of these families are grandchild-centered families.

That said, it is important to put these findings in the broader context. Many grandparents do not provide care for their grandchildren. My analysis of the HRS, presented in chapter 2, showed that grandparents who do not provide care for their grandchildren outnumber those who do. Among men and women ages 51–70, 27 percent were not grandpar-ents, 41 percent were grandparents who did not provide any hours of care for their grandchildren in the preceding two years, and 32 percent were grandparents who provided at least some care for their grand-children. Another study reported that even among grandparents who live in the same neighborhood as their grandchildren, one-half provide grandchild care but fully one-half did not provide any grandchild care.[2] Among those I interviewed who provide care for their grandchildren, most report only positive emotional impacts. About one-third of the grandmas I interviewed reported that they feared they were enabling their children, and an even smaller minority reported issues with sibling rivalry. There are emotional lows for some working grandmothers, but for the majority the mix of roles produces tremendous emotional highs.

8

Social and Health Pros and Cons

The impact of caring for grandchildren on working grandmothers' social and physical well-being is mixed.[1] Grandmothers with more resources, who are working and caring for fewer hours per week, can readily juggle multiple roles of work and grandchild care and maintain a busy social life and good health. For these grandmas, multiple roles enhance each other and their overall well-being. By contrast, grandmothers with fewer resources, or who are working and caring for grandchildren for many hours per week, often do not have enough hours, or energy, to maintain their previous social lives. Some reduce social obligations in part because their friends are also doing so and they know that grandchildren are only young once. For many, time with family is their number one social priority anyway. But many face role conflict and reduce their social lives because they are simply too stressed or tired to carry on.

Most of the grandmothers, even those who feel tired or have health problems, said caring for the grandchildren adds exercise to their life and, in general, is good for their health. Some feel they are more careful about what they eat because they are being so careful about what the grandkids eat. But many are left very tired, neglecting their own exercise and nutrition or delaying doctor visits. A few have been cautioned by their families, and by their doctors, that they need to give up their demanding schedule of work and grandchild care.

Social Lives

For those grandmothers who are in good health and only care for grandchildren occasionally, social lives tend to remain constant. But for those who are providing a lot of grandchild care and who are feeling weary from busy schedules, social activities are among the first things that are pared back.

Cherry is one of many grandmothers who can maintain an active social life, despite how much she cares for the grandchildren. She works full-time and cares for the grandchildren before work some days, after work other days, and sometimes on weekends. Nonetheless, she says she and her husband have time for plenty of social activities, friends, and hobbies.

> We have six couples that we get together every Saturday night and have been doing that for 20 years. Thursday is my husband's bowling night and it is my night home alone. I don't do a thing. We usually reserve Friday nights for our other daughter and her husband. We all go out to dinner. We have kept all of our friends from high school and we go to the reunions. It all fits in well. We have a lot of friends and we enjoy them. I read and I write children's books. And I garden. I have the grandkids help with the garden. They have a huge garden at home that they could not keep up. . . . I do family genealogy. I love to research.

Despite working full-time and helping with the grandchildren some evenings and weekends, Marta and her husband also keep a fairly active social life. They find that most of their friends are just as busy with their own grandchildren. And while they do not say no often, they like to keep the option of turning down a request for grandmother care.

> My son-in-law said at first, "Now, which night of the week are you going to take the kids?" . . . My husband and I said, "We're young, we have our own lives and we're not going to commit to taking them the same night every week. But we will help when you need us to help." We find time for each other. My husband and I have this thing where we have to do something just us at least once a month. We just find the time for each other.

However, it is not easy to find time for their marriage because even after the grandchildren are gone, there is a lot of cleaning up to do in their wake.

Every time the grandkids come over they make a mess. By the time they leave, there's always paper everywhere. My grandson likes to take a deck of cards and just throw them in the air so they're all over the place. We determine whether we have to get it done right then and there. If we don't have to, we leave it. But I have a rule that we always need to get it cleaned up before we go to work on Monday morning. Laundry and groceries we do during the week when we don't see them. We do that together and get it out of the way.

Some of their old friends have moved away and others are busy caring for grandchildren. So they still get together, but not nearly as often.

My friends my age, we generally see. We see one friend once every other month or so, but on a regular basis. Most of our friends are in the same boat we are, just about all of them. We used to have little get-togethers every week, and then it turned to every two weeks, and then once a month, and then once every other month. A group that used to be 12 is now down to 6. Lots of them have moved to other places so they're not here as often. . . . We don't see everybody half as much as we used to. Our friends are still there, but not at the forefront anymore.

But this couple is committed to having fun and to each other. They always find time for their greatest shared passion, dancing.

We still dance. My husband and I are Jitterbuggers. We both love to dance, we love to dance at weddings, or sometimes we'll go to big band events. My daughter has a friend in a band, and they play some things that are a bit more than what we're used to. But if something comes on that we can dance to, then we'll dance to it. I'll be so excited to dance with my grandsons.

Several grandmothers noted they have little time for their friends anymore. Jamica works full-time and cares for several grandchildren.

She would like to cut back on paid work but cannot afford to, and she feels she cannot reduce her grandchild care because her adult children need her help. Jamica says she hears from her customers, friends, and family that she is doing too much for her children and grandchildren and not enough for herself. They tell her she has blinders on and is not even aware how much she is doing for the others.

> There are comments, that I am doing too much for one and not enough for me. So there can be a little tension about that. I have no time for friends my own age. I call them a bit, but we rarely get together. I have no time for friends.

Some grandmothers jettison competing social obligations to focus on grandchild care and much-needed rest. Being with the grandchildren has really become the top priority for Lee and her husband. At age 60, they really wish they could stop working and spend more time with the kids. Given their financial need to keep working, they find themselves cutting back on other things they had planned to do, such as volunteering and going to church. They get tired and they want to focus their energies on the grandchildren.

> I used to go to a nursing home before my grandkids came, and I'd take people for walks and visit with them. So I can't do that anymore; they've taken up that volunteer time. This last year, we were going to church before, but they've taken that time up, too. Because when I'm not with them I just need the time to rest. I just want to sleep in instead of going to church. I don't know if it's grandparenting or just because I'm getting older. I think it's because of the working full-time and part-time jobs. I'm just more tired than the grandkids are. Or I think what it is, is that I want to be the grandparent, I want to spend that time. So I prioritize that more than volunteering or going to church. I want to spend that time with them.

They have curtailed their social life, reserving their energy for work and caring for the grandchildren. Recently their son gave them a trip to Europe and they found they were too tired, and missed the grandkids too much, to really enjoy it. Their plans for future travel have been put on hold. They are not sure they want to be away.

Our son gave us a trip to Europe for three weeks this past summer. The thing I missed most was my granddaughter. . . . We backpacked across Europe and took the train across Europe. I think I should have done it when I was 25 and not 60, because after two weeks of riding the rails I had to rest in Italy. We spent most of the time just resting because we needed to. . . . It was good but I definitely was tired after two weeks. And ready to come home to my granddaughter. It really surprised me how much I missed her. Or that she was the thing I missed most. I was ready to come home and play with her. Three weeks was too long.

Bennie would gleefully give up her entire social life for more time with the grandchildren. Bennie works full-time, supporting herself, her disabled husband, and her youngest daughter who still lives at home. After years of caring for her own parents before their deaths, she is now caring for her husband, who is only 47. But the focus of her life is caring for her grandchildren. Everything else is put on the back burner.

I would watch the grandkids any time. I would pick them up from school, so would my husband. We would take them to lunch, or go to lunch at school for grandparents' day. My husband treats my kids and the grandkids just like they are his. When my son wants to go out on a date, I will watch the kids. If I have plans, I cancel them so I can watch the kids. I take the kids apple picking, to movies; sometimes I get all three grandkids here so they can hang out together. With everyone's busy lifestyle they are not together too much. I will bring them here for the day, or go there at night and spend the night at their house, wherever they want to go. I take them when they are sick so my kids don't have to use a sick day. So I use one of my sick days to watch them. I take them for snow days, so the kids can go to work.

Her goal is to care for the grandchildren whenever their own parents cannot, so that they never have a sitter. She loves having them there and would readily allow all three children and all three grandchildren to move in with her if they wanted. The result is that she has nearly given up on any social life that does not revolve around her grandchildren. Bennie has no desire to maintain a social life other than the one that revolves around her adult children and her grandchildren.

I have canceled going to dinner, canceled movies, parties. I would cancel it all to care for the kids. I want to spend as much time as I can with them. And I want my kids to be able to go to work or to go out on a date. My husband also would rather they be with us and not with a babysitter. I don't want them with a babysitter. Now that they are getting older, I go to their games, their school things, their concerts. I have the kids as often as I can. At least twice a month. Whenever they want me, I will take them. I ask for them. I want them here. I would love to have them all, all three kids and all three grandkids, here with me all the time.

Some grandmothers find that work and grandchild care leave little time for anything else. Between working 60–70 hours a week, caring for the grandchildren after work most days and weekends, and caring for her frail older mother, Betty has reduced her social life to her own family. She has not had time for a movie or a book or sewing. She only has time for her grandchildren. If she could afford to cut back on work she would, and that would give her even more time to spend caring for her family.

I haven't been to a movie in a couple of years, can't see paying all that money to see a movie. I take the kids to church. I love to read but haven't had time. I love to sew and haven't had time to do that. It's not the kids. It's the job that makes me not have time to do things.

Natalie, a white mother of three adult children who lives in the midwest, and her husband gave up most of their social life when they were just 48 so that they could work by day and care for their two grandchildren every evening and most weekends. Natalie works full-time but has a day off a week that she also spends with the grandchildren. She used to have a fairly active social life but she rarely has time for that now. Her friends who do not yet have grandchildren are somewhat unhappy with her new focus on the grandchildren.

It does affect how much time I have to work out. I do get upset about not having enough time to work out. I do chase them. I tell myself that I do get a workout chasing them. I would like more time for a workout and more time to walk with my friends. I used to walk with a group of ladies. That is gone. I am busy with grandchildren. So getting together with friends has gone a bit by the wayside. We don't see people as much. Every once in a while I feel that a friend or two minds that I am not that available to walk or go out. They don't express it verbally, but I see it, I feel it. They don't understand.

Some grandmothers have time but not the energy for social obligations. Estelle finds that between her full-time job and her live-in daughter and grandson, she has curtailed her social life tremendously. It is not so much that she is too busy to see her friends or attend events, but it is that she is wrung out by her daughter's demanding, and sour, disposition. During our interview her phone rang but she chose not to answer it.

> I claim my time. . . . Hear that phone? I am not going to answer it during the interview. That is my daughter. She thinks that I am to be at her beck and call. If I don't have time for all my other activities, it isn't because of my grandson or the job. I do less with friends, less activities, in part because my daughter is so surly. She wears me out. If I had my house to myself right now, especially not having her surly personality there, if I did not have to deal with that. I can never turn myself off because she is so surly. I have to manage her the way I manage things at work. I don't commit to much with friends and volunteer work because I am tired of putting up with people between work and her being at my house. Sometimes I just don't have it in me to deal with people anymore at the end of the day.

A few of the grandmothers are stretched far too thin to maintain social lives. Pauline is a 61-year-old mother of four and grandmother of eight. She works full-time for a hefty salary. Though she feels it is her responsibility to help with the grandchildren and she is glad she is able to do so, the combination of employment and grandchildren often leaves her too exhausted for any social life whatsoever. Meeting the requests of her children and grandchildren is all-consuming and at times she has nothing left.

> There are times I'm, like, stop the world I want to get off. It's not all the time but it happens a lot having to deal with it all. I thought by the time I

was 61 I'd be able to relax and not worry about raising kids, but whatever. Life is what it is and you do what you have to do. I think everybody gets stressed out occasionally. And I don't think it is, well, I guess it is more stressful for me because I know other grandparents who aren't as involved in the day-to-day life of their grandchildren. You deal with the hand life deals you. Occasionally, the best way to explain it is that I say, I love to see them all come over and I love to see them all go home, too.

Though she loves caring for her grandchildren, the requests for her help are endless. And when they all seem to want help at once it is simply too much.

I do wish for a day off from all of it. There are times I'm, like, like I said, stop the world. Nobody bother me, no phone, just let me be. That's not real often but occasionally I do have days like that. Especially when they're like, several at one time have issues and are wanting help to deal with things. It gets a little too much. It's easier to deal with when only one of the grand-children, or one of the kids, wants or needs something from me. But if I'm dealing with more than one or two issues at once I'm, like, stop! Again.

Health Consequences

To examine the health impacts of working and caring for grandchil-dren on the national level, I analyzed the Health and Retirement Sur-vey (HRS) 2010. As noted in chapter 1, studies of how carework shapes working women's emotional, social, and physical health show both posi-tive and negative impacts.[2] Studies vary by the types of carework they include, working status, custodial status, and other confounding factors, but some studies suggest that working and caring for grandchildren may positively impact grandmothers' physical and mental health, in part because it increases the feelings of being needed and useful, and they lead to a more active and involved social life.[3] However, other studies suggest that working and caring for grandchildren may increase stress on the job and reduce time for exercise, rest, and proper health care.

My analyses of the HRS data show that working and caring for grandchildren had no significant impact on grandmother self-reported mental or physical health. Table A.7, which appears in the appendix, shows that having self-reported mental health problems is more likely among women ages 51–70 if they smoke or have limitations in their activities of daily living (ADL). Mental health problems are less common among women who are black and women who exercise. Most notably, mental health problems are not significantly related to either the number of working hours or the number of grandchild care hours. There is no notable difference in mental health by work or grandchild care hours when we control for other variables. On average across the nation, working grandmothers who provide grandchild care have the same level of mental health as those who do not.

Table A.8 explores the impact on physical health. It shows that self-rated health is better among those who are more educated and who exercise. Self-rated health is worse among those who are Hispanic, who smoke, who have a higher body mass index (BMI), and who have more depressive symptoms, chronic illness, or ADL limitations. Most notably, self-reported physical well-being is not significantly related to either the number of hours of grandchild care or the number of hours of paid work. There is no notable difference in physical well-being by work or grandchild care hours when we control for other variables. Thus, on the national level, working grandmothers who provide grandchild care have the same levels of physical well-being as those who do not.

The 48 working grandmothers I interviewed described a variety of positive and negative health impacts. The results are mixed because the impacts are various. There are good and bad health effects.[4] In short, for some, caring for grandchildren increases their attention to diet and exercise while for others it leaves them too busy and tired to pay much attention at all.

For many working grandmothers, taking care of the grandchildren has a decidedly positive health impact. After a full day at the office, Marta and her husband often care for the grandchildren, playing with them and feeding them dinner. Though she gets very tired, Marta said that paying attention to their health makes her pay more attention to her own.

> According to my husband it's the best thing that ever happened to me. I eat less. I eat less because I always have to be concerned about what they're eating and cut their food up for them. And it's better for me. I'm always moving. They force me to get on the floor and exercise and play with them, and roll around on the ground.

Lucinda also feels that caring for the grandchildren is positive for her health. She was one of only a few grandmothers who specifically mentioned that she intends to pass her love for fitness on to her grandchildren. She works out six days a week. The only day she does not work out is the day she drives one hour each way to spend the entire day caring for her only granddaughter. She plays on two adult soccer teams, takes ski vacations, and golfs. Her husband and friends are all equally active. Not only is she committed to sustaining a high level of fitness, but she is also committed to introducing that lifestyle to her granddaughter.

> My hobby is fitness, playing soccer, and gardening. And I have tried to carry those all over even though we have our granddaughter. And I introduce her to these things. She will be a soccer player. And I make sure I have time for all of those things. What have I given up? Sleep. I am still seeing all my friends; they all work, too, and we all still play soccer two nights a week. And we still all hike, go on our annual golf and ski trips. I just mark on my daughter's calendar if there are Wednesdays I will not be able to care for my granddaughter. She has a babysitter.

Several grandmothers reported that the mix of work and chasing grandkids leaves them feeling more energetic. Paula feels the balance of work and grandkids keeps her feeling young. A 48-year-old black woman, Paula says that taking care of the grandkids and working full-time makes her feel good. Though she works three 12-hour night shifts a week and cares for grandchildren nearly every day of the week, she likes the diverse roles.

> Doing both makes me feel younger. . . . I like the balance. I have a lot of time with the grandkids, and I like the job but not the hours, so I liked the balance. I would like to go to more of the grandkids' functions but not really take care of them more. I need to work. I like to work.

Estelle is one of a few grandmothers who found that working and caring for her grandson left her too busy to overeat. Estelle lost a significant amount of weight three years ago and had been working out immediately after work each day in an effort to keep the pounds off. She still works out every day after work except the days she goes straight home to care for her grandson. Nonetheless, she gets a lot of exercise chasing after him.

> I was babysitting him, right after work. I would go exercise after work, then pick him up . . . then take him home, feed him, play with him, put him to bed. That would get difficult at times . . . but I was able to stay on top of my dishes and laundry while he was playing. You just remember those lessons you had when the kids were little. You learn how to juggle all those things. He was better than having a dog, as far as my diet.

The more activity the better, according to several of the grandmothers. Sarah routinely swims, runs, and plays tennis. Even so, taking care of the grandchildren increases her level of activity and that is one of the things she loves most. She has played tennis with her grandson since he could hold a racket. For years she beat him but now that he is 17 he always wins. Still, she holds her own.

> Taking care of the grandkids definitely adds to my physical activity. I do really active things with the older grandkids. There was a point when I could always beat my grandson and now he runs me all over the court. I always felt good that I could play tennis with a 14-year-old boy. The active things keep you young. I enjoy doing active things with them. I think it makes me feel better about myself.

Time with the grandkids keeps several grandmas feeling younger. Reagan feels combining meaningful work and time with grandchildren keeps her spry. A 60-year-old white woman with one stepson and three grandchildren, Reagan constantly rearranges her work schedule to spend time with the grandchildren. Though she is too busy for proper workouts now, she says playing with them keeps her young and fit.

> I love seeing the grandkids. I am energized when I see them. Even if I am tired, I am absolutely ecstatic. They are energizing. It makes me feel young: I go to the water parks with them, and I am the oldest person there on the water slide. I act like a little kid. We also take them to our farm in Oregon. It was my parents' before they died. We go in the spring, for a weekend. Or

we go in the summer. We climb trees. We plant and pick at a farm. They love to play in the mud. We take mud baths; I take pictures. We take the train down there and play.

She prefers this mix of grandkids and a meaningful career and plans to work for another 10 years, until she is 70. She only wishes she had more hours in the day.

> I was hoping I would have grandkids and so I was hoping I would be involved. I want to do both. I am really lucky. Just wish I had more hours in the day. I would always choose kids first, but I need to have a job, an occupation, a project. I really want to do it all. I want more time with them but they have busy schedules. . . . I want to continue to keep spending time with the grandkids. I am very aware that the time that they have to spend with us is short. I savor every minute, every hug and phone call. It is wonderful.

Dana is one of several grandmas who said that being mindful of what the grandkids are eating keeps her mindful of what she is eating. Working full-time and then watching the grandchildren two to three nights a week until 10 pm and sometimes on weekends makes 48-year-old Dana tired. But she loves her time playing with the kids. Overall, she says it has a good impact on her health because her commitment to providing the grandchildren with healthy choices spills over into her own lifestyle.

> I feel healthier. I'm in pretty good shape, in good health anyway. But I think it makes me feel better about myself. I cook better for them than I would for myself, I know that for sure. I do watch more what they eat than I would watch what I ate if it was just me. So at least twice a week I'm probably eating better. Although we do give them sugar; their parents aren't big on giving them sugar or candy but we do. . . . I think the kids are exercise. I walk a lot anyway. And I take the kids on walks. I like to go out on walks, so I'll take them with me if I can. I'd love to have them more. I think it'd be fun. I think I miss having my own. When they were younger they were so much fun.

But the health impacts for working grandmothers are not always positive. For some the mix of responsibilities leads to a mix of health results. Carol feels that the health impacts of caring for her live-in grandson, coupled with a full-time job, are mixed. She enjoys her time with her grandson in a way she was not able to do as a mother. And caring for him makes her take better care of her own health. But it is all-consuming and leaves her exhausted and pressed for time to take care of her own business.

> I appreciate things more as a grandma through him than I could when I was younger as a parent. But I am tired. I feel at the same time that not every 22-year-old parent wants to go for a walk with a young child. So I like the chance to appreciate things that I can appreciate now. To go on walks with my grandson, and enjoy them more now that I am older and wiser now. As a grandma I want to take that walk. It makes me feel younger. I have more energy; I do things with him that I don't remember ever doing with my kids, like finding worms. Taking care of him makes me healthier. More aware of my mortality. I eat better. I am trying to teach somebody the life lessons that vegetables are just as good as cookies. But I would love a day off I could plan. I would get to the back of the linen closet, or the kitchen junk drawer, but I don't know. I would love to get a pedicure. . . . I never thought I would be working full-time and raising a grandson. This isn't what I or we pictured at all. I thought I would be a Christmas/Easter grandma. Maybe a week in the summer.

For those who noted negative health impacts, the main issues were being too stressed and tired. Grandmothering at older ages proves quite difficult for some. At 67, Mariam is eager to retire. She has been balancing full-time work and many hours of grandchild care per week for nearly two decades. As she ages, she feels more and more tired.

> I fall in bed at night. I am tired when they leave. We love to see them come and we love to see them go. I don't resent that. I am tired when they go. I think that dealing with grandkids does keep you younger, not just sitting around waiting to die. It makes me feel good to be around them and forget the things that happen as you get older. When they go home, I feel the

aches. I feel my age. The bones hurt. There are four boys and when they are
all together it is nuts. Loud. Upside down.

The positive health effects of caring for grandchildren are tempered
for some grandmothers because when they combine it with work, they
no longer have the time or finances to take care of their own health.
Jamica juggles a full-time housecleaning job with care for several grandchildren. She would love to reduce work so that she has more time for
the fun parts of grandmothering.

> I think taking care of them keeps me younger, to keep up with them. I
> have no choice but to be healthy. But it can tire me out, to get from the job
> to them, stresses me out, tires me out. No downtime. I go straight from the
> job to the grandkids, no downtime in between. There are days I want to
> go and sit for half an hour, before I have to jump into the rest of my day. I
> would like a day off, especially because I would like to go to college and see
> my boys play football. I have seen them play, but it is hard to fit it in there.
> They love it when I am there. I was surprised; I did not know they would
> care that I was there. They miss me.

Cleaning houses and chasing grandchildren provide a lot of exercise
and that can have good health effects. But having so little time and money
to care for herself has left Jamica behind. When resources are limited,
grandmothers often choose to put others' needs before their own.

> It can be difficult to take care of everything. But this year my car broke down
> and I have been walking. I cannot afford a new car with two kids in college.
> I have to run after buses. But I have lost 25 pounds. It has been good for my
> health. I don't go to the gym. But my job is physical. If I have time, I want
> downtime, not a workout. But all this walking is helpful, it is good for me.
> My job takes me up and down the steps. . . . But I have gotten behind in den-
> tal and doctor appointments. I make sure everyone else has their appoint-
> ments but not me. I had my first physical in May. I had not been to the
> doctor in eight years. I have no health insurance. Have not had any all these
> years. And I am behind on the dentist. I am more worried about getting
> physicals for the kids and the grandkids. I make choices. I don't have dental
> insurance. So do I let my 16-year-old son lose a tooth, or do I lose a tooth?

Though caring for the grandchildren has some positive impacts on a grandmother's health, particularly when it leads to an increase in joy, exercise, and healthy eating, combining grandchild care and work responsibilities leaves many too tired and struggling with other adverse health impacts. The latter was the case for Susan. For 62-year-old Susan, taking care of her four grandchildren only makes her tired when she is in charge for a few days or more. A happily married mother of two and grandmother of four, Susan works full-time as a secretary in the northeast in part because her husband is semiretired and in part because she is helping her son pay for law school. She loves taking care of her daughter's children and while she is there she also does a lot of cooking and cleaning. She takes care of the children occasionally after work but more often on weekends, sick days, and vacation days. Recently she used a week of vacation to care for the grandkids while their mother traveled. Though her son-in-law was around, her husband was not available to help. The grandkids got sick and she was very tired by the end.

> When I take time off for the kids, it is usually vacation days but sometimes sick days. We often talk during the day to sort out the schedule. Last year I took a whole week of vacation to watch some of the kids while my daughter traveled with one of them. That was hectic. . . . I got very tired. My husband was not around to help. I was by myself some of the time. I stayed all day and all night. The baby got sick, another had a cold, we took the baby to the doctor. And during that week I cooked and cleaned. Did everything she would do. My son-in-law was there but he was working. I kept telling her everything was fine. I did not want her to feel guilty. She offered to come home when the baby was sick but we said no. She needed that time away. But I was so glad when she got home. I was so tired.

Her daughter appreciates her help enormously but worries that her mother gets too tired. She encourages her mom to rest when the kids do, rather than use that time to do laundry and vacuuming.

> Sometimes I feel tired. She will say you look tired, Mom, and I will say it was hectic. She says all I want you to do is watch the kids, that I don't have to clean and pick up. She wants me to sit down and rest while the kids are

sleeping. I should sit down but don't. I try to do too much to help her. She does the same. She takes time away from herself to do for her kids.

Many grandmothers feel the need to limit grandchild care to protect their own health. Even though she gets very tired, Blake feels that time with her grandsons keeps her more aware of time passing. Blake, who is 68 and runs her own business, was caring for her two grandsons every Thursday until it became too much for her. She asked her daughter and son-in-law to rearrange the schedule and now that her shifts with the boys are shorter, she feels it keeps her younger and more alert.

> There was a point when I had them both all day Thursday and I would just get exhausted. I finally said, "I am not as young as you are. Taking care of two boys all day long is more than I can deal with." We adjusted the schedule, and they went to preschool for half of the day and then I had them the other half. And that was great, fine with me, not as exhausting. Mostly I don't feel pressure; they are old enough now that they understand when I have work to do. They are not as demanding. They can entertain themselves. I am sure that spending time with the boys keeps me younger. Being around the younger generation keeps me more focused on them and having fun and playing. That feels like staying younger. Balancing the time requires some organization so that I don't just let my days drift, so I see that as good. Some of my friends don't have work or grandchildren and their days just drift. It keeps me more alert.

When the responsibilities get too taxing, some have to reduce time at work or time with grandchildren to protect their own health. Patty has some chronic arthritis, and her husband has Alzheimer's disease. Juggling a part-time job cleaning houses, caring for the four grandchildren six days a week, and caring for her frail older mother has negative and some positive health impacts. Finding it all too much to balance, she recently reduced the number of houses she was cleaning from 13 to 3.

> I do feel stressed. Recently I have been tired and exhausted. I told another customer I can't do the cleaning anymore. So I cut back on the paid work. The thing I really like is taking care of the grandkids. I like to

do a lot of things and be around a lot of people. When I cut back on paid work I miss the visiting with the older ladies that I cleaned for. I used to go to the gym and work out, swim, lift weights. And now I clean house as my form of exercise. I have terrible arthritis. Chasing the kids is wonderful exercise. I never sit for very long. I wish for a day off but then when it happens, and I have a day of nothing and nobody, I get anxious and worried and I find things to do. I just play on the computer when I should be doing laundry. I think I want it but don't like the time on my hands. I don't always enjoy it.

For Lee, the health effects of caring for one grandchild were mainly positive, but now with two, she is feeling more of the negatives. At 60, Lee works more than 40 hours a week and cares for the grandchildren four days a week after work and on some weekends. The combination makes her very tired, but Lee does it because time with the grandchildren makes her smile. Taking care of the first grandchild was a lot easier though. Now that there are two, and the second one is exclusively breastfed, it is a lot more tiring.

Yes, definitely after I've worked all day long, if I have to babysit that night, with two it's stressful. It's much harder. One wasn't so bad. He's starting to crawl now so he gets into things. And my daughter didn't give him a bottle like she did the first one, and so when she's gone he just cries. It's hard to distract him. The 3-year-old I just put a movie in, and since I can't do both of them I don't get to play with her if her brother's upset. It makes me feel old when I can't take care of them. Like, oh, I should be able to do this! So it makes me feel younger to be with them, but old because I can't do as much. And two are harder than one.

Too many competing responsibilities make some grandmothers feel completely overwhelmed. Betty is one of many grandmothers who report mixed feelings about juggling work and grandchildren. On the one hand, time with the grandchildren is meaningful and keeps her physically active. On the other hand, she balances so many responsibilities, including caring for her frail mother, that she never really has time for herself. She is tired and years away from either retiring or having independent grandchildren.

Taking care of the grandkids is good for me. Keeps me moving, keeps me going. When you sit and don't do anything, that isn't good. But it gets tiring sometimes. For the most part I am used to it. This week I have been tired. I don't know why. . . . Only time I feel stress is when other people are begging for my time, the job, the church, my mother, my other kids. I am only one person; I can't do it all. I feel tired. . . . I really never have a day off. If I won the lottery, I would take a long vacation to North Carolina and go home for a month or two or three. I have not been there in four years. The grandkids are not coming; this is for me. I would go by myself.

Similarly, Marta gets weary. Marta did not expect to be juggling work and grandchildren. She had planned to retire before her current age of 54 so that she could spend even more time with grandchildren. Though she rates her health as excellent, she gets tired balancing all of her duties.

It definitely makes me tired. I don't want a day off but I am always glad when their parents come to pick them up. . . . I thought I wouldn't be working and I'd just be able to take care of them. I would pop in and take them out to lunch. Those things I can't do. It's a bit more scheduled and regimented because I have to work.

Natalie also gets overwhelmed. She is only 50 but she gets very tired juggling her full-time job and her nightly and weekend care of the grandchildren.

I love it but I do get tired. I don't have kids at home now; we are empty nesters. But I think I have less time now than I did when my children were home. I work all day and have the grandchildren nearly every night until about 7. I get tired. I do less at my own house because I am over there. I cook less. It gets overwhelming. But I would not have it any other way. I get behind on my laundry and my groceries; I am here less and so I can't get it done. I think it keeps me younger. I sit little. I watch TV little. I am chasing kids around. I do wish I could have a day off from everything. I need that, and I don't get that often, and there is some frustration with that. I sometimes just need a day for me and I want to take a day but sometimes I just can't.

Juggling paid work and grandchild care leaves some grandmothers without enough time or energy to take care of their own health. Tara juggles full-time work with eight grandchildren that she cares for nearly all of the time. Her boss had already warned her that she is at risk of losing her job because she misses so much work.[5] Two of her grandchildren live with her and her husband for now because their mother died of a drug overdose and their father is serving time in prison. Some of their other grandchildren are dropped off almost around the clock. Her husband helps as much as he can but he has already had several heart attacks. She says her house is a mess and she has neglected her own health while caring for everyone else.

> I have so much to do and I can never get it all done. I will start a load of laundry in the morning when I get up and then move it along. You should see my bedroom. My husband and I had a trailer and it burned down about five years ago. So we live in the garage. When we got the two girls we built a room onto the garage for them to sleep in. But they want to sleep with us. I have a huge pile of laundry on our bed. I just grab clothes out when they need clothes.

At the time of the interview an additional grandchild was living with them because her parents were facing difficulties, but she was expected to return to her father soon. Ironically, Tara, a nutritionist, rarely has time to prepare a healthy meal. She knows the importance of fresh fruits and vegetables but rarely has time to buy them.

> In two weeks when our third grandchild goes back to her dad, it will be easier. I buy groceries on the days I don't teach classes. And sometimes their other grandmother will take the grandkids on weekends and that gives me and my husband time to be alone and to get shopping done. Or I shop after work.

She has maintained this hectic schedule for years and there is no end in sight. As she put it, the grandchildren just keep arriving.

> I do sometimes get really stressed out and need a break. I do get a break. The other grandmother will take them. I get exhausted, I don't have time to

pay my bills. But I have to get the kids to bed. I have not done my taxes yet. I have not had a physical in two and a half years. I feel tired. I am missing my own appointments. I feel stressed and get migraines. I am exhausted when I get home. I don't have time to go to the doctor. My muscles ache. But I love what I am doing.

Some grandmothers have provided this level of care for years, even decades, and work hard at minimizing the negative impacts. For Calista, that means cutting down on the stress. At 54, Calista has worked full-time and cared for two grandsons from 3 to 11 every evening for over a decade now. She also volunteers at the church and helps care for her frail older mother. She has arthritis from a job-related injury and she gets fatigued. She said she used to worry about all the things she needed to do and the things she was unable to get done. But no more. She is determined to continue to meet her responsibilities but to worry less. Worrying wastes too much of her precious energies.

> I'm sure it makes me feel healthy. But I do get tired a lot of times. I still manage to go on, but stress maybe not as much as I used to. I try not to get like that because there's just too much to do. . . . It is tiring. I do get tired but it's just necessary. My daughter, she appreciates it.

Many grandmothers strive to find a way to limit how much help they are providing to protect their own health. But it is not easy to strike the right balance. Amelia is a divorced white married mother of four and grandmother of three. She works full-time in the midwest. Her daughter became pregnant at age 17 and continued to live with Amelia for the first five years. Amelia and her husband provided nearly around-the-clock care for their grandchild and paid for nearly everything. Working full-time and caring for her daughter and grandson made it difficult for Amelia to take good care of herself. Working out, which had been a daily commitment to secure a recent weight loss, becomes nearly impossible at times.

> Working out has been a challenge, having time to exercise. Every time I try to go for a walk my grandson wants to go with me. I have to sneak out, or he wants to ride his bike with me. Or I want to do the exercise programs on

TV and it is hard with others coming in to bother me while I am working out. Now that they are moving out I have done more. But for the five years they lived with us, it was hard to work out.

After five years of nearly constant help from Amelia and her husband, their daughter and grandson moved out. But they continue to live nearby and Amelia and her husband still help them nearly daily. For Amelia, the responsibilities of a full-time job and grandchild care sometimes make her too tired, even as they also keep her feeling young.

> Sometimes I feel stressed out. I just can't do it all. I feel guilty when I have to say no and I stress about that. I want to be able to do more. Sometimes I feel tired, and my job tires me out more. I would say it makes me feel young, keeps me in the circle of what is going on. I play and read books. I am 51. I am young and have grandkids and I can go play baseball and catch with them. I sometimes wish I could have a day away. . . . If I had a day I would lay somewhere quiet and read a book.

For some grandmothers, carework becomes too taxing as grandchildren grow. Estelle also gets tired sometimes, between her full-time job and her live-in daughter and grandson. In part, she finds it harder to take care of him now that he is getting older and heavier.

> My ability to carry him isn't what it was. He is a big boy, and it is a struggle to carry him, put him in the car seat, carry him up the stairs. That was a struggle. I feel frazzled nerves. When I was trying to visit someone or go to the grocery store, and he would scream in the car seat, and that would drive me crazy. I can't reach back and give him a pacifier. He would scream, and it was too hard on me. I would just stop over and over to give him a pacifier. So sometimes I would just not try to take him anywhere.

As she gets older and grows more tired from chasing a growing grandson, Estelle tries to limit the care she provides. She tries to say no more often and to protect her sleep.

> I don't sleep that much. I have no trouble telling her I will not babysit so that she can go out at night. Or telling her I am too tired, had a hard

day and can't do it. I have had times I said yes and then wished I had not because I was too tired. . . . I have started closing my bedroom door so that I am not woken up by him waking up in the night.

Some grandmothers are literally at the end of their ropes. Their situations have become untenable. Between working 50 hours a week, caring for her three grandchildren evenings and weekends, and checking on her mother with Alzheimer's disease, Candi is exhausted. More than anything, she just wants to lie down.

> It's sad, but the thing that makes me feel the best is being able to lay in my bed. My bed right now is the best friend that I have. If I had to choose between a hotel right now, just laying around, and an African safari I would choose the hotel. I'd feel like I was important enough to get some rest.

Her last comment reveals just how low on her own list of priorities she finds herself. Generally, she is so busy caring for others that she does not make sure she gets enough rest.

Connie is also at the end of her rope but her adult kids continue to ask for her help. Between working two jobs that total about 40 hours a week, and caring for three grandchildren, especially her disabled 8-year-old grandson, Connie is tired. Very tired.

> I am very much stressed, tired, totally exhausted. It somewhat keeps me young, but it never makes me feel healthier. Yes, I wish for a day off. Yes, I do. I'm striving for a day off. It hasn't happened yet; a week would be nice. No, I have no time, no me time at all. I don't do any of that. I haven't done a holiday or vacation ever. . . . I want them to learn the value of being a grandparent. Oh, I think I should be relaxing. But I want someone to take care of them. They'll be lost totally if they didn't have me to help.

Social and Health Consequences

While some grandmothers expected to be juggling work and grandkids, many did not. Among those who did not, many expected their adult children to be more independent and rely on them less, while others expected to be done working by now so they could spend even more time with the grandkids. Often those doing the most intensive grand-mothering did not expect to be providing so much grandchild care or financial assistance. Some manage to balance all of these responsibilities and to hang on to their friends, hobbies, churches, travel plans, and volunteer activities. Others readily give up social engagements and travel, eager to spend more time with the grandkids. Grandkids are only young once and they are often fountains of joy. Many grandmothers appreciate this second chance to raise small children. But a few give up social activities and retirement plans more reluctantly. I asked all 48 grandmothers if this mix of paid and unpaid work was the plan and all but four said no. They did not intend to be doing so much. Nonetheless they would not walk away from it. A *New York Times* article quoted one grandmother who also felt this way: "I did not expect this and I didn't want it, but my heart's involved now."[6] Very few of the grandmothers mentioned the lack of federal guarantees for paid time off for sick leave, vacation, childbirth, or the lack of access to health insurance, quality daycare, or preschool. They generally saw the stresses they faced as individual family matters to which they felt compelled to respond. Few mentioned the need for government programs that would support working families.

The social and health impacts of caring for grandchildren are mixed for working grandmas. Some maintain an active social life and attend to their own health readily. Others feel the time with grandchildren provides the best possible social life and a constant diet of healthier foods and greater physical exercise. But for some, the combination of duties proves to be too much for one day, let alone day after day. They are exhausted and neglecting their mental and physical well-being. Many would like a day off, or a reduction in paid work, or more days of paid sick leave and vacation days. Some wish their adult children were given more reasonable amounts of paid time for illness, vacation, and parental leave without risk of losing their jobs. While many might want a change in the balance of work and grandchild care, to better preserve their social lives and physical well-being, few want less time with grandchildren. For most of the women I interviewed, time with grandchildren is a top priority.

Conclusions

Grandmothers at Work

Working grandmothers in the United States provide a great deal of care for their grandchildren, ranging from child care, emotional supports, financial supports, and, at times, custodial care. We have not known much about how working grandmothers balance work and care of grandchildren, or what the impact of that mix of responsibilities is on their financial, emotional, social, and physical well-being. This study addresses those issues, providing a national picture by using data from the Health and Retirement Survey (HRS) 2010, and an individual picture, by using the results of the Grandmas at Work Survey. According to the HRS 2010, among women over age 50 who have grandchildren and are employed, 46 percent provided care for their grandchildren at least some hours per year. All of the grandmothers I interviewed for the Grandmas at Work Survey are included in that 46 percent.

Reliance on working grandmothers is high in the United States for several reasons. Demographic changes are notable. The proportion of children born to single mothers has risen steadily. The rate of mothers with young children working has also risen steadily. More women are working later into middle age than ever before. These trends have converged to create a high demand for child care—and a generation of grandmothers who continue to have jobs. The US welfare state has not responded to these trends. Unlike workers in most European nations, US workers do not have national guarantees for paid time off for sickness, vacation, parental leaves, or flexible scheduling. Many working parents, particularly those in lower-income jobs, do not have meaningful paid time off. Also, unlike most European nations, the United States does not have universal health care, readily available high-quality, low-cost child care, or universal preschool options. The result is greater reliance on working grandmothers. Working grandmothers love time with their grandkids, but there are only so many hours in their days.

Using qualitative data from 48 interviews with working grandmothers who care for their grandchildren, and nationally representative data of those ages 51–70 from the HRS, I have explored how grandmothers juggle their roles and the effects of that juggling. I find that the main reward of providing care to grandchildren is joy. To a woman, the grandmothers felt tremendous happiness when spending time with, or even talking about, their grandkids. Regardless how difficult the circumstances or demands, they loved time with the grandkids. For many it provided a second chance to enjoy raising kids without so many competing pressures or concerns about shortcomings. Juggling work and grandchild care gave grandmothers a great deal of role diversity and most liked that mix of responsibilities; however, for some it proved to be exhausting as responsibilities competed for limited resources.

The interviews suggest that grandmothering in the United States, like mothering, may be becoming more intensive. All but four of the grandmothers described doing more than their own mothers did, and more than they had intended to do. Though the intensification of mothering appears to be driven mainly by changing cultural expectations, the intensification of grandmothering appears to be driven in part by unmet need. In the absence of supports for working families, more are asking grandmas to help. And many grandmas make a point of saying yes. They are often prompted by joy, family legacies, a sense of duty, or the need for their intervention. All but four of the grandmothers are doing more than their parents did and more than they intended to, particularly since they are still working. Though they say their parents gave them little or no support, many are giving their adult children and grandchildren boundless supports. Especially when adult children face difficult challenges—including divorce, joblessness, disability, drug use, or prison—or when they have established goals to complete college, buy a first home, or travel, many working grandmothers provide a great deal of care and cash. Indeed, when the demands get tough, so do the grandmothers.

Many grandmothers balance paid work and unpaid carework perhaps somewhat more easily than their adult children do. After all, many had done this juggling decades earlier. And with age often comes maturity. But, perhaps most important, many have understanding bosses and lax workplace guidelines, though some must proceed with much more caution. In either case, however, nearly all of the grandmothers I interviewed frequently rearrange their work schedules, change jobs or schedules, use paid vacation and sick days, and bring work home or return to work late to be available to provide grandchild care. For some, rearranging their work schedules results in lower earnings and savings or in an end to paid vacation or sick time, pensions, and other fringe benefits.

Financial support of the younger generations is occurring at very high, and in some cases alarming, rates. None of the grandmothers I interviewed are paid for their services but nearly all provide money to their children and grandchildren. Some limit their contributions to gifts and splurges but many are paying for monthly bills and daily necessities. Some can readily afford these contributions but many are diverting money from their own retirement funds, depleting their nest eggs, or incurring new debts in their efforts to support the next generations.

Many factors limit grandchild care. Some grandmothers have actively taken steps to reduce how much care they are providing, often by working more hours or years than they want or need with the goal of being unavailable for grandchildren. Others have partners who cannot, or do not, or will not, assist in caring for the grandchildren. Sometimes there are resentments when one grandparent wants to provide more care than the other. Finally, some grandmothers are in a new sort of sandwich generation, caring for their adult children, their young grandchildren, and their frail older parents. Their roles often conflict as they attempt to stretch dollars and hours across many competing responsibilities.

The impact of balancing paid employment and unpaid grandchild care varies considerably by the amount of resources, age and health, and the quality of the relationships. The emotional impacts are mixed. Many of the grandmothers, though certainly not all, feel very appreciated and their spirits soar with the knowledge that they are providing much-needed and highly valued care. But about one-third struggle with the worry that they are providing too much care and enabling their adult children to be irresponsible. A smaller minority worry that their adult children are rivaling over whether grandmother care is fairly or properly distributed. The social and health impacts are also mixed. Some integrate grandchild care into hectic social lives while others eliminate nearly all social obligations to focus exclusively on the grandkids. Many report that chasing grandkids, and worrying about their nutrition, keep them active, fit, and eating better than they would be otherwise. Some are simply too exhausted by the demands of paid work and unpaid carework to do anything else. As a result, they neglect their own health.

Theoretical Implications

Working grandmothers who care for their grandchildren find numerous rewards and costs associated with the multiple roles they perform. Virtually all find caring for grandkids joyful and rewarding; some view it as an extension of a lifetime of carework and some view it as a second chance to provide care under less stressful circumstances. Even though the rewards may be numerous, some chafe at the gendered expectations that they should be readily available for this work. While many report that they easily balance multiple roles, others report that the competing responsibilities tax already limited hours, dollars, and sources of energy.

Carework. All forms of carework comprise a vital form of unpaid work in the United States. The care of grandchildren by grandmothers is a labor of love that fills in for the huge gaps in the US welfare state. Given that the United States does not have the sorts of supports available to working families throughout Europe, this form of carework is particularly important for families. By caring for grandchildren, grandmothers provide typically no-cost, high-quality child care. Care by grandmothers tends to be flexible in ways that paid care is not. Kids can almost always go to Grandma's for sick days, snow days, holidays, vacation days, weeknights, and weekends. For working grandmothers, however, providing this carework may bring many positive and negative consequences. For some, it comes at a fairly high price in terms of financial, emotional, social, and physical well-being.

Lifecourse Approach. Lifecourse theorists have focused on younger women balancing paid work and child care and have paid scant attention to middle-aged women who are balancing paid work and grandchild care. A lifecourse approach reveals that some middle-aged women have had brief periods of carework while others have done carework almost nonstop across their life course. Many relied on their training as working mothers to successfully juggle work and grandchild care. But they are quick to point out that grandmothering is different than mothering, or at least they feel it is supposed to be different. Though the work of grandmothering may be becoming more intense, and grandmothers have a lot of responsibility, they are often not in charge. Some are pressed to do more than they want; some are permitted to do less than they would like.

Rewards of Carework. The rewards of caring for grandchildren are numerous. Though the costs associated with carework are well documented, so are the joys. And perhaps no type of carework is more rewarding, or joy-filled, than grandmothering. The women I interviewed nearly all shed happy tears as they talked about how much they love their grandchildren, love spending time with them, love caring for them, and love feeling loved in return. Many enjoyed the mix of paid and unpaid work responsibilities and reported a positive impact on their financial, emotional, social, and physical well-being, though for some the responsibilities proved too much and the consequences were quite negative.

Gendered Expectations. Cultural definitions and expectations about who should perform carework have changed. Indeed the gender gap in carework has shrunk such that in most arenas women now provide only twice as much care as men. Nonetheless, carework in general, and caring for grandchildren in particular, is still widely regarded as work performed by women. Very few of the women I interviewed balked in any way at the expectation that as women they should care for their grandchildren. With only a few exceptions, they did not mention gender as an issue. Rather those who balked at the intensiveness of grandmothering mainly wanted to have some control over their days or wanted to be sure they were not providing too much assistance to their adult children. Those who were motivated to limit care found clever ways to do so. Indeed, not all grandmothers are suited to, or interested in, grandchild care. Some simply said no. Others failed to answer their phones. More than a few worked more hours, or more years, for pay than they needed to reduce their availability as babysitters. As a group they were not attempting to redefine gender roles, but many were trying to maintain a clear distinction between mothering and grandmothering.

Intensive Grandmothering. Just as mothering has become more intensive, these data suggest that grandmothering has become more intensive. For the most part, the grandmothers have very positive attitudes about their carework. They are joyful about the time they spend with the grandchildren and are pleased to be helping to raise their grandchildren. By providing free, high-quality, safe child care, these grandmas allow their adult sons and daughters to work more, earn more, save more, finish college, coach soccer teams, travel, perform housework, and tackle dozens of other activities. Many are sequential grandmothers, providing care for each new grandchild as it arrives; thus in many instances they have been balancing paid work and unpaid grandchild care for decades. Many are also intensive grandmothers, providing long hours of hands-on care, including feeding, bathing, driving, helping with homework, and tucking into bed. Some are replicating the patterns of their mothers and grandmothers before them; others are establishing new patterns to be sure their daughters have supports they never had. But some worry that they provide too much help and therefore enable their children to be irresponsible parents. This is the potentially darker side of intensive grandmothering. Overly solicitous support from grandmas might be doing more harm than good—or it might be providing a necessary lifeline to a grandchild whose situation is otherwise untenable.

Role Stress or Role Enhancement. Did working and caring for grandchildren lead to role stress or role enhancement? In fact, many women reported both. Many actively acknowledged how much they enjoyed the mix of responsibilities and purposely kept their work hours high so that they did not become full-time nannies. But some found the mix stressful. In particular, those who were single, with fewer resources, or in poorer health found juggling so many balls to be stressful. Those whose partners did not want to participate in, or were critical of the amount of, grandchild care often found the multiple roles too taxing.

Sandwich Generation. Role conflict was often higher for those working grandmothers who were also providing care to the older generation by stopping by after work and on weekends to help their aging parents with activities of daily living. Several found the multitude of roles more

than they could sustain. Caught up in a new type of sandwich generation, caring for their parents, adult children, and grandchildren, these
working grandmothers provide a lot of care and support to multiple
generations simultaneously.

Taken together, these theoretical perspectives suggest that the
impact of working and caring for grandchildren is decidedly mixed. To
balance all of their responsibilities, most of the working grandmothers
actively rearrange their own work schedules to accommodate the needs
of their grandchildren. For the most part, grandmothers have greater
security and flexibility through their jobs than their daughters. Though
some set limits on the amount of care they will provide, many do not.
They are at that stage of the lifecourse where they have more time to
spend with a grandchild than they did with their own children because
there are fewer competing demands. But they are also at that stage of
life where they should be preparing for their own retirement and old
age and many are not. Some grandmothers pay mortgage, daycare, and
other monthly bills on behalf of their children. Many are eating away at
their own savings; some are even accumulating debt. Concerns about
finances are forcing many to delay retirement and travel dreams beyond
what they had planned.

Policy Implications

Younger and middle-aged women in the United States are increasingly
likely to be employed and to be single mothers, yet they receive little
help from the US welfare state, given that the United States has no federal guarantees for paid vacation, paid sick leave, flexible scheduling,
paid maternity leave, universal health insurance, affordable day care, or
universal preschool. While many workers gain health and dependent
benefits through their employers, those benefits are more readily available for full-time workers with higher salaries and lengthier tenure in
their jobs. Moreover, employer-based benefits are generally shrinking.
Studies demonstrate that when employers allow more flexibility, careworkers are often able to retain employment and improve financial
security for their own old age.[1] Given the dearth of social supports, it is
not surprising that young families turn to grandmas for help with the
grandkids. Many middle-aged grandmothers are juggling paid work,

grandchild care, and parent care. Many are overflowing with joy, but some are drowning in exhaustion and debt.

Why don't we do more for working families of all ages? Public support for such programs is often high, but action by Congress is virtually nonexistent. For example, 80 to 90 percent of the grandparents interviewed in one study favor higher taxes for higher quality and more affordable daycare, stronger safety standards, and more provider training.[2] Grandparents love time with their grandkids but many would prefer that daycare was handled elsewhere, freeing them up to enjoy time with, but not necessarily provide intensive daily care to, their grandkids. Despite evidence that universal daycare throughout Western Europe fosters early childhood development, and despite evidence that readily available good child care prompts parents and grandparents to remain employed, there has been little movement by the United States toward providing universal or expanded subsidized child care. Accessible and affordable child care is one of the most important factors for improving income security, particularly for women, in the short run as they are raising their children, in the middle years as they are helping with grandchildren, and in the later years when they rely on their Social Security, private pensions, and private savings.

It seems that we do not pass federal policies that support families because we assume women will continue to shoulder carework roles, performing unpaid carework despite the consequences for their financial, emotional, social, and physical well-being.[3] Very few of the women I interviewed seemed upset about the gendered expectation that as grandmothers they should provide care for their grandchildren, whatever the economic, emotional, social, mental, or physical impacts. We have yet to meaningfully redefine supports for working families as a family, and not a women's, issue.[4] We also have yet to recognize the extent to which this is not just an issue for young working women, but increasingly an issue for women of all ages. Indeed, we are slow to realize the extent to which the need for, and provision of, carework is an issue for women and men alike, single and married alike, young, middle-aged, and old alike.

For the most part, the United States continues to define the care of family members as a private, individual responsibility. Many European nations provide considerable supports for working families and can enable parents to reduce reliance on grandparents for child care; the United States provides precious few supports, increasing reliance on grandparents for child care.[5] Nonetheless, very few of the grandmothers I interviewed criticized current policies or asked for additional governmental supports. All of them knew many other women who were juggling work and grandchild care, but they did not see it as a social issue. They were too busy addressing the individual needs of their immediate family members. When looking across families, however, it is clear that these are social issues in need of social responses. Most beneficial to US families would be federally guaranteed paid time off for sickness, vacation, family leave, and flexible scheduling. Additionally, federally guaranteed universal health insurance, subsidized high-quality, low-cost child care, and universal access to preschool would help working families, and working grandmas, enormously.

The aim is not to reduce the grandmas' time with the grandkids. That is a source of joy for both generations. But Grandma could be visiting more than babysitting, and that might have fewer negative consequences for her financial, emotional, social, and physical well-being. The aim is to temper the adverse effects on working grandmothers who provide care for their grandchildren.

APPENDIX

Grandmas at Work Survey

To assess how working grandmothers balance work and care for grand-children, including the types and intensities of care provided, and the impact of that care on financial, emotional, social, and physical well-being, I conducted in-depth interviews with 48 working grandmothers who care for their grandchildren. The women's aliases and sociodemo-graphic information are listed in table A.1.

Sample Recruitment. To be eligible for the sample, grandmothers had to be working for pay and caring for their grandchildren but both mea-sures were allowed to vary. Because there was no way to draw a ran-dom sample, this is a nonrandom convenience sample. I used snowball sampling beginning in several locations. I asked people I knew to rec-ommend a grandmother who met my criteria. Then I used a snowball method of asking each respondent to name at least two other respon-dents that did not know each other. My response rate was 100 percent; everyone I actually managed to ask to do an interview agreed to do one. Some phones and email messages were never answered, so those grand-mothers were never asked to participate.

Sample Characteristics. I emphasized variation in race, age, marital status, class, and geographic location. Ages ranged from 42 to 73, and the mean age was 57.4. The number of children ranged from 1 to 7, and the mean number of children was 2.9. The number of grandchildren ranged from 1 to 14 and the mean was 3.8. The grandmother's race, mar-ital status, education, and region of the country, work hours, and par-ent care hours are displayed in table A.2. The sample is predominantly white and married, moderately educated, living in the northeast, and working full-time.

Interviewing. Most of the interviews were done face-to-face in the grandmothers' homes or workplaces or in a coffee shop of their choosing. Some were done by phone when I could not arrange to fly to them or if they preferred a phone interview. An interview lasted one hour and I transcribed each of them verbatim. The questions were all open-ended except a few multiple-choice questions at the end. I asked about work, marital, and childrearing histories. I also asked how the women balanced work and children when their own children were young and how they were balancing their current work and grandchild duties. I also asked about the impacts of being middle-aged and working and caring for grandchildren on their physical, emotional, financial, and social health. I assured confidentiality in several ways. Grandmothers signed a standard consent form during the interviews and in it I told them that I would protect their identities. In my analysis, I have given each grandmother an alias and have been purposefully vague about where she lives and works. I have changed the names of all other family members to their roles in the family. Therefore, "George" became "my husband," "Kelly" became "my daughter," and "Ari" became "my grandson." Otherwise, the grandmothers' words appear here verbatim.

Data Analysis. After each interview I cleaned the transcripts and coded them by topics that emerged during the years of interviewing. I then created a spreadsheet to quantify some variables as well. During the writing I honed the key themes and points raised by the women, and I organized the chapters of the book around them.

Health and Retirement Survey 2010

Because the qualitative data is nonrandom and therefore nonrepresentative, I augmented those analyses with secondary analyses of a nationally representative data set on adults ages 51 and older. The HRS data is collected every two years and younger people are aged in periodically so that certain waves are nationally representative. The 2010 survey is the most recent.[1] For assistance with the analyses I am grateful to Yan Liu. For our analyses, we limited the sample to those adults ages 51–70 who did not live in a nursing home or other institution and who were not custodial grandparents.

Table A.1. Alias, age, race, marital status, and numbers of children and grandchildren for each of 48 women interviewed in the Grandmas at Work Survey

Alias	Age	Race	Marital status	Children	Grandchildren
Deanne	57	white	married	2	6
Patty	63	white	married	2	4
Betty	59	black	not married	4	14
Marta	54	white	married	3	2
Calista	54	black	not married	3	4
Candi	43	black	not married	3	3
Molly	50	black	not married	3	5
Annie	48	black	not married	5	5
Connie	50	white	married	4	3
Toni	48	white	married	4	4
Pauline	61	white	married	4	8
Dana	48	white	not married	3	4
Lee	60	white	married	2	2
Lynn	59	white	married	4	3
Carol	48	black	married	2	1
Meryl	54	white	married	3	1
Vanna	53	white	married	3	2
Madeline	53	white	married	3	1
Cherry	67	white	married	2	4
Belle	51	white	not married	2	2
Estelle	63	white	not married	3	6
Ally	56	white	married	5	9
Cally	65	white	not married	6	1
Sarah	67	white	married	2	4
Tara	42	Nat Amer	married	7	8
Amelia	51	white	married	4	3
Corey	57	white	not married	3	4
Lucinda	52	white	married	2	1
Maryann	58	white	married	2	3
Blake	68	white	married	1	2
Jamica	49	black	not married	4	3
Bennie	53	white	married	3	3

Table A.1. (Continued)

Alias	Age	Race	Marital status	Children	Grandchildren
Janelle	67	white	not married	2	2
Susan	62	white	married	2	4
Renee	66	white	married	4	4
Gillian	61	black	married	2	2
Miriam	67	white	married	3	6
Natalie	50	white	married	3	2
Christine	73	white	not married	1	2
Janet	61	white	married	2	2
Sharon	61	black	married	3	5
Karen	61	white	married	1	3
Maggie	67	white	not married	3	8
Diane	55	white	married	2	1
Leah	69	white	not married	2	2
Reagan	60	white	married	1	3
Marsha	64	white	married	1	2
Paula	48	black	not married	4	7

Previous Research. Most previous works based on the HRS have focused on the impact of grandchild care on mental and physical well-being almost exclusively for the fewer than 10 percent of grandparents who are custodial and coresidential, rather than for much more common nonresidential grandparents. Moreover, because of the emphasis in the literature on custodial and coresidential grandparents, many studies did not include the number of hours of grandchild care in the analysis.[2] Additionally, most studies explore the impact on only one health effect. Despite dozens of studies, none has adequately assessed the frequency and intensity of providing grandchild care while employed, nor how the practice, or impact on physical and mental health, varies by sociodemographic variables, including gender, race, class, marital status, and coresidence with grandchildren.

Limitations. The data set is imperfect in a few important ways that contribute serious limitations to our analyses. First, it begins with adults at age 51 but in fact one-half of all US adults are grandparents by age 50.[3] Certainly in the qualitative sample many of the grandmothers

Table A.2. Percentage of working grandmothers in each category, Grandmas at Work Survey, 2009–2012.

Race	
White	77
Black	21
Native American	2
Marital Status	
Married	67
Not married	33
Education	
Completed high school	19
Some college	38
BA	29
MA	8
PhD	6
Region	
Northeast	79
Midwest	11
West coast	8
Southeast	2
Employment hours/week	
40+	81
20–39	15
1–19	4

Source: Grandmas at Work Survey, Madonna Harrington Meyer, Syracuse University.

were not yet 51. Thus, we are failing to capture those who are most likely to be employed and the youngest grandparents who, one might argue, might be providing the most intensive support. Second, the HRS asks respondents to estimate the number of hours they have cared for their grandchildren in the preceding two years. As table A.3 shows, we have used those responses by dividing them into groups by those who provide no care, those who provide fewer than 100 hours, and those who provide more than 100 hours. In the first few qualitative interviews I asked the respondents to estimate the number of hours of grandchild care and they simply were not able to do it. Every week was different, every year was different, and the numbers tended to be enormous. It is difficult to decide, as well: Should they count the hours the grandchildren are asleep? And should we count the hours their parents are there but not actually caring for them? It is a difficult number to determine. In the HRS, many (13 percent) said they could not calculate the figure. We handled these responses two ways: by assigning them the median of 200 hours in two years, and by assigning them the value of 100 hours. The results were the same, regardless of which way we handled those who did not know the hours of grandchild care.

HRS 2010 Data Set

For these analyses we used the HRS 2010 wave core file and the RAND income and wealth imputation file, as well as the 2010 RAND fat file for weighting. We began with 15,372 respondents. Once we removed those in a nursing home or institution, and those below 51 or above 70, and those who were custodial grandparents, 7,327 remained.

Then, because the book focuses on grandmothers, we reran all analyses for only the women, N = 1,158.

Table A.3. HRS 2010 subset: Percentage for each number of hours cared for grandchildren in the preceding two years; sample narrowed to men and women, ages 51–70, noninstitutional and noncustodial.

	Unweighted		Weighted	
	Frequency	Percentage	Frequency	Percentage
No grandchildren	1,773	24	1,808	27
Didn't care for grandchildren	3,286	45	2,638	41
Don't know	988	13	825	13
Fewer than 100 hours	326	4	304	5
100 hours or more	954	13	911	14
Total	7,327	100	6,486	100

Note: N = 7,327.

Table A.4. Percentage of working grandmothers in each category, weighted, noninstitutional and noncustodial.

	Number of hours respondent spent caring for grandchildren in the preceding two years				Total
	No (0)	Yes	1–99 or Don't know*	100+	
Age					
Total	54	46	20	26	100
	100	100	100	100	100
55–59	50	50	21	29	100
	33	38	37	39	36
60–62	54	46	21	25	100
	29	29	30	28	29
63–64	52	49	19	30	100
	13	14	12	15	13
65–68	61	39	18	21	100
	19	14	15	14	17
69–70	59	41	21	20	100
	6	5	6	4	6
Association (ordinal)		Chi2 = 12			ASE = 0.165
Race/ethnicity					
Total	54	46	20	26	100
	100	100	100	100	100
White	53	47	20	27	100
	78	80	79	81	79
Black	54	46	22	24	100
	12	12	13	11	12
Hispanic	60	40	18	22	100
	8	6	6	6	7
Other	57	43	18	25	100
	2	2	2	2	2
Association (nominal)		Chi2 = 3			ASE = 0.848
Education					
Total	54	46	20	26	100
	100	100	100	100	100
Less than high school	64	36	20	16	100
	12	8	11	6	10

Table A.4. *(Continued)*

	Number of hours respondent spent caring for grandchildren in the preceding two years				Total
	No (0)	Yes	1–99 or Don't know*	100+	
Education					
High school	51	49	25	24	100
	33	36	42	32	34
Some college	51	49	20	29	100
	29	33	31	35	31
B.A.	58	42	14	28	100
	14	12	9	14	13
Postgraduate	55	45	15	30	100
	12	11	8	13	11
Association (ordinal)		Chi2 = 25			ASE = 0.002**
Total income in the past year					
Total	54	46	20	26	100
	100	100	100	100	100
0	56	44	17	27	100
	18	16	14	17	17
1–30,000	55	45	20	25	100
	46	44	45	44	45
30,001–60,000	51	49	22	27	100
	24	26	27	26	25
60,001+	52	48	22	26	100
	13	13	14	13	13
Association (ordinal)		Chi2 = 4			ASE = 0.739
Health insurance through current employer or own business					
Total	54	46	20	26	100
	100	100	100	100	100
Yes	52	48	21	27	100
	44	46	46	46	45
No	55	45	20	25	100
	56	54	54	54	55
Association (nominal)		Chi2 = 1			ASE = 0.603

Marital status					
Total	54	46	20	26	100
	100	100	100	100	100
Currently married	53	47	23	24	100
	63	65	73	59	64
Widowed	55	45	20	25	100
	12	11	11	11	11
Currently not	55	45	13	32	100
married	25	23	15	30	24
Association (nominal)		Chi2 = 19			ASE = 0.001**

Number of grandchildren					
Total	54	46	20	26	100
	100	100	100	100	100
1-2	54	47	16	31	100
	28	28	21	33	28
3-5	51	49	24	25	100
	36	40	45	36	38
6-10	56	43	19	24	100
	26	23	24	23	25
11+	55	46	22	24	100
	9	9	10	8	9
Association (ordinal)		Chi2 = 13			ASE = 0.041*

Self-rated health status (n = 8,461)					
Total	54	46	20	26	100
	100	100	100	100	100
Excellent	54	46	14	32	100
	16	15	11	19	15
Very good	54	46	21	25	100
	41	41	42	40	41
Good	54	46	21	25	100
	30	30	32	29	30
Fair	51	49	25	24	100
	11	12	14	11	12

Table A.4. (Continued)

	Number of hours respondent spent caring for grandchildren in the preceding two years				Total
	No (0)	Yes	1–99 or Don't know*	100+	
Self-rated health status (n = 8,461)					
Poor	60	40	12	28	100
	2	2	1	2	2
Association (ordinal)	Chi2 = 11				ASE = 0.220
Living within 10 miles of a child					
Total	54	46	20	26	100
	100	100	100	100	100
Yes	46	54	26	28	100
	47	62	68	58	54
No	62	38	14	24	100
	53	38	32	42	46
Association (nominal)	Chi2 = 41				ASE = 0.000***
Hours working per week					
Total	54	46	20	26	100
	100	100	100	100	100
1–19	48	52	22	30	100
	14	18	17	18	15
20–34	57	43	19	24	100
	25	22	22	22	24
35+	54	47	21	26	100
	61	61	61	61	61
Association (ordinal)	Chi2 = 4				ASE = 0.363
Mental health problem					
Total	54	46	20	26	100
	100	100	100	100	100
Yes	57	43	19	24	100
	19	16	16	16	17
No	53	48	21	27	100
	81	84	84	84	83
Association (nominal)	Chi2 = 2				ASE = 0.403

Care for parents					
Total	54	46	20	26	100
	100	100	100	100	100
Yes	47	53	22	31	100
	5	7	7	7	6
No	54	46	20	26	100
	95	93	93	93	94
Association (nominal)	Chi2 = 2				ASE = 0.446

Hours cared for parents					
Total	54	46	20	26	100
	100	100	100	100	100
0	54	46	20	26	100
	95	93	93	93	94
1–99 or DN	61	39	28	11	100
	3	2	3	1	2
100+	38	62	19	43	100
	3	5	3	6	4
Association (ordinal)	Chi2 = 12				ASE = 0.015*

Hours spouse cared for parents					
Total	54	46	20	26	100
	100	100	100	100	100
0	54	46	20	26	100
	90	88	87	89	89
1–99 or Don't know	51	49	24	25	100
	7	7	8	7	7
100+	49	50	25	25	100
	4	4	5	4	4
Association (ordinal)	Chi2 = 2				ASE = 0.719

Multigenerational					
Total	54	46	20	26	100
	100	100	100	100	100
Yes	26	74	26	48	100
	7	23	18	27	15
No	58	41	19	22	100
	93	77	82	73	86

Table A.4. (Continued)

	Number of hours respondent spent caring for grandchildren in the preceding two years				Total
	No (0)	Yes	1–99 or Don't know*	100+	
Multigenerational					
Association (nominal)		Chi2 = 80			ASE = 0.000***
Smoking					
Total	54	46	20	26	100
	100	100	100	100	100
Yes	59	40	18	22	100
	16	13	13	13	14
No	53	47	21	26	100
	84	87	87	87	86
Association (nominal)		Chi2 = 3			ASE = 0.203
Drinking problem					
Total	54	46	20	26	100
	100	100	100	100	100
Yes	56	44	19	25	100
	17	15	16	15	16
No	53	47	21	26	100
	83	85	84	85	84
Association (nominal)		Chi2 = 0.6			ASE = 0.755
Physical exercise					
Total	54	46	20	26	100
	100	100	100	100	100
Yes	54	46	15	31	100
	24	24	18	28	24
No	53	47	22	25	100
	76	76	82	72	76
Association (nominal)		Chi2 = 9			ASE = 0.010*
Obese					
Total	54	46	20	26	100
	100	100	100	100	100

Yes	52	48	2I	27	I00
	40	42	42	42	4I
No	55	45	20	25	I00
	60	58	58	58	59
Association(nominal)	Chi2 = I				ASE = 0.630

Depression

Total	54	46	20	26	I00
	I00	I00	I00	I00	I00
Yes	53	47	2I	26	I00
	50	5I	5I	5I	5I
No	54	46	20	26	I00
	50	49	49	49	49
Association(nominal)	Chi2 = 0.I				ASE = 0.932

Chronic illness

Total	54	46	20	26	I00
	I00	I00	I00	I00	I00
Yes	53	48	2I	27	I00
	58	6I	60	6I	59
No	55	45	20	25	I00
	42	39	40	39	4I
Association(nominal)	Chi2 = 0.6				ASE = 0.724

Functional limitations

Total	54	46	20	26	I00
	I00	I00	I00	I00	I00
Yes	52	48	23	25	I00
	55	59	65	54	57
No	55	45	I7	28	I00
	45	4I	35	46	43
Association(nominal)	Chi2 = 9				ASE = 0.008**

$*p<.05, **p<.01, ***p<.001.$

* "Don't know" indicates that a respondent cared for his or her grandchildren but did not know the number of hours spent on caring during the preceding two years. We combined this category with "caring for grandchildren for 0–99 hours"; therefore, we would not overestimate the number of hours. Note: N = 1,158 if not specified. Source: HRS 2010.

Table A.5. *Number of hours cared for grandchildren in the preceding two years, working grandmothers, noninstitutional and noncustodial, linear regression models.*

	Weighted		Unweighted	
Variables	Imputation Option 1	Imputation Option 2	Imputation Option 1	Imputation Option 2
Black	-61.37	-64.70	-72.67*	-77.51**
	(42.66)	(42.85)	(38.89)	(39.01)
Hispanic	45.96	42.88	38.45	34.56
	(88.73)	(89.11)	(50.24)	(50.39)
Other	-163.1***	-169.6***	-153.7	-154.8
	(50.47)	(47.66)	(110.1)	(110.4)
Education	14.17*	14.25*	14.29**	14.37**
	(7.237)	(7.264)	(6.000)	(6.018)
Married	-22.56	-25.51	-27.10	-30.81
	(46.47)	(46.61)	(34.88)	(34.98)
Widowed	-80.90*	-92.11**	-45.86	-50.83
	(43.73)	(43.85)	(47.24)	(47.38)
# of grandkids	-2.607	-2.407	0.290	0.381
	(6.564)	(6.602)	(4.970)	(4.985)
Work hours	-1.640	-1.667	0.757	0.745
	(1.724)	(1.733)	(1.047)	(1.050)
Proximity	74.32**	67.08*	57.86**	51.24*
	(36.72)	(36.85)	(28.24)	(28.32)
Mental	-32.29	-33.35	-18.52	-19.24
	(45.78)	(46.16)	(38.05)	(38.16)
Excellent	114.8	106.4	79.68	72.51
	(104.7)	(104.8)	(116.6)	(117.0)
Very good	61.76	52.55	80.75	72.54
	(99.37)	(99.46)	(110.8)	(111.1)
Good	41.28	34.28	57.65	52.67
	(81.81)	(81.72)	(106.9)	(107.2)
Fair	78.80	66.19	87.33	77.89
	(89.71)	(90.00)	(106.7)	(107.0)
Smoking	53.56	56.63	54.57	55.24
	(71.60)	(71.81)	(38.54)	(38.66)

Variables				
Multigenerational	152.2***	119.3**	148.1***	117.6***
	(56.35)	(56.81)	(40.47)	(40.59)
Drinking	-103.8***	-108.7***	-35.36	-37.46
	(38.63)	(38.69)	(42.04)	(42.17)
Exercise	33.81	38.16	36.22	38.92
	(47.84)	(48.02)	(33.31)	(33.41)
BMI	-1.331	-1.520	0.610	0.533
	(3.198)	(3.217)	(2.551)	(2.558)
Depression	-8.885	-8.147	-10.63	-10.29
	(10.79)	(10.84)	(8.541)	(8.566)
Chronic	18.68	18.75	15.62	15.50
	(19.94)	(20.09)	(15.98)	(16.03)
ADL limitations	4.386	4.407	6.867	6.988
	(11.85)	(11.88)	(7.898)	(7.922)
Constant	6.967	11.99	-173.2	-171.4
	(178.2)	(179.3)	(163.5)	(164.0)
Observations	1,067	1,067	1,305	1,305
R-squared	0.030	0.028	0.027	0.023

Robust standard errors in parenthesis. *** p<0.01, ** p<0.05, * p<0.1
Source: HRS 2010. Imputation Option 1: Missing values in dependent variable replaced by the median (200). Imputation Option 2: Missing values in dependent variable replaced by 100.

Table A.6. Number of working hours per week among working grandmothers, noninstitutional and noncustodial, linear regression models.

	Weighted		Unweighted	
Variables	Imputation Option 1	Imputation Option 2	Imputation Option 1	Imputation Option 2
Black	2.709**	2.705**	0.351	0.353
	(1.122)	(1.123)	(1.038)	(1.039)
Hispanic	-2.137	-2.139	-1.665	-1.663
	(1.717)	(1.716)	(1.339)	(1.339)
Other	4.896	4.888	3.051	3.049
	(3.957)	(3.953)	(2.937)	(2.937)
Education	0.211	0.211	0.202	0.202
	(0.204)	(0.205)	(0.160)	(0.160)

Table A.6. (Continued)

Variables	Weighted		Unweighted	
	Imputation Option 1	Imputation Option 2	Imputation Option 1	Imputation Option 2
Married	-2.134**	-2.137**	-1.302	-1.300
	(1.057)	(1.057)	(0.930)	(0.930)
Widowed	-1.757	-1.769	-2.059	-2.056
	(1.483)	(1.484)	(1.259)	(1.259)
# of grandkids	-0.239	-0.239	-0.198	-0.198
	(0.177)	(0.177)	(0.132)	(0.132)
Proximity	-0.461	-0.468	-0.161	-0.157
	(0.908)	(0.909)	(0.754)	(0.754)
Mental	-1.514	-1.515	-1.241	-1.241
	(1.280)	(1.281)	(1.014)	(1.014)
Excellent	4.389	4.381	2.769	2.774
	(4.373)	(4.376)	(3.110)	(3.110)
Very good	0.832	0.823	0.495	0.501
	(4.160)	(4.164)	(2.955)	(2.955)
Good	1.843	1.836	1.271	1.274
	(4.088)	(4.092)	(2.850)	(2.850)
Fair	1.978	1.966	1.249	1.255
	(3.996)	(3.999)	(2.846)	(2.846)
Smoking	1.099	1.102	1.648	1.649
	(1.234)	(1.234)	(1.027)	(1.027)
Multigenerational	-0.0876	-0.120	1.077	1.095
	(1.357)	(1.355)	(1.084)	(1.082)
Drinking	-2.070	-2.076	-2.129*	-2.129*
	(1.544)	(1.544)	(1.120)	(1.120)
Exercise	-3.668***	-3.663***	-2.924***	-2.925***
	(1.218)	(1.219)	(0.885)	(0.885)
BMI	-0.0442	-0.0444	0.0585	0.0585
	(0.0937)	(0.0937)	(0.0680)	(0.0680)
Depression	-0.151	-0.150	-0.173	-0.173
	(0.278)	(0.278)	(0.228)	(0.228)
Chronic	-0.541	-0.540	-0.328	-0.328
	(0.533)	(0.533)	(0.426)	(0.426)

ADL limitations	-0.215	-0.215	-0.322	-0.322
	(0.276)	(0.276)	(0.210)	(0.210)
Care hour 1	-0.00100		0.000538	
	(0.00102)		(0.000745)	
Care hour 2		-0.00101		0.000527
		(0.00102)		(0.000742)
Constant-	35.23***	35.24***	31.33***	31.33***
	(5.452)	(5.454)	(4.274)	(4.274)
Observations	1,067	1,067	1,305	1,305
R-squared	0.054	0.054	0.034	0.034

Robust standard errors in parentheses. *** p<0.01, ** p<0.05, * p<0.1.
Source: HRS 2010. Imputation Option 1: Missing values in dependent variable replaced by the median (200). Imputation Option 2: Missing values in dependent variable replaced by 100.
1 All respondents living in a nursing home are removed from the table, unweighted N = 137.
2 All custodial grandparents are removed from the table, unweighted N = 289.

Table A.7. Mental health (dummy variable) of working grandmothers, noninstitutional and noncustodial, logit regression models.

	Weighted		Unweighted	
Variables	Imputation Option 1	Imputation Option 2	Imputation Option 1	Imputation Option 2
Black	-1.482***	-1.482***	-1.402***	-1.402***
	(0.370)	(0.370)	(0.272)	(0.272)
Hispanic	-0.454	-0.454	-0.197	-0.197
	(0.354)	(0.354)	(0.271)	(0.271)
Other	-0.0744	-0.0751	-0.465	-0.465
	(0.899)	(0.900)	(0.654)	(0.654)
Education	0.0416	0.0416	0.0421	0.0421
	(0.0468)	(0.0468)	(0.0328)	(0.0328)
Married	-0.402	-0.403	-0.559***	-0.559***
	(0.249)	(0.249)	(0.185)	(0.185)
Widowed	-0.253	-0.254	-0.411	-0.411
	(0.327)	(0.327)	(0.254)	(0.254)
# of grandkids	-0.00473	-0.00467	0.0471*	0.0472*
	(0.0372)	(0.0372)	(0.0278)	(0.0278)

Table A.7. (Continued)

Variables	Weighted		Unweighted	
	Imputation Option 1	Imputation Option 2	Imputation Option 1	Imputation Option 2
Proximity	0.0718	0.0711	-0.0418	-0.0422
	(0.209)	(0.209)	(0.161)	(0.161)
Work hours	-0.0104	-0.0104	-0.00805	-0.00805
	(0.00781)	(0.00782)	(0.00583)	(0.00583)
Smoking	0.616**	0.617**	0.469**	0.469**
	(0.270)	(0.270)	(0.196)	(0.196)
Multigenerational	0.317	0.311	0.115	0.112
	(0.284)	(0.285)	(0.219)	(0.218)
Drinking	0.136	0.136	0.162	0.162
	(0.298)	(0.298)	(0.230)	(0.230)
Exercise	-0.433*	-0.432*	-0.269	-0.269
	(0.258)	(0.258)	(0.201)	(0.201)
BMI	0.00339	0.00336	-0.00199	-0.00200
	(0.0172)	(0.0172)	(0.0140)	(0.0140)
Depression	0.260***	0.260***	0.264***	0.264***
	(0.0467)	(0.0467)	(0.0394)	(0.0394)
Chronic	0.152	0.152	0.184**	0.184**
	(0.107)	(0.107)	(0.0816)	(0.0816)
ADL limitations	0.112**	0.112**	0.127***	0.127***
	(0.0514)	(0.0514)	(0.0371)	(0.0372)
Care hour 1	-0.000166		-9.42e-05	
	(0.000201)		(0.000162)	
Care hour 2		-0.000167		-9.64e-05
		(0.000203)		(0.000162)
Constant	-2.256**	-2.258**	-2.233***	-2.234***
	(0.919)	(0.919)	(0.693)	(0.693)
Observations	1,067	1,067	1,305	1,305

Robust standard errors in parentheses. *** p<0.01, ** p<0.05, * p<0.1.
Source: HRS 2010. Imputation Option 1: Missing values in dependent variable replaced by the median (200). Imputation Option 2: Missing values in dependent variable replaced by 100.

Table A.8. Self-reported health (range 1–5) of working grandmothers, noninstitutional and noncustodial, linear regression models.

	Weighted		Unweighted	
Variables	Imputation Option 1	Imputation Option 2	Imputation Option 1	Imputation Option 2
Black	-0.0993	-0.0992	-0.161***	-0.161***
	(0.0730)	(0.0730)	(0.0580)	(0.0580)
Hispanic	-0.324***	-0.324***	-0.344***	-0.344***
	(0.0995)	(0.0996)	(0.0755)	(0.0755)
Other	-0.250	-0.250	-0.197	-0.198
	(0.188)	(0.188)	(0.166)	(0.166)
Education	0.0444***	0.0444***	0.0480***	0.0480***
	(0.0118)	(0.0118)	(0.00892)	(0.00892)
Married	0.00593	0.00605	-0.0178	-0.0177
	(0.0693)	(0.0693)	(0.0526)	(0.0526)
Widowed	0.00100	0.00144	0.0847	0.0847
	(0.0911)	(0.0911)	(0.0714)	(0.0714)
# of grandkids	-3.11e-05	-4.00e-05	-0.00589	-0.00589
	(0.00964)	(0.00964)	(0.00751)	(0.00751)
Proximity	0.0222	0.0225	0.0199	0.0201
	(0.0535)	(0.0534)	(0.0427)	(0.0427)
Work hours	0.00226	0.00226	0.00128	0.00128
	(0.00196)	(0.00196)	(0.00158)	(0.00158)
Smoking	-0.256***	-0.256***	-0.203***	-0.203***
	(0.0917)	(0.0917)	(0.0580)	(0.0580)
Multigenerational	-0.0588	-0.0575	0.0784	0.0790
	(0.0833)	(0.0832)	(0.0615)	(0.0614)
Drinking	0.0112	0.0114	-0.0313	-0.0314
	(0.0724)	(0.0724)	(0.0637)	(0.0637)
Exercise	0.153***	0.153***	0.112**	0.112**
	(0.0592)	(0.0592)	(0.0502)	(0.0502)
BMI	-0.0139***	-0.0139***	-0.0142***	-0.0142***
	(0.00478)	(0.00478)	(0.00383)	(0.00383)
Depression	-0.0586***	-0.0586***	-0.0723***	-0.0724***
	(0.0164)	(0.0164)	(0.0125)	(0.0125)

Table A.8. (Continued)

Variables	Weighted		Unweighted	
	Imputation Option 1	Imputation Option 2	Imputation Option 1	Imputation Option 2
Chronic	-0.203***	-0.203***	-0.208***	-0.208***
	(0.0302)	(0.0302)	(0.0235)	(0.0235)
ADL limitations	-0.144***	-0.144***	-0.146***	-0.146***
	(0.0146)	(0.0146)	(0.0110)	(0.0110)
Care hour 1	4.03e-05		1.61e-05	
	(4.83e-05)		(4.23e-05)	
Care hour 2		4.02e-05		1.50e-05
		(4.80e-05)		(4.21e-05)
Constant	3.838***	3.838***	3.900***	3.900***
	(0.247)	(0.247)	(0.189)	(0.189)
Observations	1,067	1,067	1,305	1,305
R-squared	0.410	0.410	0.407	0.407

Standard errors in parentheses. *** $p<0.01$, ** $p<0.05$, * $p<0.1$.
Source: HRS 2010. Imputation Option 1: Missing values in dependent variable replaced by the median (200). Imputation Option 2: Missing values in dependent variable replaced by 100.

Notes to Chapter 1

1. Angier 2002; Cherlin and Furstenberg 1992; Harrington Meyer 2012; Loe 2011; NACCRRA 2008.
2. Wheelock and Jones 2002.
3. Baydar and Brooks-Gunn 1998; NACCRRA 2008.
4. Munnell 2011; Park 2006; Simon-Rusinowitz et al. 1996; Turner 2005; Wheelock and Jones 2002.
5. AARP 2002; Hogan, Eggebeen, and Snaith 1996; US Bureau of Labor Statistics 2010.
6. Munnell 2011; Population Reference Bureau 2011; US Department of Health and Human Services 2008.
7. Harrington Meyer 2012; NACCRRA 2008; Pavalko and Henderson 2006.
8. The HRS is sponsored by the National Institute on Aging (grant number NIA Uo1AGoo9740) and is conducted by the University of Michigan. We used the HRS 2010 case file, the RAND income and wealth imputation file, and the fat file for weighting (RAND 2010). My complete analysis of HRS 2010 appears in the appendix.
9. Hays 1996; Lareau 2003.
10. Coontz 2013; Lerner 2010.
11. US Bureau of the Census 2008a.
12. Lerner 2010; Martin et al. 2012.
13. Cherlin 2010.
14. Lerner 2010; Martin et al. 2012.
15. US Bureau of the Census 2012.
16. Administration on Aging 2011.
17. Coontz 2013; Lerner 2010.
18. Glynn 2012a.
19. Kochhar 2012.
20. Kochhar, Fry, and Taylor 2011.
21. Chesley and Moen 2006; Folbre 2012; Harrington Meyer and Herd 2007.
22. Hughes et al. 2007; Igel and Szydlik 2011.

23. Glynn 2012b; Harrington Meyer and Herd 2007; IWPR 2007; Lerner 2010; Mezey et al. 2002.
24. Glynn 2012b; Lerner 2010.
25. Glynn 2012b; NACCRRA 2008.
26. Glynn 2012b; Williams et al. 2010.
27. Glynn 2012b; Stone 2007.
28. Folbre 2004; Waldfogel 2010.
29. Heymann 2013.
30. Armenia and Gerstel 2006; Baum 2006; Boushey and Glynn 2012; Folbre 2012; Han, Ruhm, and Waldfogel 2009; Heymann 2013; Lerner 2010; Rudd 2004.
31. Heymann 2013; Waldfogel 2010.
32. IWPR 2007; Lerner 2010.
33. US Bureau of the Census 2011.
34. Harrington Meyer and Herd 2007; Kaiser Family Foundation 2013.
35. Federal Interagency Forum on Child and Family Statistics 2006.
36. Presser 2003.
37. Cohn 2013.
38. Giannarelli and Barsimantov 2000.
39. Lerner 2010.
40. Harrington Meyer and Herd 2007; Lerner 2010; Mezey et al. 2002.
41. Vandell and Wolfe 2000.
42. NICHD 2007.
43. Century Foundation 2000; Rich 2013; Scrivner and Wolfe 2003.
44. Bernanke 2012.
45. Folbre 2012; Harrington Meyer 2000; Harrington Meyer and Herd 2007.
46. NACCRRA 2008.
47. Elder 2006; Moen and Spencer 2006; Settersten 2003.
48. Baca Zinn and Dill 2005; England 2005; Harrington Meyer 2000; Lorber 2005.
49. Folbre 2004.
50. England 2005; Folbre 2012; Harrington Meyer 2000, 2012.
51. Bianchi, Robinson, and Milkie, 2006; Chesley and Moen 2006; Folbre 2012; Glenn 2012; Harrington Meyer 2000; Harrington Meyer and Herd 2007; Krantz-Kent, 2009; NACCRRA 2008.
52. Carmichael and Charles 2003; Heymann 2005.
53. Folbre 2004.
54. Folbre 2012; Glenn 2012; Heymann 2005.
55. Cherlin and Furstenberg 1992.
56. NACCRRA 2008.
57. Kaufman 2009.
58. Folbre 2012; Glenn 2012; Lerner 2010.
59. Hays 1996; Lareau 2003.
60. Hamilton 2013; Hays 1996; Lareau 2003.

61. Cherlin and Furstenberg 1992.
62. Blumberg, Bramlett, Kogan, et al. 2013; Centers for Disease Control 2011; Hogan 2012.
63. Cherlin and Furstenberg 1992; England 2005; Folbre 2012; Harrington Meyer 2000.
64. Dannefer 2003; Reid and Hardy 1999; Settersten 2003; Szinovacz and Davey 2006.
65. Brody 2006; Cantor and Little 1985; Folbre 2012; Glenn 2012; Neal and Hammer 2009; Rubin and White-Means 2009; Stoller and Martin 2002.
66. England 2005; Folbre 2012; Glenn 2012; Harrington Meyer 2000; Harrington Meyer and Herd 2007; Loe 2011; Pavalko and Henderson 2006; Pavalko and Woodbury 2000.
67. Aumann et al. 2010; Bittman, Hill, and Thomson 2007; Brody 2006; Cantor and Little 1985; Carmichael and Charles 2003; Folbre 2012; Glenn 2012; Heitmueller and Inglis 2007; Neal and Hammer 2009; Rubin and White-Means 2009; Stoller and Martin 2002; Wakabayashi and Donato 2006; Wang and Marcotte 2007.
68. Evandrou and Glaser, 2003; Evandrou, Glaser, and Henz, 2002; Folbre 2012; Harrington Meyer and Herd 2007; NAC and AARP 2009; Wakabayashi and Donato 2006.
69. Acker, 2006; Baca Zinn and Dill, 2005; Dannefer, 2003; Glenn 2012; Heymann 2005; Lorber 2005; McNamara 2004; Settersten, 2003.
70. NAC and AARP 2009.
71. Ashton 1996; Folbre 2012; Gladstone, Brown, and Fitzgerald 2009; Glenn 2012; Loe 2011; Waldrop and Weber 2005; Wilson 1987.
72. Harrington Meyer 2012; Loe 2011.
73. Cox 2007; Hayslip and Kaminski 2005; Reid and Hardy 1999; Szinovacz and Davey 2006; Wang and Marcotte 2007; Zamarro unpublished.
74. Baker and Silverstein 2008a, 2008b; Dolbin-MacNab 2006; Hughes et al. 2007; Nelson 2000; Presser 1989; Turner 2005.
75. Blustein, Chan, and Guanais 2004; Cohen et al. 2011; Landry-Meyer and Newman 2004; Lee et al. 2003; Ludwig and Winston 2007; McConnell 1999; Musil et al. 2006; Platt Jendrek 1993; Presser 1989; Pruchno 1999; Robinson-Dooley and Kropf 2006; Szinovacz and Davey 2006; Wang and Marcotte, 2007.
76. Baker and Silverstein 2008a, 2008b; Baker, Silverstein, and Putney 2008; Blustein, Chan, and Guanais 2004; Hayslip and Kaminski 2005; Hughes et al. 2007; Kataoka-Yahiro et al. 2004.
77. Baker and Silverstein 2008a, 2008b; Baker, Silverstein, and Putney 2008; Blustein, Chan, and Guanais 2004; Goodman and Silverstein 2002; Hughes et al. 2007; Minkler and Fuller-Thompson 1999; Minkler et al. 1997; Strawbridge et al. 1997.
78. Baker and Silverstein 2008a, 2008b; Baker, Silverstein, and Putney 2008; Baydar and Brooks-Gunn 1998; Federal Interagency Forum on Child and Family

Statistics 2006; Kataoka-Yahiro et al. 2004; Kelley et al. 2000; Moen, Robison, and Dempster-McClain 1995; Nelson 2000; Park 2006; Platt Jendrek 1994; Pruchno 1999; Turner 2005; Waldrop and Weber 2005.
79. Folbre 2012.

Notes to Chapter 2

1. Baker and Silverstein 2008a, 2008b; Dolbin-MacNab 2006; Harrington Meyer 2012; Hughes et al. 2007; Igel and Szydlik 2011; Nelson 2000; Presser 1989; Turner 2005.
2. My complete HRS 2010 analysis is presented in the appendix.
3. Hughes et al. 2007; Igel and Szydlik 2011.

Notes to Chapter 3

1. Hays 1996.
2. Lareau 2003.
3. Cline, Fay, and Raabe 1990; Hamilton 2013; Hays 1996; Lareau 2003.
4. Hamilton 2013; Schiffrin et al. 2013.
5. Centers for Disease Control 2011.
6. Centers for Disease Control 2011; Hogan 2012.
7. Hamilton 2013; Lareau 2003.
8. NACCRRA 2008.
9. Folbre 2012; Glenn 2012; Lerner 2010.

Notes to Chapter 4

1. AARP 2002; Hogan, Eggebeen, and Snaith 1996; US Bureau of Labor Statistics 2010.
2. Harrington Meyer 2012; NACCRRA 2008; Pavalko and Henderson 2006.
3. Lerner 2010; Stone 2007; US Bureau of the Census 2011.
4. Harrington Meyer 2012; Hughes et al. 2007; Igel and Szydlik 2011.
5. Stone 2007; Weber and Curlew 2009.
6. Bond and Galinsky 2006; Weber and Curlew 2009.
7. Galinsky, Bond, and Sakai 2008.
8. Dodson 2011; Galinsky, Bond, and Sakai 2008.
9. Ludwig and Winston 2007.
10. Dodson 2011.
11. Pavalko and Henderson 2006.
12. Bernanke 2012.
13. My complete analysis of the HRS appears in the appendix.
14. Many said zero, others estimated the number of hours, and some said they simply did not know. For those who did not know we imputed answers; in the first scenario we gave them the median of 200 hours and in the second scenario we gave them 100 hours. A more complete explanation for this method appears in the appendix.

15. Harrington Meyer 2012; NACCRRA 2008; Pavalko and Henderson 2006.
16. Bernanke 2012.

Notes to Chapter 5

1. Aumann et al. 2010; Bittman, Hill, and Thomson 2007; Brody 2006; Cantor and Little 1985; Carmichael and Charles 2003; Evandrou and Glaser 2003; Evandrou, Glaser, and Henz, 2002; Folbre 2012; Glenn 2012; Harrington Meyer and Herd 2007; Heitmueller and Inglis 2007; NAC and AARP 2009; Neal and Hammer 2009; Rubin and White-Means 2009; Stoller and Martin 2002; Wakabayashi and Donato 2006; Wang and Marcotte 2007.
2. Ashton 1996; Folbre 2012; Gladstone, Brown, and Fitzgerald 2009; Glenn 2012; NAC and AARP 2009; Waldrop and Weber 2005; Wilson 1987.
3. Elder 2006; Moen and Spencer 2006; Settersten 2003.
4. Baca Zinn and Dill 2005; England 2005; Harrington Meyer 2000; Lorber 2005.
5. Bernanke 2012.
6. Folbre 2012, Harrington Meyer and Herd 2007.
7. The US Congress Joint Economic Committee 2012.
8. Brown-Lyons et al. 2001: 15.
9. Ashton 1996; Folbre 2012; Gladstone, Brown, and Fitzgerald 2009; Glenn 2012; Waldrop and Weber 2005; Wilson 1987.

Notes to Chapter 6

1. Brody 2006; Miller 1981; Rubin and White-Means 2009.
2. Grundy and Henretta 2006.
3. Pierret 2006.
4. DeRigne and Ferrante 2012.
5. Brody 2006; Cantor and Little 1985, DeRigne and Ferrante 2012; Folbre 2012; Glenn 2012; Neal and Hammer 2009; Rubin and White-Means 2009; Stoller and Martin 2002.
6. The complete results are displayed in the appendix.

Notes to Chapter 7

1. Hays 1996; Lareau 2003.
2. NACCRRA 2008.

Notes to Chapter 8

1. Baker and Silverstein 2008a, 2008b; Blustein, Chan, and Guanais 2004; Cohen et al. 2011; Dolbin-MacNab 2006; Hughes et al. 2007; Landry-Meyer and Newman 2004; Lee et al. 2003; Ludwig and Winston 2007; McConnell 1999; Musil et al. 2006; Nelson 2000; Platt Jendrek 1993; Presser 1989; Pruchno 1999; Robinson-Dooley and Kropf 2006; Szinovacz and Davey 2006; Turner 2005; Wang and Marcotte, 2007.
2. Cox 2007; Hayslip and Kaminski 2005; Reid and Hardy 1999; Szinovacz and Davey 2006; Wang and Marcotte 2007; Zamarro unpublished.

3. Baker and Silverstein 2008a, 2008b; Dolbin-MacNab 2006; Hughes et al. 2007; Nelson 2000; Presser 1989; Turner 2005.
4. Folbre 2012.
5. A few months after the interview I bumped into Tara and she told me she had indeed lost her job because she had missed too much work caring for her grandchildren.
6. Associated Press 2002.

Notes to the Conclusion
1. Pavalko and Henderson 2006.
2. NACCRRA 2008.
3. Folbre 2012; Harrington Meyer 2000; Harrington Meyer and Herd 2007.
4. Coontz 2013.
5. Hughes et al. 2007; Igel and Szydlik 2011.

Notes to the Appendix
1. University of Michigan 2009.
2. Cf. Baker and Silverstein 2008a, 2008b; Blustein, Chan, and Guanais 2004.
3. Hogan, Eggebeen, and Snaith 1996.

REFERENCES

AARP. 2002. Grandparenting survey. http://assets.aarp.org/rgcenter/general/gp_2002. pdf.

Acker, Joan. 2006. *Class questions: Feminist answers*, Lanham, MD: Rowman and Littlefield Publishers.

Administration on Aging. 2011. A profile of older Americans: 2011. Washington, DC: Administration on Aging. http://www.aoa.gov/AoARoot/Aging_Statistics/Profile/2011/10.aspx.

Angier, Natalie. 2002, November 5. The importance of Grandma. *New York Times.*

Armenia, Amy, and Gerstel, Naomi. 2006. Family leaves, the FMLA and gender neutrality: The intersection of race and gender. *Social Science Research, 35*, 871–891.

Ashton, Vikki 1996. A study of mutual support between black and white grandmothers and their adult grandchildren. *Journal of Gerontological Social Work, 26*(1–2), 87–100.

Associated Press. 2002, June 4. Feds study grandparents as caregivers. *New York Times.*

Aumann, K., E. Galinsky, K. Sakai, M. Brown, and J. T. Bond. 2010. The elder care study: Everyday realities and wishes for change. New York: Families and Work Institute. http://familiesandwork.org/site/research/reports/elder_care.pdf .

Baca Zinn, Maxine, and Bonnie Thornton Dill. 2005. What is multiracial feminism? In Judith Lorber (Ed.), *Gender inequality: Feminist theories and politics* (3rd ed., pp. 202–207). Los Angeles, CA: Roxbury Publishing.

Baker, Lindsey A., and Merril Silverstein. 2008a. Depressive symptoms among grandparents raising grandchildren: The impact of participation in multiple roles. *Journal of Intergenerational Relationships, 6*(3), 285–304.

Baker, Lindsey A., and Merril Silverstein. 2008b. Preventive health behaviors among grandmothers raising grandchildren. *Journals of Gerontology Series B: Psychological Sciences and Social Sciences, 63*(5), S304–S311.

Baker, Lindsey A., Merril Silverstein, and Norella M. Putney. 2008. Grandparents raising grandchildren in the United States: Changing family forms, stagnant social policies. *Journal of Sociology and Social Policy, 28*(7), 53–69.

Baum, Charles L. 2006. The effects of government-mandated family leave on employer family leave policies. *Contemporary Economic Policy, 24*(3), 432–445.

Baydar, Nazli, and Jeanne Brooks-Gunn. 1998. Profiles of grandparents who help care for their grandchildren in the United States. *Family Relations, 47*(4), 385–393.

Bernanke, Ben. 2012. Recent developments in the labor market. Washington, DC: Board of Governors of the Federal Reserve System. http://www.c.federalreserve. gov/newsevents/speech/bernanke20120326a.htm.

Bianchi, Suzanne M., John P. Robinson, and Melissa A. Milkie. 2006. *Changing rhythms of American family life.* New York: Russell Sage Foundation.

Bittman, M., T. Hill, and C. Thomson. 2007. The impact of caring on informal carers' employment, income and earnings: A longitudinal approach. *Australian Journal of Social Issues, 42*(2), 255–272.

Blumberg, S. J., M. D. Bramlett, M. D. Kogan, et al. 2013. Changes in prevalence of parent-reported autism spectrum disorder in school-aged U.S. children: 2007 to 2011–2012. National Health Statistics Reports No. 65. Hyattsville, MD: National Center for Health Statistics. http://www.cdc.gov/nchs/data/nhsr/nhsr065.pdf.

Blustein, J., S. Chan, and F. C. Guanais. 2004. Elevated depressive symptoms among caregiving grandparents. *Health Services Research, 39*(6), 1671–1689.

Bond, James T., and Ellen Galinsky. 2006. What workplace flexibility is available to entry-level, hourly employees? *Families and Work Institute* (2006): 46. http://familiesandwork.org/site/research/reports/brief3.pdf.

Boushey, Heather, and Sarah Jane Glynn. 2012. The many benefits of paid family and medical leave. Washington, DC: Center for American Progress. http://www.americanprogress.org/issues/labor/report/2012/11/02/43651/ the-many-benefits-of-paid-family-and-medical-leave/.

Brody, Elaine. 2006. *Women in the middle* (2nd ed.). New York: Springer.

Brown-Lyons, Melanie, Anne Robertson, and Jean Layzer. 2001. *Kith and kin: Informal child care highlights from recent research.* New York: Columbia University, National Center for Children in Poverty.

Cantor, Marjorie, and Virginia Little. 1985. Aging and social care. In R. Binstock and E. Shanas (Eds.), *Handbook of aging and the social sciences* (pp. 99–112). New York: Van Nostrand.

Carmichael, F., and S. Charles. 2003. The opportunity costs of informal care: Does gender matter? *Journal of Health Economics, 22*(5), 781–803.

Centers for Disease Control and Prevention. 2011. Developmental disabilities increasing in the US. http://www.cdc.gov/Features/dsDev_Disabilities/.

Century Foundation. 2000, March. Universal preschool. New Ideas for a New Century. Idea Brief No. 5. New York: Century Foundation. http://www.tcf.org/Publications/ Education/UniversalPreschool.pdf.

Cherlin, Andrew J. 2010. *The marriage-go-round: The state of marriage and the family in America today.* New York: Vintage.

Cherlin, Andrew, and Frank Furstenberg, Jr. 1992. *The new American grandparent: A place in the family, a life apart.* Cambridge, MA: Harvard University Press.

Chesley, Noelle, and Phyllis Moen. 2006. When workers care: Dual-earner couples' caregiving strategies, benefit use, and psychological well-being. *American Behavioral Scientist, 49*(9), 1248–1269.

Cline, Foster, Jim Fay, and Tom Raabe. 1990. *Parenting with love and logic: Teaching children responsibility.* Colorado Springs, CO: Piñon Press.

Cohen, Stephen, et al. 2011. Grandparental caregiving, income inequality and respiratory infections in elderly US individuals. *Journal of Epidemiology and Community Health, 65*(10), 246–253.

Cohn, Jonathan. 2013, April 15. The hell of American day care: An investigation in to the barely regulated, unsafe business of looking after our children. *The New Republic.* http://www.newrepublic.com/article/112892/hell-american-day-care.

Coontz, Stephanie. 2013, February 16. Why gender equality stalled. *New York Times.* http://www.nytimes.com/2013/02/17/opinion/sunday/why-gender-equality-stalled. html?emc=eta1.

Cox, Carole B. 2007. Grandparent-headed families: Needs and implications for social work interventions and advocacy. *Families in Society, 88*, 561–566.

Dannefer, Dale. 2003. Cumulative advantage/disadvantage and the life course: Cross-fertilizing age and social science theory. *Journals of Gerontology, Series B: Psychological Sciences and Social Sciences, 58B*(6), S327–S337.

DeRigne, LeaAnne, and Stephen Ferrante. 2012. The sandwich generation: A review of the literature. *Florida Public Health Review, 9*, 95–104.

Dodson, Lisa. 2011. *The moral underground: How ordinary Americans subvert an unfair economy.* New York: New Press.

Dolbin-MacNab, Megan L. 2006. Just like raising your own? Grandparents' perceptions of parenting a second time around. *Family Relations, 55*(5), 564–575.

Elder, Glen. 2006. Life course. In George Ritzer (Ed.), *The Blackwell encyclopedia of sociology* (pp. 109–131). Cambridge, MA: Blackwell.

England, Paula. 2005. Emerging theories of care work. *Annual Review of Sociology, 31,* 381–399.

Evandrou, M., and K. Glaser. 2003. Combining work and family life: The pension penalty of caring. *Ageing and Society, 23*, 583–601.

Evandrou, Maria, Karen Glaser, and Ursula Henz. 2002. Multiple role occupancy in midlife: Balancing work and family life in Britain. *The Gerontologist, 42*(6), 781–789.

Federal Interagency Forum on Child and Family Statistics. 2006. *America's children: Key national indicators of well-being, 2006.* Washington, DC: US Government Printing Office. http://childstats.gov/americaschildren/tables.asp.

Folbre, Nancy. 2004. A theory of the misallocation of time. In Nancy Folbre and Michael Bittman (Eds.), *Family time: The social organization of care* (pp. 7–25). New York: Routledge.

Folbre, Nancy (Ed.). 2012. *For love and money: Care provision in the United States.* New York: Russell Sage Foundation.

Galinsky, Ellen, James T. Bond, and Kelly Sakai. 2008. *2008 national study of employers.* New York: Families and Work Institute.

Giannarelli, Linda, and James Barsimantov. 2000. *Child care expenses of America's families.* Washington, DC: Urban Institute. http://www.urban.org/Uploaded-PDF/310028_occa40.pdf.

Gladstone, James, Ralph Brown, and Kerri-Ann Fitzgerald. 2009. Grandparents raising their grandchildren: Tensions, service needs and involvement with child welfare agencies. *International Journal of Aging and Human Development, 69*(1), 55–78.

Glenn, Evelyn Nakano. 2012. *Forced to care: Coercion and caregiving in America.* Cambridge, MA: Harvard University Press.

Glynn, Sarah Jane. 2012a. The new breadwinners, 2012 update. Washington, DC: Center for American Progress. http://www.americanprogress.org/issues/labor/report/2012/04/16/11377/the-new-breadwinners-2010-update/.

Glynn, Sarah Jane. 2012b. Working parents' lack of access to paid leave and workplace flexibility. Washington, DC: Center for American Progress. http://www.american-progress.org/wp-content/uploads/2012/11/GlynnWorkingParents-1.pdf.

Goodman, Catherine, and Merril Silverstein. 2002. Grandparents raising grandchildren: Family structure and well-being in culturally diverse families. *The Gerontologist, 42*(5), 676–689.

Grundy, Emily, and John Henretta. 2006. Between elderly parents and adult children: A new look at the intergenerational care provided by the sandwich generation. *Ageing and Society, 26*(5), 707–722. http://journals.cambridge.org/action/displayFulltext?type=1&fid=458803&jid=ASO&volumeId=26&issueId=05&aid=458802&bodyId=&membershipNumber=&societyETOCSession=.

Hamilton, L. T. 2013. More is more or more is less? Parental financial investments during college. *American Sociological Review, 78*(1), 70–95.

Han, Wen-Jui, Christopher Ruhm, and Jane Waldfogel. 2009. Parental leave policies and parents' employment and leave-taking. *Journal of Policy Analysis and Management, 28*(1), 29–54.

Harrington Meyer, Madonna (Ed.). 2000. *Care work: Gender, labor, and the welfare state.* New York: Routledge.

Harrington Meyer, Madonna. 2012. US grandparents juggling work and grandchildren. In Virpi Timonen and Sara Arber (Eds.), *Contemporary grandparenting: Changing family relationships in a global context* (pp. 71–90). Bristol, UK: Policy Press.

Harrington Meyer, Madonna, and Pamela Herd. 2007. *Market friendly or family friendly? The state and gender inequality in old age.* New York: Russell Sage.

Hays, Sharon. 1996. *The cultural contradictions of motherhood.* New Haven, CT: Yale University Press.

Hayslip, Bert, and Patricia L. Kaminski. 2005. Grandparents raising their grandchildren: A review of the literature and suggestions for practice. *The Gerontologist, 45,* 263–269.

Heitmueller, A., and K. Inglis. 2007. The earnings of informal carers: Wage differentials and opportunity costs. *Journal of Health Economics, 26*(4), 821–841.

Heymann, Jody. 2005. *Inequalities at work and at home: Social class and gender divides.* New York: New Press.

Heymann, Jody. 2013. *Children's chances: How countries can move from surviving to thriving.* Cambridge, MA: Harvard University Press.

Hogan, Dennis P. 2012. *Family consequences of children's disabilities.* New York: Russell Sage.

Hogan, Dennis P., David J. Eggebeen, and Sean Snaith. 1996. The well-being of aging Americans with very old parents. In Tamara Hareven (Ed.), *Aging and generational relations* (pp. 327–349). New York: DeGruyter.

Hughes, Mary Elizabeth, Linda J. Waite, Tracey A. LaPierre, A. Tracey, and Ye Luo. 2007. All in the family: The impact of caring for grandchildren on grandparents' health. *Journals of Gerontology Series B: Psychological Sciences and Social Sciences, 62*(2), S108–S119.

Igel, Corrine, and Marc Szydlik. 2011. Grandchild care and welfare state arrangements in Europe. *Journal of European Social Policy, 21*(3), 210–224. http://esp.sagepub.com/content/21/3/210.full.pdf+html.

Institute for Women's Policy and Research (IWPR). 2007. *Maternity leave in the United States.* Washington, DC: IWPR.

Kaiser Family Foundation. 2013. *Reversing the trend? Understanding the recent increase in health insurance coverage among the nonelderly population.* Washington DC: Kaiser Family Foundation. http://kff.org/uninsured/issue-brief/reversing-the-trend-understanding-the-recent-increase-in-health-insurance-coverage-among-the-nonelderly-population/.

Kataoka-Yahiro, M., C. Ceria, and R. Caulfield. 2004. Grandparent caregiving role in ethnically diverse families. *Journal of Pediatric Nursing, 19,* 315–328.

Kaufman, Joanne. 2009, March 5. When Grandma can't be bothered. *New York Times.*

Kelley, S. J., D. Whitley, T. A. Sipe, and B. Crofts Yorker. 2000. Psychological distress in grandparent kinship care providers: The role of resources, social support, and physical health. *Child Abuse and Neglect, 24*(3), 311–321.

Kochhar, Rakesh 2012. *A recovery no greater than the recession.* Washington, DC: Pew Research Center. http://www.pewsocialtrends.org/2012/09/12/a-recovery-no-better-than-the-recession/

Kochhar, Rakesh, Richard Fry, and Paul Taylor. 2011. *Wealth gaps rise to record highs between whites, blacks, hispanics.* Washington DC: Pew Research Center. http://www.pewsocialtrends.org/2011/07/26/wealth-gaps-rise-to-record-highs-between-whites-blacks-hispanics/

Krantz-Kent, Rachel. 2009. Measuring time spent in unpaid household work: Results from the American Time Use Survey. *Monthly Labor Review,* July, 46–59.

Landry-Meyer, Laura, and Barbara M. Newman. 2004. An exploration of the grandparent caregiver role. *Journal of Family Issues, 25,* 1005–1025.

Lareau, Annette. 2003. *Unequal childhoods: Class, race, and family life*. Berkeley: University of California Press.

Lee, Sunmin, et al. 2003. Caregiving to children and grandchildren and risk of coronary heart disease in women. *American Journal of Public Health*, 93(11), 1939–1944.

Lerner, Sharon. 2010. *The war on moms: On life in a family-unfriendly nation*. Hoboken, NJ: John Wiley and Sons.

Loe, Meika. 2011. *Aging our way: Lessons for living from 85 and beyond*. New York: Oxford University Press

Lorber, J. 2005. *Gender inequality: Feminist theories and politics* (3rd ed.). Los Angeles, CA: Roxbury Publishing.

Ludwig, F. M., and K. Winston. 2007. How caregiving for grandchildren affects grandparents' meaningful occupations. *Journal of Occupational Science, 14*(1), 40–51.

Martin, Joyce A., Brady E. Hamilton, Stephanie J. Ventura, Michelle J. K. Osterman, Elizabeth C. Wilson, and T. J. Mathews. 2012. Births: Final data for 2010. National Vital Statistics Report 61 (1). http://www.cdc.gov/nchs/data/nvsr/nvsr61/nvsr61_01.pdf#table15.

McConnell Heywood, Elizabeth. 1999. Custodial grandparents and their grandchildren. *The Family Journal, 7*, 367–372.

McNamara, J. M. 2004. *Long-term poverty among older women: The effects of work in midlife* (Doctoral dissertation). Bryn Mawr College.

Mezey, Jennifer, M. Greenberg, and R. Schumacher. 2002. *The vast majority of federally-eligible children did not receive child care assistance in FY 2000*. Washington, DC: Center for Law and Social Policy.

Miller, Dorothy. 1981. The sandwich generation: Adult children of the aging. *Health and Social Work, 26*(5), 419–423.

Minkler, Meredith, and Esme Fuller-Thomson. 1999. The health of grandparents raising grandchildren: Results of a national study. *American Journal of Public Health*, 89(9), 1384–1389.

Minkler, Meredith, et al. 1997. Depression in grandparents raising grandchildren: Results of a national longitudinal study. *Archives of Family Medicine*, 6(5), 445–452.

Moen, P., J. Robison, and D. Dempster-McClain. 1995. Caregiving and women's well-being: A life course approach. *Journal of Health and Social Behavior, 36*(3), 259–273.

Moen, P., and D. Spencer. 2006. Converging divergences in age, gender, health, and well-being: Strategic selection in the third age. In R. H. Binstock and L. K. George (Eds.), *Handbook of aging and the social sciences* (6th ed.; pp. 127–144). New York: Academic Press.

Munnell, Alicia. 2011. *What is the average retirement age?* Center for Retirement Research. http://crr.bc.edu/briefs/what-is-the-average-retirement-age/.

Musil, C. M., C. B. Warner, J. A. Zausniewski, A. B. Jeanblac, and K. Kercher. 2006. Grandparents, caregiving, and family functioning. *Journals of Gerontology Series B: Psychological Sciences and Social Sciences, 61*, S89–S98.

National Alliance for Caregiving (NAC) and American Association of Retired Persons (AARP). 2009. *Caregiving in the U.S. 2009*. http://www.caregiving.org.

National Association of Child Care Resources and Referral Agencies (NACCRRA). 2008. *Grandparents: A critical child care safety net. Arlington, VA: NACCRRA.* http://www.naccrra.org/sites/default/files/publications/naccrra_publications/2012/grandparentscriticalchildcaresafetynet.pdf.

National Institute of Child Health and Human Development (NICHD). 2007. *The NICHD study of early child care and youth development: Findings for children up to ages 4½ years.* https://www.nichd.nih.gov/publications/pubs/documents/seccyd_06.pdf.

Neal, Margaret B., and Leslie B. Hammer. 2009. Dual earner couples in the sandwiched generation: Effects of coping strategies over time. *Psychologist-Manager Journal, 12*(4), 205–234.

Nelson, J. L. 2000. Contemplating grandparenthood. *Ageing International, 26*(102), 3–9.

Park, H. H. 2006. The economic well-being of houses headed by a grandmother as caregiver. *Social Service Review, 80*(2), 264–296.

Pavalko, E. K., and K. Henderson. 2006. Combining care work and paid work: Do workplace policies make a difference? *Research on Aging, 28*, 359–374.

Pavalko, E. K., and S. Woodbury. 2000. Social roles as process: Caregiving careers and women's health. *Journal of Health and Social Behavior, 41*, 91–105.

Pierret, Charles. 2006. The sandwich generation: Women caring for parents and children. *Monthly Labor Review*, September, 3–9.

Platt Jendrek, M. P. 1993. Grandparents who parent their grandchildren: Effects on lifestyle. *Journal of Marriage and the Family, 55*(3), 609–621.

Platt Jendrek, M. 1994. Grandparents who parent their grandchildren: Circumstances and decisions. *The Gerontologist, 34*(2), 206–216.

Population Reference Bureau. 2011. The health and well-being of grandparents caring for grandchildren. *Today's Research on Aging, 23*, 1–6.

Presser, Harriet. 1989. Some economic complexities of child care provided by grandparents. *Journal of Marriage and the Family, 51*(3), 581–591.

Presser, Harriett B. 2003. *Working in a 24/7 economy: Challenges for American families.* New York: Russell Sage Foundation.

Pruchno, R. 1999. Raising grandchildren: The experiences of black and white grandmothers. *The Gerontologist, 39*(2), 209–221.

RAND, H. Data, Version J. 2010. Produced by the RAND Center for the Study of Aging, with funding from the National Institute on Aging and the Social Security Administration. Santa Monica, CA.

Reid, J., and Melissa Hardy. 1999. Multiple roles and wellbeing among midlife women: Testing role strain and role enhancement theories. *Journals of Gerontology, 54*(6), S329–S338.

Rich, Mokoto. 2013, February 13. Few states look to extend preschool to all 4 year-olds. *New York Times.* http://www.nytimes.com/2013/02/14/education/early-education-far-short-of-goal-in-obama-speech.html?_r=0.

Robinson-Dooley, Vanessa, and Nancy P. Kropf. 2006. Second generation parenting: Grandparents who receive TANF. *Journal of Intergenerational Relationships, 4*, 49–62.

Rubin, Rose, and Shelly White-Means. 2009. Informal caregiving: Dilemmas of sandwiched caregivers. *Journal of Family Economic Issues*, *29*(3), 252–267.

Rudd, Elizabeth. 2004. *Family leave: A policy concept made in America*. Boston, MA: Sloan Work and Family Research Network. http://workfamily.sas.upenn.edu/wfrn-repo/object/ed5rb04oq4vm53b1.

Schiffrin, Holly H., Miriam Liss, Haley Miles-McLean, Katherine A. Geary, Mindy J. Erchull, and Taryn Tashner. 2013. Helping or hovering? The effects of helicopter parenting on college students' well-being. *Journal of Child and Family Studies*, February: 1–10.

Scrivner, Scott, and Barbara Wolfe. 2003. Universal preschool: Much to gain but who will pay? IRP Discussion Paper No. 1271–03. Madison: Institute for Research on Poverty, University of Wisconsin-Madison. http://www.irp.wisc.edu/publications/dps/pdfs/dp127103.pdf.

Settersten, Richard A. 2003. Introduction. In Richard A. Settersten (Ed.), *Invitation to the life course: Toward new understandings of later life* (pp. 1–14). Amityville, NY: Baywood Publishing.

Simon-Rusinowitz, L., C. A. Krach, L. N. Marks, D. Piktialis, and L. B. Wilson. 1996. Grandparents in the workplace: The effects of economic and labor trends. *Generations*, *20*, 41–44.

Stoller, Elenor Palo, and Lisa Martin. 2002. Caregiving, informal. In *Encyclopedia of aging*. http://www.encyclopedia.com/doc/1G2–3402200060.html.

Stone, P. 2007. *Opting out: Why women really quit careers and head home*. Berkeley: University of California Press.

Strawbridge, William, et al. 1997. New burdens or more of the same? Comparing grandparent, spouse, and adult-child caregivers. *The Gerontologist*, *37*(4), 505–510.

Szinovacz, Maxinne, and Adam Davey. 2006. Effects of retirement and grandchild care on depressive symptoms. *International Journal of Aging and Human Development*, *62*(1), 1–20.

Turner, F. J. 2005. *Social work diagnosis in contemporary practice*. New York: Oxford University Press.

University of Michigan. 2009. Sample evolution: 1992–1998. http://hrsonline.isr.umich.edu/index.php?p=sdesign.

US Bureau of Labor Statistics. 2010. *Women in the labor force: A databook*. Washington, DC: US Department of Labor. http://www.bls.gov/cps/wlf-databook2010.htm.

US Bureau of Labor Statistics. 2011a. Report 985, Table 1, Employment status of the civilian noninstitutional population by age and sex, 2010. In *Women in the labor force: A databook*. http://www.bls.gov/cps/wlf-databook-2011.pdf.

US Bureau of Labor Statistics. 2011b. Report 985, Table 7, Employment status of women by presence and age of youngest child, 1975–2010. In *Women in the labor force: A databook*. http://www.bls.gov/cps/wlf-databook-2011.pdf.

US Bureau of the Census. 2008a. Table MS-1: Marital status of the population 15 years old and over, by sex and race, 1950 to present. http://www.census.gov/population/www/socdemo/hh-fam.html#ht.

US Bureau of the Census. 2011. Maternity leave and employment patterns of first time mothers, 1961–2008. Washington, DC: Department of Commerce. http://www.census.gov/prod/2011pubs/p70–128.pdf.

US Bureau of the Census. 2012. Table 4. Poverty status of families, by type of family, presence of related children, race, and Hispanic origin: 1959 to 2011. In *Current population survey, annual social and economic supplements.* Social, Economic, and Housing Statistics Division: Poverty. http://www.census.gov/hhes/www/poverty/data/historical/families.html.

US Congress Joint Economic Committee. 2012. Retirement security after the great recession: Middle-income and middle-aged Americans feeling the squeeze. Washington, DC: US Congress. http://www.jec.senate.gov/public/index.cfm?a=Files.Serve&File_id=4bc4e022-4bc8-476c-a91a-268852d8ff0e

US Department of Health and Human Services. 2008. *Grandparents raising grandchildren: A call to action.* Administration for Children and Families, Region IV, ww.acf.hhs.gov/opa/doc/grandparents.pdf.

Vandell, Deborah Lowe, and Barbara Wolfe. 2000. *Child care quality: Does it matter and does it need to be improved?* Report to the Assistant Secretary for Planning and Evaluation, US Department of Health and Human Services. http://aspe.hhs.gov/hsp/ccquality00/index.htm.

Wakabayashi, C., and K. M. Donato. 2006. Does caregiving increase poverty among women in later life? Evidence from the Health and Retirement Survey. *Journal of Health and Social Behavior, 47*(3), 258–274.

Waldfogel, Jane. 2010. *Britain's war on poverty.* New York: Russell Sage Foundation.

Waldrop, D. P., and J. A. Weber. 2005. Grandparent to caregiver: The stress and satisfaction of raising grandchildren. In F. J. Turner (Ed.), *Social work diagnosis in contemporary practice* (pp. 184–195). New York: Oxford University Press.

Wang, Y., and D. E. Marcotte. 2007. Golden years? The labor market effects of caring for grandchildren. *Journal of Marriage and Family, 69*(5), 1283–1296.

Weber, Julie, and Mary Curlew. 2009. *The impact of the recession on work and family.* Sloan Work and Family Research Network Policy Brief, Issue 19. Boston, MA: Boston College. https://workfamily.sas.upenn.edu/sites/workfamily.sas.upenn.edu/files/imported/pdfs/policy_makers19.pdf

Wheelock, J., and K. Jones. 2002. Grandparents are the next best thing: Informal childcare for working parents in urban Britain. *Journal of Social Policy, 31*(3), 441–463.

Williams, Claudia, Robert Drago, and Kevin Miller. 2010. *44 million U.S. workers lacked paid sick days in 2010.* IWPR #B293. Washington, DC: Institute for Women's Policy Research. http://www.iwpr.org/pdf/B293PSD.pdf.

Wilson, Gail. 1987. Women's work: The role of grandparents in inter-generational transfers. *Sociological Review, 35*(4), 703–720.

Zamarro, Gema. Unpublished. Family labor participation and child care decisions: The role of grannies. Rand Corporation. http://www.sole-jole.org/12185.pdf.

INDEX

Page numbers in italics refer to figures.

ADHD. *See* Attention-deficit hyperactivity disorder

Adult children: efforts to reduce stress of, 71; enabling minded by, 202; financial support not wanted by, 135, 143; gender factor in grandchild care provided for, 201; gifts from, 174, 176, 181; irresponsibility in, 186, 192–93; meeting objectives of, 86; parenthood age in, 188; partying by, 92–93, 186–87; pressure from, 81–82, 125; sibling rivalry, 8, 201–4; tensions between adult daughters and grandmothers, 82–83; unsuitability as parents, 91, 191. *See also* Enabling

Age: employment percentages by gender and, 3; of grandchildren, 122–23; grandparent percentages and, 98; parenthood, 188; retirement, 2

Al-Anon, 154

Alcohol abuse, 196

Alzheimer's, 70, 113, 160–61

Appreciation, 8, 175–80; gifts as expressions of, 174, 176, 181

Asians, 10

Attention-deficit hyperactivity disorder (ADHD), 63, 202–3

Autism, 22, 63, 76–80, 111

Babysitters, 42, 85, 87–88

Backup parenting, 39

Births, to single mothers, 10, *11*

Black women, 101; economic impact of carework on, 25; marriage rate decline among, 10; single older, *11*

Bruising financial burden, 16

Cancer, 51, 106, 194

Career: advancement, 98; change, 111

Carework: balancing paid work with unpaid, 29–31, 100–101, 232; containing, 172–73; economic impact of, 24–25, 66, 132; grandmother responses to idea of paid, 133–34; increased demand for, 230; paid care compared to, 233; for parents and older relatives, 163–73; physical well-being impact of, 25–27; rewards, 19–20, 32–34, 37–48, 234; theories, 18–24, 233–36

Childhood disabilities rate, 63. *See also* Disabilities

Children: free-range, 180; purposive child nurturing, 21; raised by nannies, 59; unprecedented cultivation of, 62; US percentage raised by grandparents, 28, 205–6. *See also* Adult children; Grandchildren

Club sandwich, 24, 163, 173

Cohabitation, 10

Confidentiality, 28

Containment, of carework, 172–73. *See also* Limits, setting

Counseling, 82

Country comparison, for paid leave, 14–15, *15*

Courthouse employment, 107

Criticism, from partners, 194–95, 198

Cultural expectations, 22, 63

Custody, 27–28; temporary, 69, 136

Daycare: costs, 16–17; disability issue with, 121–22; quality and availability of, 16–17; subsidized universal, 16–17, 237; unsafe, 89–90

Debt, 142–51

Dependent care tax credit, 17

Developmental disabilities, 22, 63

Disabilities: childhood rate, 63; daycare and, 121–22; developmental, 22, 63; grandchildren with, 22, 63, 75–78, 91; work schedule flexibility in situations of, 111. *See also specific disabilities*

Down syndrome, 63, 77–80, 111
Duty, 79–90

Economic impact, 24–25; recession and, 132; as unacknowledged, 66. *See also* Financial support
Education: as grandchild care factor, 37; work schedule flexibility and, 99
Emergencies, work schedule flexibility and, 116, 118
Emotional impact: of enabling, 181–201; mixed nature of, 174–75, 204; parenting styles creating tensions, 179–80; partner criticism and, 194–95, 198; resentment, 190, 191; sibling rivalry and, 8, 201–4; social, physical well-being and, 25–27; stress and, 204
Employment: benefits, 13–14, 236; career advancement, 98; career change, 111; courthouse, 107; job security, 53, 102, 123–24, 126–29; job sharing, 102; men and women by age of youngest child, *12*; need for changing, 99; number of working grandparents, 2; percentage by age and gender, *3*; self-employed grandmothers, 109, 112–14; unemployment, 12, 18; work hour increase, 11; work hour reduction, 177. *See also* Working grandmothers; Working grandparents; Work schedule flexibility
Enabling, 8, 23; adult children bothered by, 202; efforts to limit, 182; emotional impact of, 181–201; financial support as, 135, 184, 193, 199–200, 203–4; interview participant percentage, 206; interview participants raising topic of, 174; scope of sample and, 22
Exercise, 37
Expectations, cultural, 22, 63. *See also* Gendered expectations

Families: family tree, 89; lower-income, 13, 17, 231; multigenerational households, 101; retirement account decline in, 132; tradition factor, 74–75, 79, 80, 96, 134
Family and Medical Leave Act, US, 15
Federal policies. *See* Welfare state, US
Fertility rate, 10
Financial support, 5, 84; adult children not wanting, 135, 143; babysitter factor in, 42; as breaking tradition, 134; burden of, 16;

enabling through, 135, 184, 193, 199–200, 203–4; gifts as, 134, 137, 138, 143; high rate of, 232; income decline and increased outgoing, 151–52; intensive grandmothering and, 131–52; limits on, 141–42, 146; nature of, 134–42; for necessities, 132, 189, 193; nest egg depletion and debt resulting from, 142–51; paid carework question and, 133–34; from parents of grandmothers, 134; rent as, 138; research on, 134; for special needs therapies, 137–38; stress from giving, 8–9. *See also* Economic impact
Free-range children, 180
Fun, focus on, 67

Gender: employment percentages by age and, *3*; grandchild care and, 201
Gendered expectations, 20–24, 83, 234–35; resistance to, 154; work schedule flexibility and, 125
Gifts: from adult children, 174, 176, 181; financial support through, 134, 137, 138, 143
Grandchild care: advance notice for, 115, 117; balancing work hours and, 100–101; education factor, 37; factors impacting provision of, 37; factors in provision data on, 37; gender factor in amount of, 201; hobbies given up for, 54; hours spent providing, 37; increasing need for, 10–13; interview participant overview of, 22; juggling work and, 98–138; paid, 133–34; partner support in, 167; percentages, 2, 35, 205–6; pressure from adult children, 81–82, 125; provider data for US, 34–37, *35*, *36*, 98; proximity factor in, 37, 202; sick days and, 13–14, 31, 88, 119–20, 130; survey, 1–2; US percentages for children raised by grandparents, 28, 205–6; vacation days for, 56, 122, 130; work hours of US grandmothers providing, *35*, *36*; work impact on, 24–27; working grandparents providing, *35*, *36*. *See also* Grandmothering; Health consequences; Intensive grandmothering; Limits, setting
Grandchildren: active, 68; brought to workplace, 107, 121; with disabilities, 22, 63, 75–78, 91; living with grandparents, 28; with special needs, 22, 74, 91, 137–38; tendency to spoil, 72; work schedule flexibility with age of, 122–23
Grandma knows best, as factor in intensive grandmothering, 84–85

Grandmas at Work Survey, 27, 230
Grandmothering: as backup, 39; as being
redefined, 204; images of, 20–21; joys of,
37–48, 60–61; lifecourse embedding of, 61;
mothering compared with, 34, 45, 48, 49,
53–54, 65; parenting styles and, 179–80,
205; policy implications, 236–38; relationship with adult children strengthened
through, 58–59; rewards from, 19–20,
32–34, 37–38, 60–61, 234; second chances
through, 48–61; tendency to spoil grandchildren, 72; theoretical perspectives on,
18–24, 233–36. *See also* Intensive grandmothering; Lifecourse approach
Grandmothers: as backup, 39; care for own
mothers by, 168–69; covering for other,
106–7, 119; custodial, 27–28; federal policy
absence not mentioned by, 31, 229; financial support from parents of, 134; grandmothers emulating own, 80–81; health
concerns of, 158–60; interview and data
overview, 29–31; leisure, 41; mothers of,
81; paid carework question responses of,
133–34; parents of, 134, 163–73; role differentiation between mothers and, 21; rules
for, 53–54, 55; as sandwich generation, 7,
23–24, 163–73, 235–36; self-employed, 109,
112–14; sequential, 84; tensions between
adult daughters and, 82–83; work hours of
US, *35*, 36. *See also* Adult children; Working grandmothers
Grandparents: age and percentages, 98;
grandchild care percentages for men and
women, *35*; grandchildren living with,
28; grandmothers emulating own, 80–81;
percentages of grandchild care provision
by, 28, 205–6; remote and uninvolved,
20. *See also* Financial support; Working
grandparents

Health, 9, 26, 163; carework limits due to,
158–60, 222, 226–27; emotional, social
and physical well-being, 25–27; insurance,
16, 30; mental, 71, 93; problems, 46; risk,
170; role enhancement and, 23; self-rated,
214–15
Health and Retirement Survey (HRS), 2,
28–29, 34, *35*, *36*, 230; health consequences
data from, 214–15; work hour balance data
in, 100–101
Health consequences, 216–28; HRS data on,

214–15; negative, 219–20; positive, 215–18;
positive and negative, 221, 223–24; social
and, 228–29
Helicopter parenting, 205
Hispanic women, 101; economic impact of
carework on, 25; education level, 99; self-
rate health among, 215; single older, *11*
Homework supervision, 72
Hours, grandchild care, 37
Household income, *12*
HRS. *See* Health and Retirement Survey
Husbands, 64. *See also* Partners

Income: families with lower, 13, 17, 231;
household, *12*; median wealth data, 12–13;
outgoing financial support increase with
decreased, 151–52; work schedule flexibility and, 99
Intensive grandmothering, 21–23, 29, 231;
active grandchildren and, 68; challenging
tasks in, 69; as expensive, 131; family tradition factor in, 74–75, 79, 80, 96, 134; financial concerns, 131–52; focusing on fun, 67;
grandchildren with disabilities, 75–78, 91;
grandma knows best as factor in, 84–85;
help from husbands, 64; as lifeline, 90–96;
as overlooked by scholarly literature, 65;
pressure from adult children factor in,
81–82, 125; prevalent attitudes towards,
235; research on intensive mothering and,
62; responsibilities in, 66–79; sense of
duty factor in, 79–90; tiredness from, 73,
178; to-do lists, 65
Interview participants: enabling topic
brought up by, 174; grandchild care overview for, 22; grandchild care percentages
and, 205; number of, 2–3; selection conditions for, 99; sociodemographics data on,
27; work hours data for, 36
Interviews: confidentiality, 28; data overview
for, 29–31; methodology and location of,
28; number of participants, 2–3; participant conditions, 99; sample description,
28

Job security, 53, 102, 123–24, 126–29
Joys, of grandmothering, 37–48, 60–61

Latinos, employment benefits of, 13, 14
Leave: maternity, 14–16, *15*, 91; parental,
14–16, *15*, 91; sick, 4–5, 13–14

Leisure grandma, 41
Lifecourse, 61
Lifecourse approach, 18–19, 29, 48, 233–34; life stages and differences, 100, 131–32
Lifelines, 90–96
Limits, setting, 7, 56, 104; enabling and, 182; financial support, 141–42, 146; health concerns requiring, 158–60, 222, 226–27; partner role in, 160–63; work schedule as excuse for, 154–57. *See also* Enabling
Lower-income families, 13, 231; tax credit eligibility, 17

Management positions, 108, 128–29; CEO, 115–16
Marital status, trends in, 10–11
Maternity leave, 91; country comparison of paid, 14–16, *15*; in US, 15–16
Mental health issues, 71, 93
Methodology, 27–29
Mother-grandmother role differentiation, 21
Mothering: grandmothering compared with, 34, 45, 48, 49, 53–54, 65; as more stressful, 45; research on intensive, 62
Mothers: grandmothers caring for own, 168–69; precedents set by, 81. *See also* Single mothers

Nannies, 59
Nonmarital relationships, sociodemographics of, 10–11

Paid carework, 100–101, 133–34, 233
Parental leave, 91; Census Bureau data on, 15–16; comparison of different countries, 14–15, *15*
Parenting: backup, 39; styles, 179–80, 205
Parents: adult children age of becoming, 188; adult children unsuitability as, 91, 191; of grandmothers, 134, 163–73; in prison, 69, 94–96; single, 2, 5, *11*, 65, 236; working grandmothers caring for older relatives and, 163–73
Partners, 64; criticism from, 194–95, 198; limits set by, 160–63; support from, 167
Partying, adult children, 92–93, 186–87
Physical well-being, carework impact on, 25–27
Policy. *See* Welfare state, US
Poverty, 10, 145
Preschool programs, 17, 30

Prison, 69, 94–96
Protectiveness, 53
Provider data, 34–37, *35*, *36*, 98
Proximity, 37, 202
Public support, for federal programs, 237
Purposive child nurturing, 21

Recession, 132
Relatives, care for older, 163–73
Rent payments, 138
Residence, 37, 111
Response rate, 27
Responsibilities, intensive grandmothering, 66–79
Retirement, 6–7; age at, 2; altered plans for, 57; delayed, 119, 123, 146–47, 150–51; nest egg depletion, 142–51; percentages and account decline of, 132. *See also* Health and Retirement Survey
Rewards, 19–20, 32–34, 234; joy as, 37–48, 60–61
Rhetoric of choice, 21, 96
Role enhancement: health and, 23; theory, 23; work schedule flexibility and, 129–30
Roles: diversity, 63, 103; mother-grandmother differentiation of, 21; role conflict, 235–36
Role stress, 18, 23, 235; work schedule flexibility and, 129–30

Sandwich generation, 7, 23–24, 163–73; role conflict and, 235–36
Second chances, 48–61
Self-employed grandmothers, 109, 112–14
Self-rated health, 214–15
Sequential grandmothers, 84
Sibling rivalry, 8, 201–4
Sick care, 65
Sick days, 13–14, 31, 88, 119–20, 130
Sick leave, 4–5, 13–14
Single mothers, 71; birth percentages, 10, *11*; increasing number of, 65; lack of federal support for, 236
Single parents, 5, *11*, 65, 236; rise in number of, 2
Social impact, 25–27, 31, 54, 207, 208–14; health and, 228–29
Social Security, 4, 25, 145
Sociodemographics: interview participant, 27; percentage of births to single mothers by race, *11*; trends, 10–13, 37; working

grandmother, 37; work schedule flexibility and, 99

Special needs, grandchildren with, 22, 74, 91; financial support for therapies, 137–38

Stress, 172, 204; in adult children of grandmothers, 71; financial support causing, 8–9; mothering as more stressful, 45; role, 18, 23, 129–30, 235

Substance abuse, 196–97

Summer care, 65

Supermoms, 60

Tax credits, 17

Temporary custody, 69, 136

Theoretical perspectives, 18–24, 233–36

Time-use research, 14

Tiredness, 39, 40, 73, 178

Underappreciation, 8, 174

Unemployment, 12, 18

United States (US): grandchild care provider data for, 34–37, 35, 36, 98; marital trends in, 10–11; maternity leave in, 15, 15–16; percentage of children raised by grandparents, 28, 205–6; work hours of grandmothers in, 35, 36; working grandparents by age and gender, 3. See also Health and Retirement Survey; Sociodemographics

Universal daycare, 16–17, 237

Universal preschool, 17, 30

US. See United States

Vacation: days, 56, 122, 130; paid, 5, 13, 30, 31, 56

Wealth, median, 12–13

Welfare state, US, 61; absence of support from, 230–31, 236; grandmothering policy implications, 236–38; grandmothers as not mentioning support lack, 229; as intensive grandmothering factor, 66, 96; policy absence, 31, 229; preschool programs and, 17, 30; support from employers and, 13–18

White women: births to single mother percentages, 10, 11; marital status data for, 10

Work: balancing unpaid carework and paid, 29–31, 100–101, 232; grandchild care impact of, 24–27; grandchildren brought to workplace, 107, 121; juggling grandchild care and, 98–138

Work hours: balancing grandchild care hours and, 100–101; increased, 11; reduced, 177; of US grandmothers, 35, 36. See also Hours, grandchild care

Working grandmothers: grandchild care percentages, 2; job security of, 53, 102, 123–24, 126–29; parents and older relatives cared for by, 163–73; sociodemographics, 37. See also Work schedule flexibility

Working grandparents, 34; grandchild care percentages, 35, 36; likelihood of providing grandchild care, 98; number of, 2; percentage by age and gender, 3; work hour balance in grandchild care provided by, 100–101

Work schedule, 2, 4; excuse for limiting grandchild care, 154–57; flexible and inflexible, 101–26; rearranging, 83–84, 88, 94

Work schedule flexibility: age of grandchildren impacting, 122–23; availability, 99; career and residence changes to obtain, 111; CEO position affording, 115–16; changing jobs to achieve, 109–10; childhood disability situations demanding, 111; covering for other grandmothers at work, 106–7, 119; coworkers and, 102, 118–19; emergencies and, 116, 118; employers and, 14; flexible grandmothers and, 129–30; gendered expectations and, 125; grandchildren brought to work, 107, 121; income and, 99; job security and, 53, 123–24, 126–29; job sharing as, 102; management positions as offering, 108, 115–16, 128–29; role enhancement and role stress in, 129–30; self-employment and, 109, 112–14; vacation days, 56, 122, 130

Madonna Harrington Meyer is Professor of Sociology at Syracuse University. She is a coauthor, with Pam Herd, of *Market Friendly or Family Friendly? The State and Gender Inequality in Old Age* (2007) and the editor of *Care Work: Gender, Labor, and the Welfare State* (2000).